Understanding Social Research:

Perspectives on Methodology and Practice

Edited by

George McKenzie, Jackie Powell
and Robin Usher

 The Falmer Press

(A member of the Taylor & Francis Group)
London • Washington, D.C.

UK   Falmer Press, 1 Gunpowder Square, London, EC4A 3DE
USA Falmer Press, Taylor & Francis Inc., 1900 Frost Road, Suite 101,
         Bristol, PA 19007

First published in 1997

**A catalogue record for this book is available from the British
Library**

ISBN 0 7507 0721 6 cased
ISBN 0 7507 0720 8 paper

**Library of Congress Cataloging-in-Publication Data are available
on request**

Jacket design by Caroline Archer

Typeset in 10/12 pt Times by
Graphicraft Typesetters Ltd., Hong Kong.

Printed in Great Britain by Biddles Ltd., Guildford and King's Lynn on
paper which has a specified pH value on final paper manufacture of
not less than 7.5 and is therefore 'acid free'.

Contents

Series Editor's Preface   vii

1   Introduction   1
    Robin Usher

2   The Age of Reason or the Age of Innocence?   8
    George McKenzie

Part 1: The Nature of Enquiry   25

3   Telling a Story about Research and Research as Story-Telling:
    Postmodern Approaches to Social Research   27
    Robin Usher

4   Challenging the Power of Rationality   42
    Pat Usher

5   Being Economical with Politics   56
    Alan Hamlin

6   Family Behaviour and the Economic Method   71
    George McKenzie

Part 2: The Nature of Disciplines   85

7   The Search for the 'Discipline' of Information Systems   87
    David E. Avison

8   Nursing Research: A Social Science?   101
    Sheila Payne

9   The Case for Research into Practice   112
    Joan Orme

10 Scientific and Statistical Hypotheses: Bridging the Gap   124
    David J. Hand

Part 3: Research Practice   137

11 Researching Social Work and Social Care Practices   139
    Jackie Powell

Contents

12 Qualitative Approaches to Data Collection and Analysis:
Examinations and Schools   155
David Scott

13 Grounded Theory — Its Basis, Rationale and Procedures   173
Dean Bartlett and Sheila Payne

14 Action Research in Information Systems   196
David E. Avison

15 Issues in Participant Observation — A Study of the Practice of
Information Systems Development   210
Joe Nandhakumar

16 Enigma Variations: Uncertainty in Social and Economic Research   221
George McKenzie

Notes on Contributors   233

Index   236

Series Editor's Preface

The purpose of the *Social Research and Educational Studies* series is to provide authoritative guides to key issues in educational research. The series includes overviews of fields, guidance on good practice and discussions of the practical implications of social and educational research. In particular, the series deals with a variety of approaches to conducting social and educational research. Contributors to this series review recent work, raise critical concerns that are particular to the field of education and reflect on the implications of research for educational policy and practice.

Each volume in the series draws on material that will be relevant for an international audience. The contributors to this series all have wide experience of teaching, conducting and using educational research. The volumes are written so that they will appeal to a wide audience of students, teachers and researchers. Altogether the volumes in the *Social Research and Educational Studies* series provide a comprehensive guide for anyone concerned with contemporary educational research.

The series will include individually authored books and edited volumes on a range of themes in education including qualitative research, survey research, the interpretation of data, self-evaluation, research and social policy, analyzing data, action research and the politics and ethics of research.

The last five years have witnessed considerable discussion and debate about the shape and scope of research training for postgraduate students in general, and social science postgraduates in particular. The contributors to this volume provide a wide ranging discussion of issues and themes that are of central concern for the education and training of those engaged in social and educational research. The papers offer a starting point for new researchers that will guide their work and promote discussion and debate in 'graduate seminars'. It is to be hoped that all together these papers will stimulate a range of new thinking and new work among those engaged in social and educational research at graduate level and beyond.

Robert Burgess
University of Warwick

1   Introduction

Robin Usher

This collection comprises the thoughts of individual social researchers who approach their work from a variety of perspectives. The diverse approaches represented here reflect the diversity of socio-economic problems which are likely to be found amongst any group of social scientists. If this collection has any one single theme that stands out above all others, it is that in the realm of social and economic research there is no single correct practice and no superordinate methodology. This theme is exemplified in the papers. Their diversity and variety both in terms of research methods and disciplinary focus, far from being a sign of weakness, is rather a sign of difference at work. Far from being a matter of regret, it is in our view a matter of celebration and a mark of the sophistication and complexity of the process of social research. Our hope is therefore, that these papers will stimulate processes of exploration and interrogation amongst social researchers.

In order to express this diversity, contributors were left free to develop their chosen topic in their own way, subject only to the condition first, that their contribution should be rooted in their own practice as researchers but that they should try to be as reflexive as possible about this, and second, that they endeavour to highlight the epistemological commitments embedded in their research practice and the methodological choices that follow from these commitments. The hope is, that as a consequence, readers will be better able to understand the connection between epistemology, methodology and research practice, and in doing so enrich their own research. However, it is important to emphasize that this is no DIY manual of research methods since the message that emerges very clearly, taking the contributions collectively, is that there can be no such manual. Methods are not part of some universal algorithm of 'how to do research' but are a function of concrete research practice, rooted in research traditions and paradigms.

What can be achieved, and this is clearly revealed in the contributions, is that research methods need to be, and indeed can be, subjected to critical scrutiny. This critical scrutiny is, however, somewhat different from what would be normally understood by this term, for what is most in need of scrutiny is not the outcomes of research (which is the way methods are usually assessed) but also the epistemological commitments of any research. Even if researchers feel confident methodologically and see no need to review their methods, it is increasingly the case that social research now demands not only an evaluation of outcomes, but a reflexive analysis of the research process and of the place of the researcher within that.

Epistemology, in a disciplinary sense, belongs to philosophical discourse where it is understood as the way in which claims to knowledge are justified — to ask epistemological questions is to ask questions about what is to *count* as knowledge. However, epistemology is not, as it is commonly understood, simply a set of rules about how to decide what is to count. Epistemology itself has a history and is itself socially located. Historically, it evolved as part of the struggle against the medieval Church with its monopoly over learning and its construction of truth in terms of the authority of divine texts. Epistemology constituted a different way of grounding knowledge through the emerging natural sciences and its 'democratization' of knowers. Experiment and observation replaced tradition and the divine text, validation became a function of measurement and intersubjective testability, and experience mediated by rationality, the source of knowledge.

Inasmuch as research involves finding out about the world, it is unavoidably about the making of knowledge claims. In making a claim there is an implied preparedness to justify the claim by pointing to the ways in which one knows — in other words, the putting forward of good reasons for knowing so that claims can be intersubjectively tested and thus publicly licensed. Traditionally, these 'good reasons' have been defined epistemologically as the 'objective' and 'systematic' differentiation of valid or legitimate knowledge from apparent knowledge or mere belief. The 'best' or strongest kind of knowledge has been taken as that which is the outcome of using scientific method and hence scientific method came to be seen as a set of universal rules for conducting research and the making of publicly licensable knowledge claims — claims guaranteeing that the world was known truly.

Any research, whether in the natural or social sciences, in making knowledge claims inevitably raises epistemological questions. Very often however these are not made explicit, in fact most of the time they are taken for granted. Most researchers in the social sciences (particularly those at the more quantitative end of the spectrum) tend to think only in terms of *methods* or particular techniques for gathering evidence and very rarely consider the epistemological assumptions of their research. Or if they do, they do so purely in terms of whether they are working 'scientifically' or being sufficiently 'objective'. This is taken as the 'natural' thing to do in research, without any recognition that by so doing certain epistemological assumptions are being implicitly made. Thus for instance, being 'objective' is implicitly understood in terms of being unbiased, value-neutral and ensuring that personal considerations do not intrude into the research process. Yet to accept this definition of objectivity unproblematically is to implicitly accept a certain epistemology and all the commitments and assumptions that go with that.

There is a powerful tendency in social research either not to take account of epistemology at all or to think of it purely in its positivist/empiricist form — the descendant of philosophy's struggle against the medieval Church and the authority of tradition. A positivist/empiricist epistemology contains the following assumptions:

1   The world exists independently of knowers, i.e. it is 'objective'. It consists of events and phenomena which are lawful and orderly. Through systematic observation and correct scientific methods, i.e. by being 'objective', it

is possible to know this lawfulness — to explain, predict and control events and phenomena.

2 There is a clear distinction between the 'subjective' knower and the 'objective' world. There is also a clear distinction between facts and values, with the former belonging to the objective world, the latter to the subjective knower. Subjectivity (the concerns, values and particularity of the researcher) must not interfere with the discovery of truth.

3 There is order and reason in the social world, social life is patterned and this pattern has a cause-effect form. Things do not happen randomly and arbitrarily. The goal of research is therefore to develop general and universal laws that explain the social world.

4 Knowledge is arrived at through the use of the senses and the application of reason, through observation enhanced by experiment and measurement. Both experience and language are transparent, thus the senses provide unmediated access to the world and there is a clear correspondence between the world and the words we use to represent it. Sensory experience must, however, be filtered through rationality and since reason is a universal characteristic, different observers exposed to the same data should be able to come to the same conclusions — this is known as intersubjective verification.

5 All the sciences or disciplines are based on the same method of finding out about the world. Thus the natural and social sciences share a common logic and methodology of enquiry.

6 Enquiry and critique into epistemological-ontological commitments that underlie the use of methods is a pointless exercise.

A positivist/empiricist epistemology of research emphasizes determinacy (that there is a certain truth that can be known), rationality (no contradictory explanations, convergence on a single explanation), impersonality (the more 'objective' and the less 'subjective' the better), the ideal knower (that anyone whose senses are not impaired and whose faculty of reason is fully functioning can be a knower), and prediction (that research should aim for generalizations from which predictions can be made and events/phenomena controlled). In order to be seen as valid, knowledge has to be dehistoricized, detached from its source in experience (since experience could only become knowledge when acted upon by reason) and from the place where it was made. Furthermore, research need not be reflexive or self-critical since the focus is exclusively on methods and outcomes rather than the research process itself. This ignoring of reflexivity leads to seeing research as a 'technology' or technicized process.

As we have noted, traditionally epistemology has been concerned with answering questions about who can be a knower, what are the means by which beliefs can be tested in order to count as knowledge, and what kinds of things can be known. The answers that positivism gives to these questions is first, that the 'ideal knower' is the rational, value-neutral, transcendental person — for which read 'man', for as feminist writers have pointed out women did not count as knowers since their rationality was considered to be impaired (Harding, 1987); second, that the tests for what is to count as knowledge involve the application of scientific method; third, that the kinds of things that can be known are those that are directly observable and quantifiable.

This seems to imply that scientific method is an abstract set of logical rules, independent of the world and its social practices (as it were, 'made in heaven'), and universal in their applicability, i.e. all knowledge claims can be differentiated in the same way. Critics of positivism argue however, that not only is there no one single epistemology, no one single test or set of rules of what is to count as knowledge, but that epistemology should not be understood as defining a set of universal logical rules. Instead, whatever rules there are should be seen as a cultural artefact, historically-located and value-laden. Rationality is neither universal, culturally neutral nor invariant in its form. Scientific method, as we have seen for instance, has itself evolved historically with the growth of the natural sciences and of Western philosophy. Furthermore, there is no *single* scientific method, rather it is more aptly understood as ways of working specific to particular research paradigms and to particular disciplinary pursuits.

Different epistemologies provide different versions of how things can be known. Epistemologies in this sense are linked to disciplines with different disciplines having different ways of knowing the world. They are also linked to ontologies, different versions of what kinds of things exist in the world. Any research paradigm or tradition has its own epistemology, its own way of validating its knowledge claims (as the contribution by McKenzie on economic method and Hamlin on political economy show very clearly). Disciplines are located within a paradigm (or in the social sciences more than one paradigm as many of the contributions show). Paradigms delineate what questions can be asked, what can be researched, what is an appropriate methodology, what constitutes data, and what kind of tests enable beliefs to be counted as knowledge. Any research method or procedure is therefore inextricably embedded in commitments to particular versions of the world and to particular ways of knowing it, and the researcher, by using these methods and procedures rather than others, reproduces and strengthens these commitments. Epistemology is not just a technical philosophical procedure but a commitment to a particular way of understanding the world and acting within it through research. It follows from this that there is no means of carrying out research which is neutral and self-validating, any method in the final analysis being dependent on its location in disciplinary paradigms and research traditions and on an epistemological-ontological rationale and position.

Of course, this is not to say that the situation in the disciplines of the social sciences is one of easy-going plurality and the ready toleration of difference. On the contrary, epistemologies in the social sciences are sites of struggle and this is particularly the case in newly emerging disciplines. The contributions by Payne on Nursing and Avison on Information Systems, both newly emerging disciplines, make this very clear. By highlighting the question of where disciplines are to be located within the spectrum of the social sciences, issues to do with boundaries and exclusions are raised in an acute form, both within disciplines and between disciplines.

Some epistemologies have more credibility and dominance that others and this is not so much a matter of their natural goodness in describing the world but because they are powerful. The most powerful is still a positivist/empiricist epistemology that holds up the methods and procedures of the natural sciences as the model for all research and which implicitly understands itself as a universal epistemology. The consequences of the dominance of positivist/empiricist epistemology are by now well-known but are still worth mentioning in this context. First, in the social sciences and in social research a pre-eminent place has been accorded to the production of generalizable knowledge and the discovery of law-like regularities. Second, there has been a privileging of the language, methods and quantification which supposedly characterize research in the natural sciences (Scott's chapter on qualitative research in education clearly demonstrates the taken-for grantedness and therefore power of quantitative approaches). Third, feminist research has shown that the influence of positivist/empiricist epistemology in the social sciences has been to focus mainly on 'questions about social life that appear problematic from within the social experiences that are characteristic for men' (Harding, 1987; p. 16). Hence the tests to which knowledge claims are subjected are always gendered, male definitions prevail of the things in the world that can be known and, as a consequence, the experience of women becomes invisible. In more general terms, Hand in his chapter shows clearly the significance for the research process of the initial question asked.

Of course, the dominance of positivist/empiricist epistemology has not gone unchallenged and the contributors show that there are now a number of counter-epistemologies in the disciplines of the social sciences. For example, hermeneutic/interpretive epistemology argues that the model to be followed is not an idealized and universal logic of scientific discovery and justification because this is an inappropriate model for the social sciences. In social research, it is argued, the test of knowledge should not be generalization and prediction but interpretive power, meaning and illumination. The focus should be on human action and interaction which by its nature is meaningful and hence has to be interpreted. An idealized logic drawn from the natural sciences and a limiting of what can be known to the empirically 'given' cannot hope to elucidate these meanings and thus cannot hope to portray the rich diversity of the social world.

Yet concluding from this that an unbridgeable chasm exists between the natural and social sciences may not be the only possibility. Kuhn's view of natural science as it is actually practised, rather than how it understands itself and is itself understood, emphasizes the importance of normative consensus and commitment within research communities as the means by which a paradigm is maintained and realized in practice. In effect, this means that the natural and social sciences are actually not that different although in a reverse way to that which is normally assumed. The social sciences need not strive to be more like the natural sciences, since the latter might actually be more like the former than we might at first think. Kuhn (1970) helps us to see that the way research in the natural sciences is practised does not follow a positivist/empiricist epistemology — on the contrary, there is a significant hermeneutic/interpretive dimension. The difference, for example, between the natural sciences and the social sciences is not that the former are more 'objective' whilst the latter are 'subjective'. Since any research practice has a hermeneutic dimension, the natural sciences are just as subjective in this sense as the social sciences. Here, it is important to note however that 'subjective' does not refer to individual subjectivity but to the subjective as socially defined.

Paradigms are frameworks that function as maps or guides for research communities, whether in the natural or the social sciences. They provide ways of looking at and ways of working in the world. As we have noted earlier, they define the objects, direction and methods of research. To this extent, they provide a 'social subjective'. Knowledge is not the product of an individual consciousness nor is the latter the means by which knowledge is validated. Rather than research or finding out about the world being a matter of epistemological individualism, we should see it as the outcome of active and historically evolving communities. Furthermore, if research is a social practice carried out by research communities this means that what constitutes 'objectivity' and the 'objective' will be defined by the community and the paradigm which shapes its work — in other words, it is the community rather than the world or a set of universal rules which decides what is 'objective'.

Research in the positivist/empiricist mode proceeds from hypothesis formation to data collection and to the verification or disconfirmation of hypotheses in the light of the data. More interpretive approaches such as grounded research and action research (discussed by Avison, Bartlett and Payne, Powell, Payne, Scott and Nandhakumar) start with data and generate hypotheses or theory from the data in a backwards and forwards, or dialectical movement, between theory and data. Here the emphasis is more on searching for order rather than assuming it is already there as a positivist approach does. The feminist approach (as discussed by Pat Usher, Orme and Payne) is concerned with critiquing all research traditions by exposing their roots in androcentrism and patriarchal control and exclusion. This however does not lead to a rejection of existing research methods but rather to a more open-ended and critical approach where a diversity of methods can be employed within an inter-disciplinary environment.

Postmodern research (as discussed by R. Usher) on the other hand, whilst recognizing that there is no postmodern method(s) as such, questions both the assumption of, and the search for, a pre-existing order by highlighting the privileging and exclusion characteristic of all research paradigms and traditions. This emphasizes the need for reflexivity, a recognition of the way in which research 'constructs' a world to be researched. Furthermore, in contrast to the positivist's narrow empiricism, the postmodern 'empirical' is much wider, and one with greater potential for the social scientist. Here empirical testing can relate to practice in close and fruitful ways. When the test of a theory is not its correspondence with the empirical but its correspondence with the practical, the empirical includes, rather than excludes, the practical. The merit of a theory then is found in its practical implication and efficacy in solving problems of the discipline. By questioning the hierarchically structuring and rigid binary oppositions, for example between theory and practice, the universal and the local, the abstract and the specific, the rigorous and the relevant, postmodern researchers seek therefore to replace order, homogeneity and determinacy as the prime goal of research with diversity, difference and indeterminacy. By foregrounding the power inherent in all disciplinary-based research they draw our attention to the very ambivalence of 'discipline' — that it is at one and the same time, both knowledge and social control.

References

HARDING, S. (1987) 'Introduction — is there a feminist method?', in HARDING S. (Ed) *Feminism and Methodology*, Buckingham, Open University Press.

KUHN, T. (1970) *The Structure of Scientific Revolutions*, Chicago, University of Chicago Press.

2   The Age of Reason or the Age of Innocence?

George McKenzie

Introduction

Research is a response to a challenge. It is undertaken in an attempt to solve a problem. We undertake research everyday whether in our personal lives, as students or as part of out professional career. We may need to find the best route to travel from Southampton to Birmingham or the cheapest food market. Natural scientists may undertake research with the view of developing more efficient means for generating electric power or methods for increasing farm productivity. As social scientists we are concerned with identifying the causes of unemployment, poverty and drug abuse and for designing policies which seek to alleviate these social problems and improve the quality of life. Whatever the nature of the problem, the challenge and response process is similar. There is a problem. We may have a vision as to how to deal with that problem and this might take the form of some conjectures or prior theories as to the best way to proceed. That is, we may have some idea as to the cheapest shop or about the chemical makeup of farm soil or the causes of unemployment. Information is gathered, prices are compared, experiments or interviews are undertaken. Conclusions are drawn and decisions taken.

But this sounds too easy. Wouldn't it be nice if we really could follow the procedure of theorizing and data collection to solve the problems that we face. If this were the case then all that would be involved is time and effort which, of course, we are all prepared to expend. Unfortunately, the process of research is embedded with a terrible anxiety: how do we know that our conclusions are the correct ones? I may not have time to compare all prices in all shops. That would be a very expensive activity, so I may simply guess on the basis of limited information. A more efficient means of generating electricity may be designed but it may have unforeseen effects on the environment. Or a policy designed to alleviate unemployment may lead to higher taxes for those employed who in turn as the majority seek redress through the ballot box. How do I know when I am correct? What criteria can I use to decide?

The research process is further complicated by the fact that in the face of uncertainty others may have reached different conclusions. One member of the family may prefer one shop over another because their father always shopped there. They do not want to look elsewhere. One group of researchers may argue that coal-based electricity generation is to be preferred to nuclear-based because it preserves the traditions of the mining communities. Some policy makers may argue that unemployment is not as important as inflation. Not only may we be unsure as to the results of our research activity, we have to justify it in the face of competing claims which not only arise from different interpretations of available information but different prejudices on the part of the researcher. What criteria can be used to choose between the competing claims?

The implication is that the process of research is embedded in a churning vortex of constructive and destructive tensions. In other words, the research process is itself problematic. Constructive energy is generated through the creation of new modes of doing things or new ideas which enable us to live and work in more satisfying ways. But in the wake is left destruction. Traditional modes of production which are part of a way of life for many are destroyed. Researchers who may have devoted a lifetime to developing and refining a particular idea now find that this idea is no longer valued. As we seek to improve our understanding of the world in which we live, we are inevitably drawn to conclusions that challenge or destroy the current orthodoxy. Thus research openly seeks to be destructive.

But what about the new propositions? If they are widely accepted and turn out to be reasonably correct then it is possible that many people, possibly everyone, can be made better off. But of course the propositions may not be correct. Disastrous errors could be made as a result. And even if the propositions were true, they could be misused by unscrupulous individuals. Nuclear power offers many a cheap source of electric power but it also has huge destructive potential that can be used to threaten national or ethnic control at the expense of others. New sources of cattle feed that were both cheaper and more nutritious are today found to be the cause of disease in both cattle and humans. While we may like to think that our research could lead to blissful order, it can and does cause chaos. Because this possibility is not fully appreciated, there exists a tension between those who seek to impose upon the process of research rules which seek to preserve order, and those who argue that research is itself inherently chaotic and can never be ordered.

This tension is not new. It is not a product of the Industrial Revolution of the eighteenth century or of the Electronic Revolution of the late twentieth century. It has been recognized and discussed since the times of the ancient Greeks at least. Despite the fact that the world of 2000 AD is remarkably different from the world of 400 BC, the debate about what we know and how we know it has continued unabated, basically focusing on the same questions: is it possible to establish rules which define objectively our knowledge and hence define the process whereby we search for that knowledge? Or is it impossible to separate the search for knowledge and, indeed, the very concept of knowledge from our sensory experience. What is the relationship between what we see and understand and that which is reality? In other words, how do we go about creating knowledge about the world in which we live?

Inevitably, those who sought to develop rules found themselves continually pressed to explain exceptions to the existing rules. The uncertain nature of the world and the uncertain nature of the research process itself were addressed through the use of closure statements which enabled gaps in reasoning and interpretation to be bridged. Conclusions could then be drawn by reference to metaphysical concepts such as the soul, as with the ancient Greeks, with God, as in medieval times, or with the rational mind as during the Enlightenment of the seventeenth and eighteenth centuries and subsequently in modern times. By their nature, the closure rules involved leaps of faith and consequently disbelievers would be marginalized. Clubs in the form of the Academy, the Church and modern disciplines, such as economics and sociology, would seek to provide fora in which the believers could refine their ideas and methods. Perhaps not unsurprisingly they would also seek to monopolize the process of knowledge creation.

Throughout recorded history the sceptics have argued that recognition of the impossibility of creating universal truths is an important part of any research process designed to enhance understanding, whether by an individual or by society as a whole. Our world today is markedly different from that of the ancient Greeks, yet the same issues are being addressed today as they were 2300 years ago. Thus, although the development of this chapter will appear to be linear and historical, it really concerns the ebb and flow in the continuing debate as to what human understanding is about.

I begin with the attempts by ancient Greek thinkers to define the nature of existence (ontology). This is followed with a discussion of the approach taken by Descartes who shifted the emphasis away from studying the meaning of existence to the process of knowledge formation (epistemology). His work is credited with laying the foundations for the Age of Enlightenment during the eighteenth century when it came to be believed that rational human thought could provide the basis for all human endeavour. From this era, the modern natural and social sciences, as we know them, evolved. More recently, however, postmodern and feminist scholars have argued that there is an inconsistency between what we claim that we are doing in our research and what we actually do. These inconsistencies are discussed in the later sections of the chapter.

The Academy

At the heart of Greek thinking was the relationship between reality and perception. This can be illustrated by the following simple but classic textbook example. Consider a stick which is partly submerged in water. Viewed for the first time, we would be inclined to conclude that the stick was bent. In reality, of course, the stick is straight. The proposition that the stick is bent can be verified or falsified by removing it from the water. This is, of course, a very simple problem. Suppose instead that we are interested in the process whereby the water causes wood to rot. To understand that, we would not only need to see how all the atoms and molecules move and are linked to each other but to explain why they are linked and why they move. We would need to get inside the wood. Similarly, no such experiment is available to those researchers trying to identify the causes of war, poverty or financial collapse. To fully comprehend such problems would require investigators to put themselves in the shoes of all persons, politicians, the poor, the rich, investors, *et al.*, in order to understand their circumstances and motivations in responding to those circumstances. But of course this is impossible. Others may give us answers to our questions, but these answers may not reflect what they are actually thinking. They may have reasons for trying to mislead us either by lying or selectively choosing the information provided. Or their subconscious mind may be influencing their answer in some way unknown even to themselves. Whereas, we could remove the distorting effects of the water in our experiment so as to verify that the stick is straight, it is impossible to remove the gap between what we may say to others and what we actually think and do. No matter how hard we try to understand and appreciate another person's actions, it is impossible to crawl into their mind. This impossibility defines in large measure the limits of our research enterprise and creates a tension between any claims to objective research and what is actually being achieved.

Such issues were addressed by Plato's Academy, devoted to understanding the reasoning mind. It was based on the ideas of Plato (circa 427–347 BC) and involved his pupils, including Aristotle, and their successors until around 240 BC. The focus of the Academy was the essence of existence. In *Theaetetus* and *The Republic*, Plato sought to advance the view that knowledge must be unchanging. According to his thinking, experience derived from the senses could not count as knowledge since objects viewed in this way were subject to change. Knowledge could only be achieved through the use of reason. This would enable generalizations based on mathematics and logic to be drawn about the world around us. The method involves two steps. First, it is necessary to search for unchanging objects and when they are identified to describe them. Second, it is necessary to illustrate how they could be known through the use of reason. This would be achieved by identifying necessary and sufficient conditions that would define or delimit an object. This search for knowledge takes the form of trying to identify counter-examples to a proposed definition. When a definition is immune to counter-examples, it becomes knowledge for it must then satisfy the criteria of being unchanging. These steps provide the basis of modern research methodologies that began to evolve rapidly in the seventeenth century and in the eighteenth century during the Enlightenment. First, the process involves the establishment of universal propositions or knowledge. Second, the process involves the assumption that those searching for knowledge were rational, although it was argued in ancient times that not everyone could achieve this lofty endeavour. In other words, these intellectual activities could only be undertaken by the Academy. Only certain kinds of men could achieve the status of a learner and the power associated with it. Closure would be achieved by restricting discussion as to what is or is not knowledge to an elite. The Academy was thus a forerunner to the modern disciplines such as physics or sociology.

The objects that satisfied Plato's criteria of knowledge are severely limited — they refer to form: triangularity or whiteness are properties of objects that may change. The definition of a triangle or of the colour white does not change and therefore they count as knowledge. Plato's search for definitions represents his search for knowledge, which itself required definition. Although it may be possible to follow the method of providing counter-examples to eliminate particular propositions for their failure to satisfy the criterion of being unchanging, it is not the same as falsification, which Plato argued was impossible. In *Theaetetus*, Plato defines knowledge as justified true belief. It is impossible to falsify beliefs. You may think that you know something, but this is only thinking that you know, without actually knowing. Justification for a belief must be provided. Unfortunately, Plato was unable to provide us with an idea as to what the process of justification involves.

Aristotle (384–322 BC) pushed the ideas of his teacher further and in so doing attempted to identify more clearly the limits of our ability to know and understand. Basically Aristotle argued that research was a circular process. Observations of phenomena would be made and from these explanatory principles would be derived through induction. Then on the basis of these principles further characteristics of the phenomena would be deduced. Aristotle stated four criteria that such premises or assumptions should satisfy. First, they should be true. Second, premises should be indemonstrable. Third, they should be better known than the conclusion. Fourth, they should be better known than the conclusion.

In explaining his approach, Aristotle emphasized that it was highly subjective and hence the search for knowledge was not straightforward. First, observations would be made on the basis of sensory experience, sight, sound, taste, smell, touch. As Plato had emphasized, sensory perception was not necessarily objective. Two individuals might perceive the same phenomena in different ways. Inductive reasoning could then take two forms. One could enumerate or catalogue observations and then seek to draw generalizations from the results, or one might seek to draw generalizations on the basis of insight. Some unexplained intuitive process enabled the investigator to identify generalizations. Aristotle was quick to point out the limitations of the inductive-deductive process. First, he recognized that a particular phenomena could be deduced from several sets of premises. Thus he excluded as valid arguments those statements which have true conclusions but false premises. Second, Aristotle recognized that scientific enquiry must accept that some premises are not capable of verification, otherwise there would be no end to any investigation. Thus uncertainty is a fundamental property of the research process. This recognition of uncertainty then leads Aristotle to conclude that knowledge resides in the mind and that the mind is part of the soul. The concept of the soul whose existence can neither be proved or disproved serves as a mythological construct to fill a gap in understanding what exists and what is knowable. This is analogous to Plato's concept of true belief.

Warning flags have been hoisted deliberately. If knowledge claims are restricted to propositions based on immutable concepts such as 'white' or a 'triangle', then it would seem that there is little that we can do to enhance our knowledge about contemporary social and economic problems. For example, let us take a brief diversion and consider the problem of unemployment. One measure of unemployment is the difference between the amount of time that individuals desire to work and the amount of time that employers actually offer at current wages. However, this definition is based on human desire which is changeable and differs across individuals. Not everyone will desire to work the same amount of time. Another definition is based upon the difference between the amount of work that is socially just and that which is actually offered. But since everyone has different notions of justice this definition also fails Plato's criterion. Yet another definition involves the difference between the amount of work which would be offered by a free competitive market where labour demand and supply were equal and that actually offered. However, since we can never observe such a free market equilibrium this definition fails as well. In other words, it is impossible for contemporary social scientists to agree on a definition of unemployment.

Over subsequent years, many sceptical voices emerged, perhaps inspired by the statement by Socrates (469–399 BC) that the only thing that he knew was that he knew nothing. A vacuum was being created because of the failure on the part of thinkers to develop concepts of knowledge creation which satisfied their criteria based upon a dichotomy between the object of investigation and the perceptions of the investigator. Theological precepts began to be used to fill the gap. St. Augustine (354–430 AD) claimed that human knowledge would be impossible if God did not enlighten the human mind and thereby allow it to comprehend ideas. In pursuing his vision he sought to demolish the ideas of the New Academy, intellectual descendants of The Academy. These ideas were characterized by propositions advanced by Cicero (106–43 BC), namely that since we can never know what is true, we must act according to what seems probable. Augustine thereby characterizes Cicero as someone for whom knowledge is uncertain. In attempting to deal with this position which was unacceptable to him, Augustine sought to revive Platonic criteria: knowledge must be timeless, immutable and accessible to the mind. However, the human mind was itself immaterial to the process except in the sense that it was enlightened by God. Indeed, Augustine proposed that the human mind was part of God. This doctrine was to apply to all knowledge creation. In a sense what Augustine sought to do was very much what both physical and social scientists do today when they reach an impasse. A conjectural story or myth is created to fill some gap. In this case, the impasse was the understanding of the process of knowledge creation and the role of the individual which through Augustine's epistemology could be brought to the forefront as part of God. Although such stories could never be proved or disproved, provided that people believed them on faith and their structure was not completely inconsistent with the worldly environment, then such myths could provide a basis for stable societies. Inconsistencies were characterized as mysteries, themselves the product of God's enlightening influence. The role of reconciling the inability to define knowledge in some universal had shifted from the Academy to God.

The Age of Enlightenment

Beginning in the twelfth century, Aristotle's works on scientific enquiry began to be translated from Greek and Arabic into Latin thereby making them accessible to a wider European audience and for the following four centuries scholars interpreted and debated the meaning of Aristotle's thoughts and those of the Academy. By the seventeenth and eighteenth centuries the fruits of scientific enquiry were being more widely enjoyed. The world was no longer conceived as being flat. Trade with the New World and Asia was leading to increased prosperity. Demand for new and better consumption goods increased and this led to pressures on productive processes and this challenge led to the Industrial Revolution. Many believed that the scientific principles which were transforming both industry and agriculture could be used to transform society and the way in which it was organized. The Enlightenment began.

Some historians have sought to date the Enlightenment as the period between the English Revolution of 1688 and the French Revolution of 1789, roughly the eighteenth century. However, two of the most prominent and enduring influences on the Enlightenment were thinkers from the early seventeenth century, René Descartes (1596–1650) and Francis Bacon (1561–1626). Both were influenced by the writing of Aristotle. Both sought to overcome the limitations on the search for knowledge which Aristotle had identified. In their thinking we can identify the seeds of the positivist and interpretivist methodologies which dominate social and economic research today.

Descartes was a mathematician whom many credit with the invention of analytical geometry (e.g. the so-called Cartesian co-ordinates). Like Plato, he believed that the essence of science was the discovery of relationships that could be expressed in mathematical form. In his mind, mathematics provided the structure for the creation of certain knowledge. Descartes argued that deductive reasoning based upon mathematics should be the basis of all human enquiry. Such propositions are not produced by sense experience but independently by reason, he argued. Descartes expressed this approach in the form of rules which he believed would expand the realm of human understanding. Basically these rules stated that research should only be undertaken when it was known that a certain outcome was feasible. As with Plato, Aristotle and Augustine, the emphasis is on the search for truth and certainty. Any research that produces knowledge which is uncertain is to be avoided.

However, rather than elaborate extensively on Cartesian logic, I am going to turn to a much earlier debate between St. Anselm of Canturbury (circa 1033–1109) and the monk Gaunilo. Few contemporary philosophers, I suspect, will attach much importance to this. However, to my mind, it pre-emptively identifies the limitations of rational thought that underpinned the Age of Enlightenment and Modern Times. Descartes was a believer in the proof of the existence of God advanced by St. Anselm of Canterbury in his *Proslogion*. This is a masterpiece of deductive reasoning. Assumptions are made and a result is derived, entirely in the spirit of contemporary economic and sociological analysis. St. Anselm's proof is about a page long and is well worth studying. Its argumentation is based on the axiom that God is the thing than which a greater cannot be conceived. If a thought exists in the mind, then it exists in reality. Since there is no greater thought than God, then God must exist. Anselm argued that his proof was so transparent that it had to be accepted by any fool who denied God's existence. In retort the monk Gaunilo argued in his *A Reply on Behalf of the Fool* that Anselm's reasoning could be used to prove anything. In essence, propositions based upon deductive reasoning are conditional upon assumptions. Although the logical process of reasoning involved may be invariate, as in mathematics, the assumptions may not. Of course if the underlying assumptions are shared by many people, then they may form the basis for a religion based upon those shared beliefs. However, such thoughts need not exist for everybody. Deduction could not enable a particular idea to be advanced as universal. This was Gaunilo's conclusion.

If Descartes' deductive approach can be characterized as bottom-up in the sense that one works from assumptions to conclusions, then Bacon's inductive approach is very much top down. With Descartes and Bacon, we have the destruction of Aristotle's inductive-deductive circle. Like Descartes, Bacon believed that the rational human mind was capable of knowledge creation. However, this would not take the form of rational, deductive thought, but of rationally conceived empirical investigations. Organized experiments would be undertaken with a systematic recording of results. Attempts at replicating results would be undertaken continuously. When sufficient information was available, it would be used to establish laws. Induction would then be used to identify basic axioms supporting these laws where the axioms themselves would be subject to empirical investigation. In this sense, Bacon was very much influenced by Aristotle. However, he gave much greater emphasis to the role of observation than the latter and it is in this spirit that much statistical enquiry is carried out in the social sciences today. Bacon argued that scientific enquiry should seek to free itself of prejudices. However, his approach was widely criticized on the grounds that it could not be free of assumption. The choice of data to gather implicitly involved some hypothesis. It was argued that such hypotheses needed to be made explicit. Nevertheless, the empirical approach of Bacon brought about rapid advances in human understanding of physical phenomena and particularly, gravity, electromagnetism and the solar system. This then put pressure on investigators to understand the causes of such apparently systematic events.

In this environment, many began to believe that rational enquiry could lead to progress in all spheres of human life, including law, art and literature. Undoubtedly great advances were made in the way in which we organize and govern ourselves. However, there were also massive excesses. Attempts to create universal propositions led to great absurdities. Reason was defined as common sense. But what was common sense? The utilitarian proposition of the 'greatest happiness of the greatest number' could not stand up as a widely accepted proposition underpinning human action. Plato's point about being unable to come up with a unique definition of justice is relevant here. In the opinion of the economist Joseph Schumpeter (1954, pp. 122–123), the Enlightenment was hokum. In his view, this epoch involved '. . . applying reason to a heap of nonsense inherited from the past'.

Sceptics such as John Locke (1632–1704) and David Hume (1711–1776) appeared early in the Enlightenment project. Locke, like the thinkers that we have discussed so far, was concerned with the necessary conditions for knowledge. However, he argued that there was an unbridgeable gap. Although we might develop scientific theories based on the existence of atoms it was not possible to discuss atomic structure since this was outside the realm of our experience. He claimed that only by divine revelation could we understand the causes and effects of atoms. Subsequently, Hume argued that even if we could visually see how atoms were connected and how they moved we would still not possess complete knowledge. The reason is that we could still not say anything about cause and effect. We might see the atoms move but we cannot explain why they move. We might see atoms connected but we cannot explain why they are connected. This problem is very real for the social scientist. He or she may see that there exists extensive poverty in Africa but be unable to come up with a universal explanation for that poverty or an effective way of alleviating it.

Modern Times

Despite the doubts and questions raised above, many thinkers have continued in their attempts to advance the use of rational/deductive and empirical/inductive methods to the study of society with a view to bettering the human condition. The search was on for a world of certainty, optimism and a rationally constructed social order. The edifice of Descartes and Bacon was being extended. Adam Smith (1723–1790) and Karl Marx (1818–1883), as examples, both applied deductive argumentation in their attempts to understand the evolution of society. So powerful are some of their propositions that they continue to dominate economic and social policy formation implicitly if not explicitly some 200 years later. For example, Adam Smith utilized deductive argument to advance the case for the abolition of monopolistic organizations and for free international trade. His theorem concerning the benefits of free trade, though refined over the years by economists, forms the basis for the European Community, the North American Free Trade Area, US and European anti-monopoly legislation and many policies being implemented in the former Soviet Union. As a result many have argued that free competition should be the universal norm governing all societies. But wherever we see claims to universality, we know that there will exist some equally strong counter argument. In this case, free trade argument says nothing about how the gains from trade are distributed, a concern which continues to provide the basis for considerable political debate in most countries.

Auguste Comte (1798–1857) sought to lay the foundations for a new discipline which he called 'social physics' and ultimately labelled 'sociology'. He advocated a 'positive method' involving the correlation of facts in an attempt to understand the nature of society. He viewed this positive science as the third and final stage of human development. The first stage involves the interaction between the theocracy and the secular state. In the second or metaphysical stage, there is rebellion against secular and religious authorities out of which change emerges. This is followed by a positive period during which the scientific method forms the basis for a durable and ordered society. However, in 1844 Comte began to reconsider his ideas when he became friends with the journalist Clotilde de Vaux and they both developed the thesis that rational thought needed to be subordinated to love of people, and that only motivated in this way could scientific enquiry promote progress.

Max Weber, however, argued that the subjective and objective aspects of research needed to be kept separate even though subjective concerns were driving the research endeavour, viz.

> What is really at issue is the intrinsically simple demand that the investigator and teacher should keep unconditionally separate the establishment of empirical facts (including the 'value-oriented' conduct of the empirical individual whom he is investigating) and his own practical evaluations, i.e. his evaluation of these facts as satisfactory or unsatisfactory (including among these facts evaluations made by the empirical persons who are the objects of investigation.) These two things are logically different and to deal with them as though they were the same represents a confusion of entirely heterogeneous problems. (1949, p. 11)

Whereas Descartes and Bacon claimed that deductive or inductive methods could be used in all areas of human inquiry, Weber would argue that there is a difference between the natural and social sciences involving the nature of the object of research. While care would need to be taken in distinguishing between the subjective and objective, Weber argues that once this is done, then the scientific method can be applied. For many researchers, however, the subjective and objective cannot be compartmentalized in this dichotomous fashion. Knowingly or unknowingly, we build our individual prejudices into our research.

Another attempt at trying to identify a universally applicable research methodology is associated with Karl Popper (1902–1994). He argued that the purpose of research is to falsify. Indeed he argued that rules should be established which only admit hypotheses which are falsifiable (1965, p. 49). In a sense he is applying the logic of Descartes. He seeks certainty and universality in falsification. For Popper, the only interesting propositions are those that are falsifiable. Consider his classic example based on the proposition that 'all swans are white'. Either it is true or it is false. As soon as a black swan is observed, the proposition is falsified. There is complete certainty. Indeed we have a proposition that would satisfy Plato. Unfortunately, problems of interest in social and economic research are never posed in such clearcut terms. For example, many believe that government policies to curb inflation by strictly controlling the availability of money is the prime cause of unemployment. This proposition can never be falsified because it would involve a detailed modelling of all aspects of human life including the interrelationships between the financial sector, the industrial and service sectors and labour markets. This has proven to be impossible.

The existence of such tensions were noted by Baudelaire. In 1863 he sought to define modernity as 'the transient, the fleeting, the contingent. It is the one half of art, the other being the eternal and the immutable'. Modern social research seeks to develop claims which are eternal and immutable. In contrast, we need to be aware of the transient and contingent nature of our understanding. It is the tension in this duality which in this writer's opinion needs to be drawn out and made explicit as we pursue our research projects.

But where does this leave us in our search for a unified scientific approach to research? This is the theme which the physicist and philosopher of science, Thomas Kuhn (1922–), sought to develop in his *History of Scientific Revolutions* (1962, 1974). He argues that science itself is a social process in which scientists solve puzzles posed by the dominant methodology of the particular scientific community in which they participate. Each community has its paradigms or modes of thought which define a research tradition. Expressed in such terms, scientific enquiry is bound to appear to be very conservative. Thus Kuhn argues that progress in understanding can only be achieved if existing paradigms are destroyed. The challenge of an anomaly in accepted reasoning should lead to a response urging change,

> Because it demands large-scale paradigm destruction and major shifts in the problems and techniques of normal science, the emergence of new theories is generally preceded by as period of pronounced professional insecurity. As one might expect, that insecurity is generated by the persistent failure of the puzzles of normal science to come out as they should. Failure of existing rules is the prelude to a search for new ones. (pp. 67–8)

Postmodern Perspectives

Postmodernism is a rejection of modernity and its emphasis on reason, science and rationality that was spawned after the Age of Enlightenment. It rejects modern attempts at identifying universal rules applicable to the organization of society and, in the context of this volume, to the undertaking of research designed to understand the problems of that society. It thus denies any possibility of constructing rules which define knowledge in a unique and enduring way. This does not mean that research should not be undertaken or that it should be unsystematic. In my view, postmodern perspectives assist us in focusing upon problems we had not thought existed. It is not a universal method because such a method does not exist. Rather, it is one of many ways of thinking. It suggests that greater account needs to be taken of behaviour that has not been defined as rational, that research is an uncertain process which is only capable of enhancing understanding and not developing universal laws, and that research necessarily requires the use of diverse methodologies. It suggests that whenever we appear to identify regularities in human behaviour, we should also devote effort to seeking to understand why some individuals or groups do not conform to the pattern. If we return to the duality used by Baudelaire to characterize modernity, we might conclude that modern social science has been obsessed with identifying propositions which are 'eternal and immutable' whereas postmodernism concentrates on the 'the transient, the fleeting, the contingent'.

It is impossible to do justice to the diversity of postmodern perspectives. Some are discussed by Robin Usher in Chapter 3, hence I will focus on only a few ideas that are related to the themes that I have raised in previous sections. We have seen how thinkers from the times of the Greek Academy have queried our ability to establish universal propositions about the world about us. But then what is it that we are doing? We have moved very quickly over the past decades from the latter stages of the Industrial Revolution into the early stages of the Electronic Revolution. Productive processes now require fewer workers on the production line. However, they now require more people to process the information necessary to design this machinery and to monitor its output. Financial capital has become a major ingredient in the Electronic Revolution, with the result that even more information is being created about the complex properties of diverse financial instruments. If we cannot hope to develop universal propositions about this data, what then can we do with it? Derrida (1930–) has suggested that what we are really doing is creating texts based upon our own interpretation. These texts are read by others who in turn may give them another interpretation. These texts and their interpretations then form a complex and unexplainable, uncertain dynamic within and around which we make judgments and decisions. In the social sciences, the rapid growth in the number of data bases would seem to offer more opportunities for understanding our world, yet all this new information will tax our capability to tell stories about it. Hence the continuing search for some universal rule or filter (e.g. statistical analysis) which will tell a story for us. Literally, we are writing formula novels since the assumptions and style are unchanging.

Gadamer also seeks to understand the nature of what we write and how we interpret what we read. He proposes that there is an overarching discipline *hermeneutics*, the theory and practice of interpretation. One of his major theses is that the dichotomy between subject and object which is the basis of the natural sciences has limited validity for the human sciences. Fundamental to an appreciation of his reasoning is the recognition of the role of *prejudice* and *tradition*. Gadamer argues that contemporary society has a prejudice against prejudice. He suggests that we should recognize the impossibility of eliminating prejudice from our work and instead should seek to make its basis explicit. To do this, he argues that every statement must be seen as an answer to a question and it is the question which first must be understood. In Gadamer's hermeneutics the notion of an unbiased subject investigating an object is no longer a valid dichotomy. In the human as well as the natural sciences, our perspective is influenced by the thinking which has preceded it as well as by our individual perspective. In the human sciences the subject and object are intertwined through different or similar prejudices and traditions. Gadamer admits that this process of unwinding is problematical. First, it is in principle endless. Second, there is a limit to what we can understand about the role of the unconscious in influencing our research efforts.

A second theme, already alluded to, of postmodernism is the existence of binary oppositions. Derrida argues that the systems of thought upon which text construction and interpretation are based is trapped in a world of binary oppositions. He shows that one term in each pair is always given a privileged position over the other which is marginalized or excluded. He therefore proposes to examine the term which is marginalized and in so doing seeks to show that the position of the superior term over the marginalized term is untenable. The privileged term achieves its status by what it suppresses. In this way power is achieved. The process by which binary oppositions are unwound is called *deconstruction*. In the context of social and economic research, this critique suggests that instead of, or in addition to, seeking to identify generalizations about human behaviour, we should also study difference. Instead of focusing on the average or representative person, efforts should also be made to understand those who have been categorized as marginal. Where binary oppositions appear, we should seek to identify reasons why one of the terms is marginalized. But care needs to be taken. This is not a method but a way of thinking.

This dichotomy is particularly apparent in the binary pair involving the *subject*, or investigator, and the *object*, the investigated. Traditionally, it has been the investigator who has been privileged, developing theory, designing questionnaires and undertaking the empirical investigation of the objects who are treated as separate, independent entities in the manner suggested by Weber, as noted previously. The procedure of grounded theory and action research, in contrast, involve the object in the process of project design. For example, this might involve consulting with the objects as to their concerns and enabling them to formulate questions to be included in any survey. Critics suggest that the objects may be prejudiced and that this will render the results of the survey invalid. However, this implies that the investigator (subject) is objective.

Similar themes are also apparent in the work of Foucault. His systematic studies of the marginalized, those labelled as mad or deviant from what is considered to be the norm, illustrate how madness or deviancy are relative concepts used to control the contradictions in society in a manner so as to create a society which is governable. Disciplines create the concepts of madness and deviancy and thereby create subjects both normal and by comparison abnormal. For Foucault, disciplines and methodologies, including those upon which social and economic research are based, are discourses of power which classify, process, label and position people.

Disciplines are a system of control or rules which fix the limits of enquiry. These rules are the myths that replace the concepts of the Aristotelian soul, the Augustinian God, Cartesian certainty and the rational mind as the unifying influence which empowers the individual, in this case as a researcher, and provides order to the research process. Those who do not adhere to the agenda and methods of the discipline are marginalized. The message which Foucault is delivering is that by working entirely within the walls of a discipline, valid problems and methodologies for dealing with them are bound to become excluded. The preservation of the rules of the discipline becomes a prime task absorbing the efforts of the researcher, rather than actual research. For Foucault, it is necessary to identify modes of living, including modes of research, which minimize the risk of domination by institutions such as the disciplines of scientific inquiry. Power and freedom are therefore not incompatible. In order to reduce the one-sided dominance of the institutions that we have inherited, modified or created and within which we work, Foucault would argue that we as individuals and as researchers must seek to exercise power. It is not the Academy or discipline which exercises power, but the individuals who belong to these institutions. They as individuals choose whether or not to submit themselves to the rules.

Feminist Perspectives on Research

All of the thinkers referred to so far are male. This is not an oversight but simply a statement of the fact that those recognized as major contributors to epistemology are male. This has led women, particularly over the past fifty years, to call attention to the patriarchal foundations of research programmes and methodologies. Basically, social and economic research has been undertaken by men about problems facing men. This protest has led to greater emphasis on the provision of equal opportunities for women in higher education and research and to the recognition that funding needs to be given to projects designed to improve understanding of problems facing women. The particular notion of equality underlying these developments can be traced back to Plato who sought to develop the dichotomy that one's rational mind and body were independent; thus although women possessed different physiologies their mental capacities were identical to those of men. Consequently, there exists no basis for discrimination. In contempoary language research could be gender neutral and expressed in gender neutral language.

However, over the past fifteen years, many feminist researchers have questioned the validity of equal opportunities in general, and in particular, the context of research initiatives. They argue that this approach perpetuates the patriarchal nature of universities and their research activities. The problem is that to be equal, women must be like men. In other words, there is a privileging of the male perspective, thereby marginalizing women's issues in the university research agenda. Indeed the subject/object dichotomy is often used to exemplify this point. In the past, it has been men who have set the research agenda for women's studies without the participation of women in the identification of their problems or in the design of research strategies. Sawicki (1991) illustrates this point in respect of health policy and research.

This has led to an alternative approach involving the recognition of difference as a basis for action. Women have different problems from men for a variety of historical, cultural, social and physiological reasons. It is not surprising, therefore, that many feminist researchers have sought to integrate postmodern perspectives into their research agenda. They seek greater awareness about the prejudices that influence education and research. This involves recognition that social structures (including those within educational and research institutions) whether based along gender, racial, religious or ethnic lines are designed to perpetuate the power of the relevant establishment, that there is no representative woman, let alone representative man, that the role of the unconscious (as opposed to the rational, conscious self), is important and that progress needs to be made in unwinding the subject/object dichotomy prevalent in university activities. As such, contemporary feminist research strategy is increasingly emphasizing the validity of diverse research methodologies, thereby enabling the use of whatever concepts are required to understand a particular problem. The question is posed 'what are the best ways to understand a problem?' rather than 'I have a method — what problems can I apply it to?'. (The reader is referred to the chapters in this volume by Pat Usher and Joan Orme and to the thoughts of feminist scholars such as Hekman (1990), Flax (1990) and Lather (1991)).

There are no rules or strict agenda associated with the feminist project, hence it is not a discipline in the conventional sense. Like postmodernism, it is a perspective. Feminist research focuses upon the problems facing women and from a perspective that is impossible for a male. In so doing it challenges the patriarchal discourse of the traditional disciplines. Because feminist research strategy does not consist of rules that would enable it be classified as a discipline, feminist scholars leave themselves open to criticisms from those to seek to defend and advance the patriarchal views that emanated from The Enlightenment. But, any such defence is bound to fail. In my opinion the open-endedness of feminist research practice offers a solid basis for all contemporary social and economic research. It explicitly recognizes the tensions that have been the subject of so much discussion over the centuries. Attempts to create rules delimiting the creation of knowledge have been shown to be incapable of providing solutions to the major contemporary socio-economic problems of unemployment and poverty. Feminist researchers thus recognize the futility of more than 2500 years of search for universal propositions governing the process of knowledge creation. By adopting such an open-ended approach to my own research, I am able to draw upon whatever methodologies and methods which seem appropriate to me when trying to understand a particular problem. The focus of my research is the problem rather than the methodology.

References

ANSELM OF CANTERBURY (1077/78) *Proslogion*, translated by Charlesworth, M.J. (1965), London, Oxford University Press.

ARISTOTLE (1994) *Posterior Analytics*, translated by Jonathan Barnes, Oxford Clarendon Press.

AUGUSTINE (1950) *Against the Academicians*, translated by O'Meara, J. London,

BACON FRANCIS, (1878) *Novum Organum*, Oxford, Clarendon Press.

BAUDELAIRE CHANLES, (1992) *Selected Writing on Art and Literature*, London, Peugvin.

COMTE AUGUSTE, (1830/1842) *Course on Positive Philosophy* in ANDRESKI, S. (Ed.) *The Essential Comte*, London, Croom Helm.

DERRIDA J. (1976) *La Voix et le Phenome*, Paris, Presses Universitaires de France.

DESCARTES, RENÉ (1628) *Regulae ad directionem ingenii*, translated by COTTINGHAM, J. STOOTHOFF R., and MURDOCH, D. in *Descartes: Selected Philosophical Writings* (1988), Cambridge University Press.

FLAX, J. (1990) *Thinking Fragments: Psychoanalysis, Feminism, and Postmodernism in the Contemporary West*, Berkeley, University of California Press.

FOUCAULT, M. (1972) 'The Discourse on Language', in *The Archaeology of Knowledge*, New York, Pantheon Books.

GADAMER, H-G. (1981) *Reason in the Age of Science*, Cambridge, Mass., MIT Press.

GAUNILO (1078) *A Reply on Behalf of the Fool*, translated by M.J. Charlesworth, published with ANSELM's *Proslogion*, London, Oxford University Press.

HEKMAN, S. (1990) *Gender and Knowledge*, Cambridge England, Polity Press.

KUHN, T. (1962, 1974) *The Structure of Scientific Revolutions*, second edition, Chicago: University of Chicago Press.

LATHER, P. (1991) *Getting Smart: Feminist Research and Pedagogy With/In the Postmodern*, London, Routledge.

LYOTARD, J-F. (1992) *The Postmodern Explained to Children*, London, Turnaround.

MARX, KARL (1974) *Das Capital*, London, Peugvin.

PLATO, (1883) *Theaetetus*, translated by Campbell, L. Oxford, Clarendon Press.

PLATO, (1976) *Republic*, translated by Liusay, A.D., London, J.M. Dent

POPPER, K. (1965) *The Logic of Scientific Discovery*, New York, Harper and Row.

SAWICKI, J. (1991) *Disciplining Foucault*, New York, Routledge.

SCHUMPETER, J. (1954) *History of Economic Analysis*, New York, Oxford University Press.

SMITH, A. (1950) *The Wealth of Nations*, London, J.M. Dent.

WEBER, M. (1949) *The Methodology of the Social Sciences*, New York, The Free Press of Glencoe.

Part 1

The Nature of Enquiry

This first group of chapters addresses many of the philosophical issues embedded in social and economic research. In Chapter 3, Robin Usher pursues the theme that research is really a form of story telling and that the search for 'deep realities' underlying the modernist perspective is misleading. He focuses upon the postmodern perspective which questions many aspects of research which many take for granted, for example that data is independent of its interpretations or that there exist universally accepted criteria for discriminating amongst theories. In the second part of his chapter, Usher develops the theme that research is a social practice which expresses itself in textual form, and that the autobiography of both the researcher and the reader are essential to the interpretation of the text.

In Chapter 4 Pat Usher also questions the modernist project with its emphasis on rationality, order and certainty. In so doing she argues that it is patriarchal in nature and suggests that various themes should form the basis of feminist research. These include, amongst others, recognition that: a) gender is a pervasive influence that guides the questions and criteria involved in research projects, b) that all theories are a product of historical and socio-political influences, and, c) that a multiplicity of research methods should be used within an interdisciplinary environment. Chapters 5 and 6 examine the application of the economic method to disciplines other than economics, namely politics and sociology. The economic method involves deductive theorizing which takes as given that economic agents, i.e. individuals and firms, act rationally so as maximize their individual objectives. As Alan Hamlin points out, such objectives need not be narrowly conceived and could include a wide range of altruistic aims. He seeks to develop this mode of thought as a basis for researching public policy. In Chapter 6, George McKenzie lays out some of the formal structure of the economic method against the background of Gary Becker's analysis of family behaviour. His prime objective is encourage the reader to work through an important, modern mode of analysis as a basis for understanding it as a truth producing practice within the discourse of a particular discipline.

3   Telling a Story about Research and Research as Story-telling: Postmodern Approaches to Social Research

Robin Usher

In his postmodern text 'America', Jean Baudrillard writes that 'the point is not to write the sociology or psychology of the car, the point is to drive . . . that way you learn more about this society than all academia could tell you' (Baudrillard, 1988; p. 54). For Baudrillard, participating in American driving behaviour is a better way to understand contemporary American society than through 'research' as conventionally understood.

Although we can understand what Baudrillard is getting at, it's very likely that we find his remarks disturbing. We are so used to thinking of research as providing a special kind of methodologically validated knowledge about society which 'merely' driving could not possibly provide that we suspect Baudrillard of not being entirely serious in his remarks. For the same reason, it's not easy to accept the notion of research as story-telling. We think of story-telling as 'unserious', as fictional, whereas our image of research is that it is about 'truth' and is therefore an altogether more serious business. Equally, it's not easy to accept that an account of research is an example of telling a story. To attempt to explicate the 'nature' of research through a story does not somehow seem appropriate.

However, another and different reading of Baudrillard's remarks, would be that the task of understanding or finding out about something is best approached indirectly and obliquely. It is this 'message' which informs my starting-point because I want to present postmodern approaches to research, initially at least, through a reading of Umberto Eco's novels — *The Name of the Rose* (Eco, 1984) and *Foucault's Pendulum* (Eco, 1990). This may seem a rather indirect and oblique way of proceeding but my argument is that a postmodern understanding of social research is best secured in this way. Thus I will try to exemplify through the approach itself something important about the postmodern. I will try to show the textuality, 'fictionality', and narrativity or story-telling dimensions of research. I shall present research as story-telling by first telling a story (Eco's) which although not about research can nonetheless help us to understand research from a postmodern perspective.

The stories that unfold in Eco's novels have often been seen as a metaphor for the epistemological quest of the modernist project, a quest for knowledge of the deep underlying causes of events, for unitary meaning and the total explanation of phenomena. In *Foucault's Pendulum*, the three protagonists through their work as publishers of esoterica, become intrigued by conspiracy theory writings that purport to explain history in terms of a grand 'plan' cleverly hidden by its authors — the epistemological quest taken to its ultimate (and irrational) end. On the assumption that the more unlikely the connections made the more convincing the plot which ensues, they set out to devise a plan of their own using random computer-generated associations. When a group committed to a conspiracy theory of history hears of the plan it proceeds to hunt them down for their hidden 'knowledge'. The more they protest that there is no 'plan' in reality, the more the group believes that there is. They end up meeting bizarre deaths at the hands of this group for a knowledge which does not 'exist'.

At one level, *Foucault's Pendulum* is questioning the modernist separation of knowledge from power. For its authors, the plan is nonsense, the knowledge it purveys fictional and 'harmless'. Yet in the event it is powerful in its effects and in ways not obvious to those concocting it. The message then is that knowledge which purports to 'explain' reality in terms of its deep underlying meanings is dangerous and must be treated with caution lest it overwhelm those who create it and those who become subject to it — in *Foucault's Pendulum* these are one and the same.

More generally, *Foucault's Pendulum* is also a cautionary tale to all those in the social sciences whose objective, in line with their commitment to the modernist project (the search for deep underlying 'realities'), has been the development of explanatory 'grand designs'. The story of the 'plan' can be read as an allegory of all the grand designs that have sought to erect structures and systems, overarching theories — designs which fabricate the world to the extent that this is what the world ends up becoming. The thinking that lies behind this is that if only the jigsaw can be constructed from the pieces of data randomly strewn around we can have the 'big picture' which will explain and give a meaning to the disorder and contingency of the world. Armed with this deep knowledge, the world can then be controlled and changed and we, through this, can become empowered. This is the totalizing dream of the modernist project, a dream which in the end has nothing to do with reason but everything to do with desire — the desire for mastery and ultimately control — and hence is itself totalitarian.

In *The Name of the Rose* a monk, William of Baskerville, is called in to solve a number of inexplicable murders at a monastery with a library which contains the most extensive collection of books and manuscripts in the Christian world. This quest then becomes entangled with a quest for the book whose identity is unknown yet whose possession is the motive for the murders.

The plot of the novel is centred on the library — a library which is itself a labyrinth with many hidden secrets, the foremost being the mysterious book around which the action revolves. The library is where all knowledge is to be found — if you know how to find it — and only someone like a detective, the epistemological searcher par excellence with deeply penetrating observation and highly developed powers of reasoning can unlock the secrets of the library-labyrinth and thereby know the 'truth' (the identity both of the murderer and the book).

As McHale (1992) points out the essence of the modernist project is encapsulated in the question 'how can the world be truthfully known'? The detective is therefore an apt metaphor for the modernist social researcher. He (and Eco deliberately makes him a 'he') seeks the truth usually in the form of a quest for a missing or hidden item of knowledge and does not rest until this item is found and the truth discovered. The problem, then, which both the detective and the researcher grapple with is *epistemological*, a problem of the accessibility and circulation of knowledge where the individual mind, aided only by its power of reasoning, has to grapple with an elusive, hidden reality to find the deep hidden meaning that underlies chaotic and disordered events.

Yet, William of Baskerville, the epistemological hero, the prototype detective-scientist, ultimately fails in his quest. He discovers the 'truth' (or rather *a* truth because the library contains many truths) but only by stumbling upon it rather than by a successful chain of reasoning. As he himself finally admits, there was no mastermind, no plot, and no pattern underlying the murders.

Thus the champion of empiricism and reason only 'solves' the mystery through constant misinterpretation of the evidence and even then only through irrational associational leaps prompted by a dream and a grammatical error, both recounted by his adolescent sidekick. This element of the irrational (or the non-rational) in William's detective work represents a challenge to the very adequacy of and faith in systematic reason and scientific method. In the novel, it subverts the detective story's epistemological structure and in the parallel world of the modernist project it subverts the epistemological quest at the very heart of that project. What takes its place is another, alternative concern — a postmodern concern — displacing the modernist concern with how the world is to be truly known with the ontological question — what is this world and what is to be done in it?

It is this ontological notion of 'constructed worlds' which mark Eco's novels as postmodern. In *Foucault's Pendulum*, the three protagonists by putting together a story construct a world which becomes murderously real. In *The Name of the Rose* there are a plurality of largely incommensurable worlds created at a variety of different levels which confront each other. Both texts embody the very postmodernist notion that different languages, different registers of the same language, different discourses each construct the world differently; in effect, different worlds are 'knowledged' or 'languaged' into being.

At the same time, however, just as these worlds are created they are destabilized — in other words, their status as constructed worlds is laid bare and the very process and strategy of 'world-making' is thus foregrounded. In *The Name of the Rose* there is a doubling or mirroring of a world within a world. The structure of the library for example is a scale model of the known world, its floor plan reproducing the map of the world. It is a labyrinth that represents a labyrinthine world. This doubling of worlds opens up an abyss of a potentially infinite regress which destabilizes the world constructed by the text and by so doing foregrounds the concern with 'world-making' and the role of language in the construction of worlds. The text becomes self-referential or self-reflexive by drawing attention to its own world-making through the use of textual strategies such as doubling.

It is perhaps worth remembering at this point that stylistically postmodernism is often said to have its origins in architecture. Modernist structures are homogeneous, oriented within right-angled grids and sharply bounded, displaying the 'tyranny of the straight line' (Kvale, 1992; p. 37); they are meant to be triumphs of reason aptly reflecting the epistemological project of modernity. Postmodernist structures, on the other hand, are skewed and distorted, displaying shifts and transformations, ambiguous and unpredictable, with no fixed boundaries. They suspend the notion of a clear final ordering and instead emphasize ambiguity, the intermixing of orders and styles in a general irony, pastiche and playfulness. Above all, they reflexively *draw attention to themselves* as built structures. In *The Name of the Rose* Eco projects, through the 'space' of the library, a reflection of this postmodern conception of the world. As readers, we experience it as both an interior and physical space of uncertainty, complexity and disorientation. In Eco's texts there are spaces where worlds are both made and subverted. Like postmodern structures, we become aware of complexity, are plunged into uncertainty and disoriented. Yet this in itself is productive because it draws our attention to the process of world-making and directs us towards a reflexive stance.

Jameson (1991) suggests that postmodern spaces should be read as allegories of the contemporary ontological condition, the almost unthinkably complex, interrelated and interactive, global system of multinational capitalism, the information superhighway and the condition of 'hyper-reality' where the signs and symbols of reality have become more 'real' than reality itself. Postmodernist 'space' points to the ungraspable of this world and thus as it can be seen as standing for the futility of our attempts to master it through totalizing knowledge and the discovery of deep underlying meanings. This is the 'lesson' that both William of Baskerville and the protagonists of *Foucault's Pendulum* learn.

Some Features of a Postmodern Approach

As we have seen therefore postmodernism displaces epistemology. There is a general postmodern scepticism about epistemology's traditional aim of distinguishing true, certain knowledge through a general account of the nature and limits of knowledge. Epistemology privileges scientific method as the methodological guarantee of a true and certain knowledge. It seeks to formulate universal rules as to what can be counted as scientific knowledge, a set of universal characteristics that qualifies a practice as scientific, a theory or explanation as adequate. Postmodernism therefore questions epistemology's dominant positivist/empiricist conception of scientific knowledge which traditionally sets the standard and provides the model for all knowledge claiming to be scientific. In particular, it challenges the leading assumptions of the positivist/empiricist research tradition that:

- observation is value-neutral and atheoretical,
- experience is a 'given',
- a univocal and transparent language is possible,
- data is independent of its interpretations, and

- there are universal conditions of knowledge and criteria for deciding between theories.

In the postmodern, there is a questioning of whether knowledge is established through systematic empirical observation and experiment, or whether a necessary first step requires a shifting of the way the world is seen and the construction of a new world to investigate. In other words, ontology precedes epistemology.

On the other hand, a postmodern approach does not simply embrace the alternative hermeneutic/interpretive research tradition since it sees this as still implictly operating within the terms and discourse of the positivist/empiricist tradition — in other words, the emphasis on the 'subjective' instead of the 'objective' is merely a reversal which still works within a framework of 'objective-subjective' as polar opposites. Instead, a postmodern approach seeks to subvert this dichotomy and suggest alternatives which radically challenge and critique the dominant epistemological discourse in all its various forms.

One of these alternatives is to turn to the actual historically located practices of the various sciences, natural as well as social. This historical approach, that for example informs the work of Kuhn (1970), displaces the essentialist and transcendental view of science which is to be found in both the positivist/empiricist and hermeneutic/interpretive traditions and instead argues that all sciences are social practices. This emphasis on the actual practice of a science highlights its specificity and situatedness and the practice-constituted criteria for judging the validity of knowledge-claims and theory choice. I shall say more about this later.

Another postmodern alternative arises as a consequence of the displacement of epistemology and the foregrounding of ontology. This has two important aspects. The first, which we have touched on when discussing Eco's texts, is to do with 'world-making' through language, discourses and texts. Postmodernism sees knowledge-generation as a practice of 'languaging', a practice of textual production. Here, language is not conceived as a mirror held up to the world, as simply a transparent vehicle for conveying the meaning of an independent external reality. Since there is always an already existing structure of significations which gives rather than reflects meaning, referents are an effect of language. No form of knowledge can be separated from language, discourses and texts at work within culture. The structures, conceptuality and conventions of language, embodied in discourses and texts — language as a meaning-constituting system — govern what can be known and what can be communicated.

One consequence of this is that knowledge, being relative to discourses, is always partial and perspectival. Thought and experience, the positivist/empiricist bedrock, are not independent of socio-cultural contexts and practices. As we have seen already when considering epistemological research traditions, they are coded by language and discourse in terms of binary oppositions, e.g. masculine-feminine, subject-object, rational-irrational that constitute identity through powerful and oppressive hierarchies.

The second aspect of the postmodern is a decentring of the knowing subject, the epistemological subject with a universal and essential human nature — unitary, rational, consciousness-centred and the originary point of thought and action. This essential nature is conceived as allowing subjects to be autonomous of the world and to occupy an Archimedean point that transcends their own subjectivity, history and socio-cultural location. This stance of 'objectivity', where the subject is a pure experiencer and reasoner transcending particularity, partiality and contingency, is the condition for the interchangeability of knowing subjects and hence the public verifiability of scientific knowledge (Code, 1993).

Postmodernism challenges and displaces this abstract, transcendental subject arguing instead that subjects cannot be separated from their subjectivity, history and socio-cultural location. In the postmodern, there are no Archimedean points, the subject is instead decentred, enmeshed in the 'text' of the world, constituted in inter-subjectivity, discourse and language. Equally, the separation of subject and object, objectivity and subjectivity, is itself a position maintainable only so long as the knower is posited as abstract and decontextualized and the object known posited as the 'other' unable to reflect back on and affect the knower (Acker *et al.*, 1991).

The need to take account of the status of knowers-researchers and their socio-cultural contexts, the intimate inseparability of knower and known, the known and the means of knowing, the impossibility of separating the subjects and objects of research challenges the epistemological assumption of an 'objective' world and the foundational systems of thought which secure, legitimate and privilege 'objective' ways of knowing that world.

As I have noted earlier, knowledge is never absolute and universal. In the postmodern, there is a foregrounding of complexity, uncertainty, heterogeneity and difference. There is a questioning of the powerful notion that there is 'one true reality', stable and ordered, that exists independently of knowers, which can be experienced 'as it really is' and which is best represented in scientific models of research. Instead, postmodernists argue that the 'real' is unstable, in flux and con-tingent. Although we can sense the real, knowing it is only possible by representing it through a signifying system. But in representation, the real is not simply being reflected 'as it really is' but is being constructed or shaped in a way particular to the codings of the signifying system. As we have seen, these codings take the form of binary, hierarchical and oppressive oppositions.

What this implies is that social events, processes and phenomena are indeter-minate. Knowledge in the form of predictive generalizations requires a closure which itself requires a determinate, orderly 'real'. Hence the closure that is neces-sary can only be *imposed* — it is not something that exists naturally in the real and is simply reflected in the form of predictive generalizations. It is not that closure is impossible but since it can only be imposed then the very status of this know-ledge becomes questionable. Closure since it involves violence raises questions of power which are not supposed to be relevant in 'scientific' research. Once ques-tions of power do become relevant, however, then the 'objectivity' of the research process becomes highly problematic.

The need to take account of the dimension of power challenges the possibility of 'disinterested' research and value-free knowledge. Science is both constituted by a particular set of values and itself is value-constituting yet the scientific attitude is one that continually attempts to suppress the place of values and conceal the workings of power. Research can be seen as an enactment of power relations. By denying the place of values and power, science becomes a form of mystification and a source of oppression. As Foucault has argued, power is always present in any attempt to know, indeed power works its effects through its intimate interconnection with knowledge. It is for this reason that a postmodern approach to research highlights the need to consider not only outcomes and methods but also the implication of research with power and unspoken values.

The dependence of knowledge on socio-cultural practices and contexts, unacknowledged values, tacit discourses and interpretive traditions means that research is embedded in unconscious fore-structures of understanding, the 'unsaid' and 'unsayable' that is the condition of any methodical knowing. All knowledge of the real is textual, i.e. always already signified, interpreted or 'written' and therefore a 'reading' which can be 're-written' and 're-read'. Hence there is neither an originary point of knowledge nor a final interpretation. However, as I have just noted, some readings are more powerful than others. The most powerful readings are those imposed by the violence of closure and the 'metaphysics of presence' — the claim to a direct and unmediated knowledge of the real that can only be provided by scientific method. Yet given that all readings are subject to contingency and the historical moment in which they are read, and given that the object of scientific research is always open to contest, then all claims to presence, to unmediated knowledgeability, are always problematic.

Postmodernism challenges foundationalism, the position that knowledge is founded in disciplines, and the consequent boundary-defining and maintenance that is characteristic of disciplinary knowledge. There are two aspects to this. The first is that social scientists located as they are in the modernist epistemological project, want to give 'reasoned', connected and totalizing accounts. But as we have seen, the world they investigate and seek to explain is not one that can readily be *reflected* in their theories and accounts. It is, in other words, not organized naturally into disciplinary compartments. They are therefore always as (Acker *et al.*, 1991; p. 149) point out in the business of attempting to systematically 'reconstruct social reality and to put these reconstructions into the form of a social theory'.

The social sciences conceive of themselves as representing the real whereas what they are actually doing is 'writing' it. Social reality does not exist as an extra-discursive context, rather the real and the discursive are intimately interwoven . . . 'the social is written . . . there is no extra-discursive real outside cultural [i.e. meaning] systems . . . the social world does not consist of ready-made objects that are put into representation' (Game, 1991; p. 4). If disciplinary theorizing is itself a practice of writing, then theory cannot be tested against the real. The question then becomes by what discursive strategies does a discipline maintain its claims to the status of knowledge. In the case of the social sciences, this is done through a privileged representation of social reality based on the binary opposition 'real-representation' and the consequent repression of the fictionality or textuality of the social sciences.

Social Research in a Postmodern Mode

Text

Earlier on, I introduced the idea that all research is a social practice. I want to argue that all social research is located in knowledge-producing communities. Although these are not exactly communities in the Kuhnian sense with a single and settled research paradigm and a single disciplinary matrix (Kuhn, 1970), the production of any kind of systematic theoretical or 'scientific' knowledge (as against informal or craft knowledge) always takes place and indeed requires a knowledge or research community of some sort, no matter how flexible and loosely structured it may be.

This inseparability from a knowledge-producing community is what makes research a *social* practice. One consequence of this is that it is never a matter of researchers 'doing their own thing', although this individualistic conception is a powerful one. Even though it is not always carried out collectively, research is always collective in two important senses. First, in the sense that it is intertextual (I shall discuss this further later). Second, that it is a delimited set of activities legitimated by a relevant community where certain activities are judged appropriate and function as criteria for validating knowledge outcomes, whilst others are ruled out of order and excluded. Communities define rules of exclusion, set boundaries and impose closures. This narrows what can be done and what will count as legitimate research, valid knowledge outcomes and 'truth'.

The existence of a knowledge-producing community is a taken-for-granted 'background', implicit yet largely unacknowledged in specific research activity. As researchers, our awareness of the activity of research is normally in terms of a 'process' systems metaphor, e.g. that research is a process or system with the following stages — literature search, hypothesis generation, generation of field data, analysis of data (usually by quantitative means), validation of hypothesis, conclusions and recommendations. Of course, the notion that research is a 'system' does have a certain heuristic value but it is also very limiting because it makes research seem a mechanistic and algorithmic, a step-by-step linear, teleological and finite activity. Most significantly, it projects a model of research as both disembedded — an essentially ahistorical, apolitical and *technical* activity, a transcendental, contextless set of procedures and methods — and disembodied in the sense of being carried out by abstracted, asocial, genderless individuals without a history or culture.

If instead we see research as a social *practice* we are better able to recognize that it is not a universal process of applying a set of general methods or of following an algorithmic procedure. Rather methods and procedures are themselves a function of the knowledge-community's practice, its 'culture', its networks of implicit beliefs and pre-suppositions, whose rules, boundaries and exclusions, no matter how flexible, legitimate and sanction certain kinds of activity and exclude others.

Consider for a moment one of the effects of a practice's exclusions. Let's take as an example the fact that social and educational research cannot be presented in the form of a literary text. This may seem a wild example but it demonstrates an important point through its very extremeness. If research is a social practice, a practice of producing knowledge that is socially validated, then it is the socially located activity of research that *constructs* a world to be researched. Research can be seen as 'knowledgeing', with the implication that what's going on is not simply a matter of representing, reflecting or reporting a world that already exists. Research therefore does not passively reflect, it actively constructs — but it does so in a particular way.

Now, of course, literature (or 'fictioning') is also a social practice where worlds are created. We have seen examples of this earlier in considering Eco's texts. In this sense, research is just as 'fictional' as literature even though both are equally 'real'. Presenting research in the form of a literary text is just as much creating a world, albeit a very different one, as presenting research in terms of the linear process model. I'm not arguing that social research is the *same* as literature but I am saying that both are 'world-making' social practices. More specifically, both are textual practices, examples of world-making through particular ways of 'reading' and 'writing', interpreting and understanding, the world. Social research is therefore a textual practice which, however, cannot be presented in the form of a literary text because that is outside the boundaries of what is constituted as acceptable by the knowledge communities of social science.

The 'world-making', constructive quality of research can either be denied — as it is, for example, in the positivist/empiricist tradition — or it can be acknowledged. To acknowledge it involves laying bare the activity of knowledging — 'in our action is our knowing' (Lather, 1991; p. xv) — and foregrounding what is involved in 'world-making'. It is in a sense to *research* the research, to bend the research back upon itself, to ask 'by what practices, strategies and devices is world-making achieved?'. By asking this question, the research act is made self-referential or *reflexive*. This is an activity which is familiar enough in literary texts (as we have seen with Eco's texts) but the positivist/empiricist tradition that is dominant in the knowledge-producing communities of social research denies it through its own textual practices. Yet since all research, including positivist/empiricist research, is a textual practice and since reflexivity is a function of textuality then any denial of reflexivity misses out an important dimension of the activity of research (Usher, 1993).

Traditionally, reflexivity has been seen as a 'problem' to be dealt with through 'scientific method'. It is in this way that claims to 'presence', of direct and unmediated knowledge of the world, could supposedly be established. Yet since the activity of knowing is not simply a passive representation of the world and since *how* the world is known influences *what* is known, then presence is itself a function of those activities. In other words, presence can only be achieved by 'presencing' practices — hence a direct and unmediated knowledge of the world is impossible. The world always comes already interpreted — in other words, as a text. As such, it has an openness, an indeterminacy which as we have seen earlier can only be closed, made determinate, measurable, lawful, by violence.

To foreground the textuality of research and the 'absence' of presence leads immediately to the question 'why do research if you cannot say anything about what is out there and all research is self-reflexive?' (Steier, 1991; p. 10). But this is to assume that because the knower is constitutively inseparable from the activity of knowing then reflexivity must always be a *problem*. There is, however, an alternative which is to see reflexivity as a *resource*, to acknowledge and work with it, but doing so requires foregrounding research as a textual, presencing practice rather than a neutral, technicist process. Another way of putting this is that reflexivity can be a resource when the place of the active researcher is recognized — 'why do research for which you must deny responsibility for what *you* [i.e. the researcher] have found?' (Steier, ibid). Yet we are hesitant to see reflexivity as a resource since it seems to make research 'subjective', a subtle form of writing the self; a different, non-literary way of writing one's autobiography?

I want to argue that a postmodern approach to social research highlights the need for researchers to be reflexive and to subject themselves, as 'knowledgers', to critical self-scrutiny. Being reflexive is not a lapse into 'subjectivity', it involves more than laying bare one's psychological self or revealing one's biases. Hence research is more than just writing the self in an individualistic sense. Here I want to suggest that an autobiographical stance which on the face of it appears to enshrine research as 'writing the self' actually helps us to see reflexivity differently (in a socio-cultural rather than an individualistic sense) and thus provides critical conceptual resources for interrogating the production (writing) and consumption (reading) of research texts.

Con-text

If research is a textual practice, a textualizing of the world through the production and consumption of authoritative knowledge-claims in the form of texts, then these always have a 'con-text', in the sense of that which is *with* the text. What is 'with' the text in this sense is the situated autobiography of the researcher/reader.

Here, what is being highlighted is the socio-cultural subjective, the contextual self or to put it another way, the embodied and embedded self. By asking reflexive questions about con-text we can scrutinize the 'knowledging' effects of the self that researches (writes) and the self that 'reads' research, a self with an autobiography marked by the significations of gender, sexuality, ethnicity, class, etc. These significations are socio-cultural products that effect, through writing, the very forms, outcomes and consequences of research and the way in which research is 'read'. They are not simply biases which can be eliminated by first admitting them and then placing ourselves under methodological control. These are 'biases', ineliminably part of us, which can be recognized but not willed away. They are the marks of the trajectory of our desires and emotional investments in the research act.

Pre-text

If research is a textual practice, then language as a signifying system assumes a central place. Here language needs to be seen not simply as a neutral vehicle for conveying representations but as an activity of 'languaging', the means through which the representational work of research is carried out. Consequently, research texts have a 'pre-text' in the sense of that which is *before* the text; language as the repository of meaning, discourses as particular ways of organizing meanings, the textual strategies, literary conventions and rhetorical devices of writing. As Shotter points out:

> It is by the use of such rhetorical devices — as reference to 'special methods of investigation', 'objective evidence', 'special methods of proof', 'independent witnesses', etc. — that those with competence in such procedures can construct their 'factual statements' and claim authority for them as revealing a special 'true' reality behind appearances . . . (Shotter, 1993; p. 25)

This is an aspect of research that we pay little attention to — we focus on methods and outcomes and don't ask how meanings are created and received. As Game (1991; p. 28) points out 'if research is understood as writing, critical attention is drawn to the process of textual production which *is* research, as opposed to a final writing-up of research results'. This is due to the academic form that most research reports take and which actually functions to conceal their own textuality; the pre-text repressed by the form itself.

However, it is by asking reflexive questions about pre-text that we can better understand that the self as researcher writes within prescribed forms (and this is why, to answer an earlier question, research cannot be presented as a literary text) that create the meanings of the textualized world that is researched and of the texts that make knowledge claims about that world.

Sub-text

I referred earlier to research as a practice of 'presencing', of the making of authoritative claims to unmediated knowledgeability in the form of truthful representations of the world. What this implies is that claims to presence are implicated with the operation of power, the ability to claim and establish presence. Thus research texts have a 'sub-text' in the sense of that which is *beneath* the text; the operation of research paradigms and traditions and the power/knowledge discourses through which they are expressed and have their effects (Foucault, 1980). The research act is constituted by power relations between researcher and researched whose outcome is the production and consumption of 'powerful' texts, texts which frequently become part of regulatory mechanisms in the domain of governmentality.

This is something we often find it difficult to accept since given the traditional separation of knowledge from power, we tend to think of research, particulary our personal research, as innocent, 'power-less', perhaps even useful and emancipatory. A reflexive questioning of the sub-text enables us to better interrogate the implication of our practice within discourses of power and how it becomes part of oppressive and dominant discourses through a 'reflexive', in the sense of a taken-for-granted, acceptance of the neutrality of research, its pragmatic usefulness or its emancipatory potential — and how as writers and readers of research we become part of such discourses despite our best intentions.

Inter-text

Research in the scientific mode generally takes the form of decontextualized knowledge claims which are made through and against other textually-embodied claims. To paraphrase Kuhn, researchers do not match up their claims against an independently existing objective reality but against other claims. Thus research texts have an 'inter-text' in the sense of that which is *between* texts. Intertextuality refers to the inhabiting of any particular text by 'the structure of the trace . . . the interlacings and resonances with other texts' (Wood, 1990; p. 47) and which works both at the conscious and unconscious levels. In effect, intertextuality points to the place of history in textual production — the way in which history is inserted into the text and particular texts into history.

At the conscious level, intertextuality works through citations that are actually 'present'. Unconsciously, intertextual traces are always present both between the researcher's own 'different' texts and and between the researcher's text and other texts. As Barthes puts it:

> a text is not a line of words releasing a single theological meaning [the author's meaning] but a multidimensional space in which a variety of writings, none of them original, blend and clash. The text is a tissue of quotations drawn from the innumerable centres of cultures. (Barthes, 1977; p. 146)

These traces, the 'tissue of quotations' are citations that although not physically present are present as 'absences'. They speak *through* the text in an endless referability and are potent in their effects even though they are not spoken about *in* the text.

Intertextuality means first, that texts have a referability, they can be cited authoritatively without the 'presence' of their author. Secondly, it means that texts are productive in the sense that they both transform prior texts (texts can be 're-read' through new texts) and make possible new texts (a text can only be written if there is a culture of writing and discourses which 'reveal' a world to be researched). However, this productivity is bounded, socially and culturally constrained and subject to relations of power (Fairclough, 1992). Researchers are never fully the 'authors' of their texts.

A Postmodern Approach to Research: an Example

I shall now try to show what it means to do research in the postmodern mode by presenting an example drawn from Patti Lather's account of her research 'Staying dumb?: Student resistance to liberatory curriculum' (Lather, 1991). Here she explores what it means to do research differently although on the face of it the research is conventionally empiricist. She collects data from interviews, research reports and entries from her own reflective diary. The research was a three-year enquiry into student resistance to a liberatory curriculum in an introductory women's study course.

Her aims were to:

1 Create a space from which the voices of those not normally heard could be heard,
2 Move outside conventional research texts, and the unacknowledged textual devices found in 'scientific' research,
3 Ask questions about the way she as researcher constructed her research text and organized meaning,
4 Challenge the myth of a found world in research and its effective communication outside the intrusion of language and an embodied researcher,
5 Explore a complex and heterogeneous reality which does not fit neatly into pre-established categories,
6 Be concerned with the politics of research by recognizing that categorizing is an act of power which always marginalizes and,
7 Put the researcher back into the picture. The researcher is a social subject in relation with others. The specificity of the researcher, for example Patti Lather's interest in emancipatory pedagogy, shapes the process and product of her enquiry.

What is particulary interesting for me about this research is that Patti Lather analyzed and presented her data not simply in a conventional form but in the form of four tales:

1 A *realist* tale — a tale based on the assumption of a found world knowable through adequate method and theory. In other words, a conventional account.
2 A *critical* tale — a tale based on the assumption that there are powerful determining structures underlying the world which are invisible to everyday understandings. The researcher's job is to bring these out into the open and and by so doing challenge their dominance.
3 A *deconstructive* tale — a tale that attempts to undermine powerful tales, such as the two above, that appear to, as it were, tell themselves. This tale discloses the constructed nature of other tales (that the story they tell is not simply a reflection of the world 'as it really is') and in this way foregrounds its own constructed nature.
4 A *reflexive* tale — a tale which brings the teller of the tale (the researcher) back into the narrative. Here the idea is to show that the author/researcher does not exist in a transcendental realm but is embodied, desiring, and herself invested in contradictory privileges and struggles.

Robin Usher

A Postmodern Approach to Research: Some Questions

To conclude, I want to set out some of the implications of a postmodern approach to social research. I present this in the form of a number of questions rather than a list of certainties:

Is it more useful to see research as a practice rather than a process? What follows from seeing research this way?

If we do see research as a practice, then what it would mean to see it specifically as a *textual* practice, a practice of *writing*?

As a practice of this kind, is it not then akin to a 'fictional' text in the sense that it too, like the latter, is in the business of constructing a world or worlds? If this is the case, then doesn't research always raise questions of *reflexivity*?

Does the existence of reflexivity suggest that all research, whatever else it may be, is autobiographical? But what is 'autobiography' and what is its relation to the self who researches?

Does being reflexive also mean taking account of the effects of the 'situatedness' of research — in other words, asking where is it 'coming from'?

What about the part played by language, textual strategies and conventions in achieving 'objectivity' and 'truth'?

Do we need to be careful about what is 'underneath', the operation of power and its effects through particular discourses?

If research is textual, then are research texts arguing against other texts rather than reflecting the world?

If our concern is that research contributes to domination and oppression should research be aimed explicitly at emancipation? But do we then need to be careful that our desire for this might merely lead to another form of oppression, of 'speaking for others'?

Post-text

In the text that has unfolded I have tried to tell a story about social research and one of my ways of doing this has been to recount Eco's story — a story which on the face of it is not about research. Yet as we have seen, by reading Eco in a particular way we can gain an understanding (a 'different' understanding?) of research which might otherwise not have been possible. This is one way of following a deconstructive strategy — a strategy with which postmodernism is commonly associated.

The lesson here (and Patti Lather's research shows this very clearly) is that such a strategy is not an alternative paradigm for research, let alone a new method for doing research. What it is, if it is anything at all, is an injunction to be constantly vigilant, to take nothing for granted in doing research. By being vigilant we are reminded to always ask not only — what is my research finding out? — but also — where is it coming from?; what is it doing?; and with what is it implicated? In this way, we become aware that research is not a transcendental activity or merely the application of an invariant technical process. Most of all, we become aware that research is both a 'constructed' and a 'constructing' activity.

Furthermore, in telling this, a postmodern story, about research we can better understand research as story-telling — as 'constructed' and 'constructing'. An advantage of this approach is the emphasis on research as illuminative, insightful and emancipatory. But what is also revealed, as Eco shows only too clearly, is that story-telling can also be powerful, oppressive and dangerous. There are always two sides to the text of social research.

References

ACKER, J., BARRY, K. and ESSEVELD, J. (1991) 'Objectivity and truth: problems in doing feminist research', in FONOW, M. and COOK, J. *Beyond Methodology*, Bloomington, Indiana University Press.

BARTHES, R. (1977) *Image-Music-Text*, New York, Hill and Wang.

BAUDRILLARD, J. (1988) *America*, London, Verso.

CODE, L. (1993) 'Taking subjectivity into account', in ALCOFF, L. and POTTER, E. *Feminist Epistemologies*, London, Routledgc.

ECO, U. (1984) *The Name of the Rose*, London, Picador.

ECO, U. (1990) *Foucault's Pendulum*, London, Picador.

FAIRCLOUGH, N. (1992) *Discourse and Social Change*, Oxford, Polity Press.

FOUCAULT, M. (1980) *Power/Knowledge*, Brighton, Harvester Press.

GAME, A. (1991) *Undoing the Social*, Milton Keynes, Oxford University Press.

JAMESON, F. (1991) *Postmodernism: The Cultural Logic of Late Capitalism*, Durham, NC, Duke University Press.

KUHN, T.S. (1970) *The Structure of Scientific Revolutions*, Chicago, University of Chicago Press.

KVALE, S. (1992) *Psychology and Postmodernism*, London, Sage.

LATHER, P. (1991) *Getting Smart: Feminist Research and Pedagogy With/In the Postmodern*, London, Routledge.

McHALE, B. (1992) *Constructing Postmodernism*, London, Routledge.

SHOTTER, J. (1993) *Conversational Realities*, London, Sage.

STEIER, F. (1991) 'Introduction: research as reflexivity, self-reflexivity as social process', in STEIER, F. (Ed), *Research and Reflexivity*, London, Sage.

USHER, R. (1993) 'From process to practice: research, reflexivity and writing in adult education', *Studies in Continuing Education*, **15**, 2 pp. 98–116.

WOOD, D. (1990) *Philosophy at the Limit*, London, Unwin Hyman.

4   Challenging the Power of Rationality

Pat Usher

Each chapter in this reader is attempting to provide insights on the relationship between producing knowledge or meanings about the world, theoretical foundations in which disciplines are embedded and the actual practice of doing research. Regardless of which discipline each of us is working within, all of us are socialized into a methodology — by which I mean a theoretical framework that derives from a research tradition. In order to justify our choice of methodology, I would argue that we need to be able to articulate its characteristics, analyze the categories of analysis that it takes for granted, be alert to the ways that these categories structure our opinions and provide us with criteria to make judgments about social experience; in short we need to be aware of how our choice of research methodology forms a context and rationale against which we evaluate other research approaches.

In this chapter I am looking at how one kind of critical theory — feminism — is raising questions about the relationship between knowledge creation and the search for objective truth. Who is it that creates meanings about the world, what criteria are used to decide what constitutes valid truth and does gender come into any of this? In the first section of this chapter I will outline the kind of critical analysis which radical feminist theory is making of the assumptions around which modernist thought has been structured, in particular the privileging of rational discourse and a particular model of knowledge exemplified by the scientific method of the natural sciences which is regarded as the guarantor of truth. I will then move on to elaborate the constructive approaches which radical feminism is advocating in seeking to expand the criteria for what is considered to be true, rational or valid.

But before I move into the main body of this paper's argument, I want to identify the assumptions I am making about the purposes and nature of research in the social sciences.

Breaking with Traditions of Knowledge-making

It is now commonplace to allege that Western thought is engaged in a crisis of legitimation and that the social sciences are questioning the epistemological foundations of the Enlightenment legacy that underpins modernist thought as we know it. My arguments are challenging the defining characteristics of modernism: namely that disciplinary knowledge can be objective, impartial, innocent in intention and effect and neutrally discovered; that there is only one, true method by which knowledge is acquired; that knowledge can be discovered by a rational subject that is distanced from its object and who can separate herself/himself from emotions, personal self interests and political values in creating innocent knowledge. I am arguing that it is not the task of the social sciences to discover absolutes in the way that the Enlightenment defined epistemology — (i.e. the relationship between knowledge construction and truth) — but rather the task is the interpretation of social meaning and not a search for scientific truth; the search is for understandings of the social world and not for scientific laws about human beings.

In other words I am challenging the view that has been derived from Enlightenment thought that the purpose of research in the social sciences is to separate universal truth from historical and cultural influences, which by implication, warp human thought. I am advocating an approach to research which recognizes that all knowledge is produced out of a relationship between human thought and human existence: that in producing knowledge one cannot make a distinction between objective and subjective knowledge, that all knowledge is shaped by a mixture of historical and cultural influences.

Drawing on the work of Foucault and Gadamer I am arguing that modern science, far from offering the one true model of knowledge, is rooted in certain historically specific assumptions about the way the world is; assumptions which are not universally valid but related to specific contexts. This approach to knowledge undermines the universalistic claims of scientific, objective knowledge, reveals the historical specificity of Enlightenment thought and illustrates a further important assumption which I make in this paper — that values, politics and knowledge are intrinsically connected. If, as I am arguing, understanding is always from a particular perspective, researchers must acknowledge that their values and prejudices are implicated in what they create as knowledge. So as well as acknowledging the influence of socio-historical conditions and the interpretive role of social research I am also arguing for a reflexivity that seeks to understand that power is not exterior to knowledge or to social relations but is embedded within their very conditions of existence. My aim is to illustrate this in the sections that follow.

Feminist Theory and the Challenge to Orthodoxies

The last three decades have witnessed an enormous breadth in the development of feminist theory. The construction of theory has always been allied to a politics and each phase has defined the focus differently and so the emphases within theory have been different. In the 1960s feminism was largely concerned with removing barriers to women's participation in all aspects of public affairs and to arguing for a greater share for women in the rights, duties, privileges and responsibilities of men. This egalitarian politics was accompanied by forms of theory which sought to challenge sexist practice. Sexism was defined as the unwarranted differential treatment of women: it was identifiable in empirical terms and could, it was argued, be removed. If men and women were treated equally in the political, social and personal sense, there was the rational possibility that women's views and activities could be invested with the same degree of significance as men's: equal but different was the sound-bite of the egalitarian paradigm.

In the 1970s, feminists were attempting to integrate their approaches into mainstream radical theories such as marxist, liberal or psychoanalytic, only to find them particularly resistant to such challenges or incapable of being broadened to include women. These experiences of being rejected and alienated, facilitated a growing awareness of the patriarchal nature of such discourses. Even if sexism was eliminated and both sexes participated fully, the patriarchal nature of structures and value systems would still ensure that men and women were positioned in unequal positions of power, and female activity defined as marginal and of lesser significance to male experience. Even if women were incorporated into patriarchal discourse, it was on the basis of their sameness to men, their specificity as women could not be recognized. In other words women began to assume the role of surrogate men.

Many feminists came to realize that the political project of women's inclusion as male equals could not succeed and the 1980s have witnessed the development of a more radical feminism responding to the failure of egalitarian aspirations. The focus of study became the phallocentric nature of all systems of representation; that whenever the two sexes are represented in a single model, the specificity of the female or the feminine is always collapsed into a single, universal model that is represented in male or masculine terms. In theoretical terms, feminists have analyzed how the general concepts, assumptions and categories of western thought have been organized around hierarchies which, by association privilege masculinity and devalue femininity. Regardless of which academic discipline radical feminists are working within, there is widespread recognition that philosophy has exerted a powerful influence on concepts, ideals and values in everyday life and that the way we make sense of the world is through broad categories and central questions to do with the nature of reality, subjectivity, how knowledge is constructed, morality/ethics and political rights and responsibilities. As feminist theory has developed, it has developed a dialogue with postmodernity and psychoanalytic approaches; this has led to questions about how philosophy is implicated in defining masculinity and femininity, how it defines the 'nature' of people, the values attached to their skills and capacities and how gender difference is a category of analysis around which every society is structured.

Radical feminism is joining with postmodern critiques to undermine the traditional model of creating knowledge developed since the Enlightenment. For as long as it was held that there was only one truth, that its discovery was guaranteed by objectivity and the rigorous pursuit of a scientific methodology, the gendered nature of this discourse and its privileging of masculinity was disguised. Postmodern approaches are asking us to be sceptical about traditional beliefs about truth, knowledge, power and the self, all of which have served as legitimation for contemporary Western culture. They question the following beliefs derived from the Enlightenment:

   i)   the existence of a coherent, unified self that is capable of using reason to understand its own processes as well as the laws of nature;

   ii)   reason and its application through science can provide an objective, reliable and universal foundation for knowledge,

   iii)   that knowledge acquired through the right use of reason will be true and unchanging irrespective of time or culture,

   iv)   reason has a universal and transcendental quality and is not contingent,

   v)   by grounding all claims to truth and authority in the application of reason, conflicts between truth, knowledge and power can be overcome. By privileging reason, truth can serve power without distortion; by utilizing knowledge in the service of power, both freedom and progress can flourish. As a result knowledge can be neutral because it is grounded in reason and its effects are beneficial. Finally,

   vi)   the scientific paradigm is the framework to guarantee truth and its methods are neutral and its contents socially beneficial.

Radical feminists have entered into a dialogue with postmodernist discourses as they have begun to deconstruct notions of reason, knowledge and the self to reveal the gendered nature of concepts and analytic categories which had been seemingly neutral and universal. Scholars such as Hekman (1990) and Flax (1990) have argued that knowledge is structured through a number of fundamental dichotomies such as rational/irrational, subject/object, nature/culture which constitute a hierarchical view of knowledge. The way that knowledge is constructed privileges certain concepts over others and rather than being a peripheral issue, the study of epistemology is central to the way the social sciences examine the relationship between human thought and social existence.

Hekman and Flax argue that the rationalism which is the source of modernist epistemology is a specifically masculine mode of thought. They argue that the positivists' claim that only rational, objective, abstract, universalistic thought can lead to the truth is in fact a specifically masculine claim. Further, they argue that each of the dualisms on which modernist thought rests is the product of the fundamental dualism between male and female. In each of the dualisms mentioned above rational/irrational, subject/object, culture/nature the male is associated with the first element, the female with the second. In each case the male element is privileged over the female and maintains its position by its capacity to define itself as a universal standard against which the subjective, the emotional, the aesthetic, the natural, the feminine must be judged. In the very dualities of modernist thought women's significance is defined as inferior to the rational, objective, abstract qualities of the scientific method which not only guarantees Truth but positions masculinity and 'man' as capable of finding the Truth. Once this kind of analysis is accepted all the other common sense stereotypes which we constantly attempt to counter fall into perspective. As Jane Flax comments, 'woman' is defined as a deficient man in discourses from Aristotle to Freud.

There are some interesting parallels between feminist analyses of modernist dualities and the irresolvable disputes between positivist and interpretive approaches in the social sciences. Many people working in an interpretive paradigm do not challenge the subjective/objective dichotomy on which positivism rests because they believe that the strength of social science research is that it can be objective in a subjective kind of way. Despite all their efforts however, the objectivity of the natural sciences remains the gold standard against which all other variants — qualitative/interpretive approaches are judged. By not challenging the dichotomy, the privileged concept maintains its power of definition. For feminists the same dilemma apply. Many feminists try to exalt the virtues of 'female nature' and the related concepts of community, care, relatedness, as opposed to the 'male' values of control, mastery, rationality and abstraction. But as the dispute in the social sciences reveals, these arguments are not convincing because such feminists cannot succeed in privileging the female over the male because they have not challenged the very dichotomy through which the female is defined as inferior in the first place. Equal but different simply cannot succeed in a world where knowledge is constructed through hierarchical meanings. Not that the reverse argument of valorizing femininity over masculinity works either. What does emerge is the insight that if particular dualisms cannot be reversed, perhaps the aim should be to dissolve them.

At this point in the paper it might be helpful to review how radical feminism has developed as a perspective and where it stands in relation to other discourses.

As I indicated above radical feminism is critical of liberal feminist discourse because the latter is tied to the dichotomies and grounding in absolutes which I analyzed above as the characteristics of Enlightenment epistemology. Anything short of a rejection of the rationality and dualisms of Enlightenment thought and the research methodologies which derive from it, will not prove a successful strategy for women.

In developing its analysis that a commitment to modernist categories is in effect a commitment to the production of gender specific theory that privileges masculinity rather than gender neutral theory, radical feminists have been greatly helped by the work of Thomas Kuhn on paradigm shifts. His work established the notion that science should be examined within a specific cultural and historical context and that its statements were not the universals they often were presented to be. Meaning and interpretation were part of the scientists' world. Although Kuhn may not have intended it, his work challenged the idea of a fixed, absolute reality against which we test our notions about the natural world. Given his approach to science, what appears according to scientists as objective reality does in fact change with changing paradigms. Theory can be argued as being grounded in distinct contexts — social, historical and political — and there are not fixed, universal criteria for determining one as more correct than the other. This hermeneutic or interpretive dimension to science is very important for all social scientists but particularly so for feminists. If the model of knowledge embodied in the scientific method of the natural sciences is not the only paradigm of knowledge then all the dualities which have disprivileged women can be exposed to critique and displacement.

The way is opened up for radical feminists to argue that a commitment to reason, perspectiveless truth, objective and neutral forms of knowledge, separation of the subject from the object of knowledge are all commitments to the production of male theory in which reason surreptitiously defines itself by excluding categories associated with femininity — subjectivity, the emotions, desire and specificity. Through such definitions, the masculinity associated with theory control and its production has not been recognized because no other theory or knowledge has emerged with which it could be compared. Men have been able to assume the role of neutral thinkers and producers of ideas because the categories of analysis they employ have repressed all traces of their sexual specificity. By universalizing their knowledge they successfully tag feminism with the label of specific, personal, incomplete, partial knowledge which can be easily dismissed and pushed to the margins.

Feminist Approaches to Epistemology

In the earlier sections of this paper I have sketched out the kinds of critique which radical feminism offers of patriarchal discourses. If women working in the disciplines are to achieve a measure of autonomy and self determination it is important that they acquire a thorough knowledge of the orthodox paradigms in which their discipline is located and their phallocentric/patriarchal nature. It is part of the feminist project to practice reflexivity about the power relations assumed within such theoretical frameworks and engage in a deconstruction of the phallocentric models which reduce women to a necessary dependence on men. However, feminism's project cannot remain solely a reactive and critical one. To be so would imply an affirmation of the very paradigms it wishes to critique: to remain an anti-sexist project only means that feminism accepts its location with a politics of sameness or equality with men. Moving on from an anti-sexist approach, feminist theory has been developing alternatives to patriarchal discourse which are not merely adaptations of existing orthodoxies. How it develops alternative epistemologies now becomes a crucial issue.

As I outlined earlier, radical feminism is critical of both positivist and interpretive approaches because although they differ in the scope, the latter methodology allows for the role of subjectivity, both approaches accept the power of reason to apprehend the truth — that it emerges out of an objectively conducted method of separating subject from object in research. If radical feminism offered alternative approaches which implicitly accepted these rival accounts, it would implicitly be affirming the very categories which patriarchal discourses offer. So by engaging in conversation with postmodern and psychoanalytic approaches, radical feminism is adopting a strategy which starts from the premise that all knowledge is contextual and historical and does not need to be grounded in the absolutes which other methodologies endorse. The production of knowledge then becomes the creation of perspectives about the social world — points of view — all of which have to acknowledge their own partial and limited insights as well as respect the position that other views and perspectives are possible and can offer intelligible meaning about the world. In attempting to develop alternative discourses, radical feminism had drawn on the work of Michel Foucault and in particular his discussion of discourses and power-knowledge.

He presents a critique of rationality that is particularly relevant to both post-modernism and feminism. His objects of investigation were not fixed and established bodies of knowledge but the rules of formation and the conditions of possibility created by a specific discourse which allowed certain statements to be made as if they spoke the truth. Objects of investigation were madness, prisons, desire, sexuality, asylums, poor homes, hospitals, institutions because he wished to understand and illustrate the intricate and highly variable forms of power in discursive practices. Not only does a discourse permit certain statements to be regarded as the truth but the rules which govern a discourse also determine who may speak, what conventions they need to use and with what authority they may speak.

His view that discourses create subjects as well as objects goes further than interpretive social science. The latter has long argued that the object of social scientific enquiry differs from that of natural scientific, but he shows how a particular discourse creates a kind of subject — who is defined as mad, criminal, deviant, unreasoned.

His second great insight is that knowledge and power are inextricably linked in discourse. His basic claim is that power and knowledge are fused in the human sciences. His theory of power differs radically from the humanist/Marxist accounts in three basic ways:

power is exercised rather than possessed,
power is not primarily repressive but productive, and
power is analyzed as coming from the bottom up.

He is distancing himself from a preoccupation with power as a possession in order to account for how subjects are constituted by power relations. He rejects a repressive model of power in order to show how individuals actually obey repressive and coercive forms of power — in other words how individuals police themselves.

What he is arguing is that in the human sciences disciplinary power has been exercised over the bodies and minds of individuals — docile bodies and obedient souls. Disciplinary power has spread through the production of certain forms of knowledge such as positivist and interpretive human sciences and through the emergence of disciplinary techniques such as surveillance, examination and discipline which facilitate the process of finding out about individuals. Thus ways of creating knowledge in the social sciences are equated with ways of exercising power over individuals. The different disciplines of medicine, psychiatry, criminology, psychology are therefore in a powerful position to create the divisions of healthy/ill, sane/mad, legal/delinquent, normal/deviant and are implicated in effecting the means of normalization and social control.

He convincingly argues that the relations of power and knowledge are internal to knowledges and that each discipline has a political investment in enhancing its view of the world. His 'bottom-up' analysis shows how all of us at the micro-level of society become part of dominant networks of power relations. By being engaged in disciplinary enquiries the power of individual researchers is enhanced within the rules of its discourse in relation to the objects of their study: their power to define people and the nature of their 'problems' is exercised through their actions as researchers.

All of these upsetting and disturbing categories of thought are immensely helpful for radical feminists. Firstly they allow a challenge to be made to philosophy's orientation around oneness, unity or identity — one truth, one method, one logic. There is opened up scope for perspective and a diversity in the models on which philosophy can develop. This insistence on perspectives is advocated as a relational, not a relativist theory of knowledge (Grosz, 1987).

Instead of being committed to truth and objectivity as privileged by both positivist and interpretive perspectives, feminism can argue for the insight that all discourses create subjects, objects, regimes of power and truth. Instead of being for or against the regimes of any one research tradition, one asks what conditions facilitated the development of a particular discourse and what criteria and assumptions does each discourse use to present itself as speaking the truth and disguising its own desire to dominate. Knowledges must be reflexive in coming to understand their own self development as knowledges. Feminism must therefore accept its own status as context-specific, the product of socio-economic and historical movements. It has no more claim to speak *the* truth than any other discourse but must own up to its own points of view, specific aims, desires and political position within power relations. No discourse can openly disassociate itself from a political position. Thus the political is always personal. Feminist theory is neither subjective, nor objective, neither absolutist or relativist: it strives to occupy the middle ground excluded by these dichotomies: it argues that all theory is relational and connected to other practices (Grosz, 1987). Radical feminism rejects the 'add women' and 'stir' approach of many interpretive approaches to research. Gender divisions are fundamental categories around which all social structures are organized and meanings created. This should be the understanding which underpins the development of all human thought and men as well as women should internalize the dominant conceptions we all have about masculinity and femininity. The context for thinking about gender is that we see it as a social relation rather than a set of opposite and different characteristics. In so dong we can illuminate how our thinking becomes implicated in power/knowledge relationships both between the sexes and within each category — how men treat other men, women treat one another.

The sub-text for such an approach is that we consciously admit the potential in our enquiries for both expressing and uncovering relations of dominance. This may often imply the writing of histories or giving expression to voices and views that have been suppressed, unarticulated or denied by traditional discourse. Models of investigation which assume homogeneity as their starting point fail to acknowledge the variety of human beings and are oppressive in their phallocentric assumptions — that women can be represented as having the same characteristics and interests as men. For these kinds of reasons, radical feminism argues that one cannot accept the separation of the subject and object of knowledge. In accepting objectivity one must accept a knowing subject free of personal, social, political and moral interest — a positivist subject unimplicated in a social context or uninfluenced by prior ideas and knowledge. Feminism as I represent it must reconceptualize the inter-relationship between subjects and objects so that reason and knowledge include a recognition of history, context and specificity.

Instead of organizing thought through dichotomies which separate and exclude — subject/object, reason/emotion, culture/nature, masculinity/femininity — a feminist position would argue for these terms to be regarded as continuities and for discourses to be created that avoid dualities, essences and the temptation to privilege the feminine over the masculine. The dualisms of masculine thought need to be displaced by a pluralism and fluidity that transforms categories which have continually positioned and named women as inferior. The modernist move of trying to incorporate women into the masculine definition of rationality should be avoided in favour of deconstructing the dualism on which it rests. Radical feminists argue that we don't need new 'truth' but a plurality of perspectives. Joan W. Scott's discussion of equality-versus-difference illustrates the point well. Instead of accepting categories in fixed opposition to one another such as unity/diversity, identity/difference, presence/absence, universality/specificity, we argue for their interdependence so that we reverse and then displace the binary opposition. In this context we can refuse to place equality and difference in opposition to one another and argue for a respect for differences 'as the condition of individual and collective identities, differences as the constant challenge to the fixing of those identities, differences as the very meaning of equality itself' (1988). Challenging the way knowledge/power is constructed from the ground of difference seems to me a crucial insight not only for all women but for all social scientists as well if they are to arrive at valid understandings about the relationships between human thought and the nature of existence. Only by following this approach can women or any other subordinated group avoid being defined as inferior against the universalizing categories of rationality, objectivity and masculinity.

What are the Implications for Feminist Method?

In this chapter so far I have been looking at the relationship between epistemology and methodology. I have defined epistemology as the study of how knowledge is constructed about the world, who constructs it and what criteria do they use to create meaning and methodology in the sense used by Harding (1987) as a theoretical and conceptual framework with which research proceeds. In this final section I want to consider whether the themes I have identified amount to such a thing as a feminist method — by which I mean distinctive techniques of evidence gathering or pursuing inquiries.

I have argued that feminism is a perspective which asks all methodologies to recognize that they too are perspectives. Arising out of this I want to argue as Reinharz (1992) does that feminist researchers do not consider feminism to be a method; rather they see it as a perspective that can be infiltrated into all disciplines as a means of developing innovative methods. Feminist social research uses the methods supplied by the discipline — both quantitative and qualitative — and adds its own perspective in order to create diverse and innovative approaches to analyzing human activity. At an earlier stage in the development of feminist theory it was argued that qualitative approaches were the hallmark of feminism because of their respect for the inclusion of women's experience which interpretive research methodologies advocated. However for reasons I analyzed earlier, feminist scholarship has identified the contradictions of methodologies which do not challenge dichotomies which label women's experience as of lesser significance. Theories and methodologies which attempt to valorize the 'essential' nature of women and their experience were seen to pose no challenge at all to the phallocentric nature of both positivist and interpretive methodologies and so feminist theory now uses the full range of methods and implicates itself in the greatest range of subject matters, challenging the false homogeneity of much that passes for understanding of the social world.

The following themes are those characteristic of feminist research which should guide the development of new approaches.

a) Acknowledge the pervasive influence of gender as a category of analysis and organization. Each of us understands our own identity through the meanings we learn to attach to gender difference: society's institutions and structures are organized around divisions that have a gendered nature. Irrespective of the area of research in which we work, feminism would argue that as a strategy in designing research one should be asking how meanings about gender are implicated in the questions and criteria that guide one's thinking. These are not the peripheral questions which can be added on after a long list of more important questions have been asked; not to address questions of gender difference is to adhere to patriarchal theoretical norms which collapse all issues of difference into unitary, homogenized categories. Such approaches cannot lead to intelligible meaning about the diversity of experience in the social world; patriarchal discourses disguise their own specificity by portraying their frameworks and questions as universally significant.

b) Deconstruct the traditional commitments to truth, objectivity and neutrality: reverse and then dissolve the binary oppositions which structure thought and subordinate all the categories — the subjective, the privately emotional, community, practice-based — that are associated with the feminine and females. The aim is to expand and multiply the criteria for what is considered to be rational and true and to be critical of norms which are discriminatory in their assumptions.

c) Adopt an approach to knowledge creation that recognizes all theories are perspectival: that each methodology is the product of a specific combination of historical, socio-political influences — whether it is positivism or post-modernism — all of them are making claims about the truth but none should be regarded as telling *the* truth. Feminism itself must be treated in this light: it is not telling a better story about social relations but in making its own claims, it expects each claim to be equally self-reflexive. This does not mean that each perspective is equally valid but each of them has a point of view and should be interrogated from a stance that accepts that no perspective is producing disinterested knowledge and each of them represents particular positions within power relations.

d) Utilize a multiplicity of research methods. Feminist research reaches into all disciplines and uses all the methods; it does not concern itself solely with the study of gender but is concerned that research about any area of social practice is sensitive to the differential experience of female and male. Reinharz (p. 245) agrees with a number of writers who suggest that feminism is accumulating stages in scholarship. The current emphasis on multiplicity of methods is because in her view feminists value inclusiveness more than orthodoxy. The outpouring of scholarly feminist literature has contributed to what Jessie Bernard calls the Female Renaissance or Feminist Enlightenment. A multiplicity of methods allows women to study the broadest range of subject matters and reach a broad set of goals. Their approaches may include interview and oral history methods, case studies, cross-cultural research, ethnography, surveys or experiments. Giving voice to experience, understanding variations within populations or measuring behaviours and attitudes are only a few of the methods utilized by feminists.

e) Be open to inter-disciplinary work. The organization of knowledge into discrete disciplines is a thorny issue that feminist researchers cannot avoid. Each of us is shaped by disciplinary approaches but given feminism's critique of the dualities of modernist thought which disprivilege the feminine, it follows that feminists must be alert to the ways that disciplines function as discursive networks to ignore or deny female experience. As I said earlier, by presenting theory as universally applicable those working within disciplines can successfully disguise the specificity of their theory. Disciplines function as phallocentric discursive systems and collapse the differential experience of the sexes into universal models with homogenized categories. Anna Yeatman's discussion of sociology's resistance to the feminist challenge illustrates the extent to which the social sciences including sociology, economics, psychology and political science are all structured by modernist dualisms.

> Its own particular versions of these dualisms — for example, structure/agency, social structure/culture, social/psychological, family/society — are logically derivative of the basic dualistic structure of the modernist consciousness: individual/society; subjective/objective; reason/emotion, and so forth. Sociology cannot change this modernist framework of reference which has governed it as a specific intellectual enterprise without abandoning its whole tradition and approach, without, that is, becoming something other than itself. Yet it is precisely the nature of the contemporary feminist challenge to require sociology, as all expressions of modern science, to move beyond this dualistic ordering of reality in the direction of integrating what have been regarded hitherto as opposing terms (p. 286).

Resistance to change is deepest in those disciplines quoted above that have a role in preserving and gate-keeping modernist conventions of ordering reality through hierarchical dualities.

Feminist approaches are challenging the taken for granted assumptions made by disciplines about a coherent self and the nature of the social world. Foucault's work has sensitized us to the connections between knowledge claims and power. For him power is not held centrally but is reproduced in disciplines at every point where someone who 'knows' is teaching someone who does not know.

In producing knowledge about the social world, feminism is refusing to be defer to the truth claims of disciplines which exclude and suppress voices and discourses different from themselves. It is a key aim of any feminist research to blur and undermine the rigidity and distortion of disciplinary based power/knowledges.

f) Involvement of the Researcher and the people being researched. As I explained earlier, feminism challenges the claim that valid knowledge is only produced through a commitment to truth and objectivity and that in order to achieve this objectivity, a gulf is necessary between the researcher and the object of research. This gulf presupposes that researchers are subjects in the Cartesian sense — capable of forming rational knowledge in the face of personal, social, political and moral interests and standing outside the social context of the 'objects' of research. Instead of accepting such dichotomous structures which separate subject and object, teacher and pupil, supervisor and student, feminism regards the terms as continuities and does not think of objectivity and subjectivity in confrontation with one another.

Such an approach acknowledges the importance of personal experience and expects researchers to analyze how their own experience is implicated in defining research questions, organizing its data collection, interacting with others. Far from being a distorting influence, experience is seen as an asset. The important point is that the researcher should develop a self-reflexive stance towards his/her own relation to the research: she/he must be accountable for his/her own cultural prejudices and disciplinary allegiance and be alert as to how these implicate themselves in the choices made in research practice.

Unlike patriarchal approaches to research, feminists need to develop an intersubjectivity, a shared or collective response to research, with those they study. It demands that the researcher establish an empathic understanding with the people s/he studies in a non-exploitative manner. Relations of respect, shared information, joint involvement in the commentary and evaluation of their own lives, openness, are all the goals of a feminist researcher. Clearly these themes are not without ambiguity and controversy but if the task is to represent the complexity of social reality, researchers need to form relationships that allow for those who are the researched to express what is significant to them in their everyday lives. It is this which provides for the validity of the research not pseudo-objectivity.

Summary

In this chapter I have tried to draw distinctions between epistemology, methodology and methods. Epistemology is concerned with philosophical approaches to what counts as knowledge and truth; methodology refers to the conceptual framework within which research as a practice is located and methods are the techniques employed to gather research materials.

I have argued that feminism is challenging the epistemological foundations of western thought by questioning the dualities and hierarchies through which modernist thought has constituted femininity and women as inferior.

I have analyzed the characteristics of feminism as a perspective drawing on the postmodernist discourse theory of knowledge. In arguing that truth is constituted through discourses, I am asking for a critical reflexivity towards the characteristics of all research methodologies so that one can understand that all knowledge is the product of historical and contextual circumstances.

In arguing that discourses create knowledge, I have also drawn attention to the power hierarchies that are created within knowledge and in particular to the way that subjects and objects are constituted through categories privileged within the discourse. It is in this respect, that radical feminism is such a fundamental challenge to traditional intellectual values because it rejects the Cartesian subject that creates knowledge through rational abstraction. Feminism is arguing that it is these Englightenment assumptions that have prevented the development of new modes of subjectivity and discourses which can resist the power of phallocentric research traditions.

Feminism has encouraged a research practice that reveals difference because that speaks of the the diversity of men and women and is a basis from which male domination of theory can be effectively challenged. It advocates the use of a multiplicity of methods in all the disciplines so that the boundaries of what constitutes research can be opened up and new ways of knowing, new forms of analysis and new texts can be created.

References

BERNARD, S. (1987) *The Female World from a Global Perspective*, Bloomington, Indiana University Press.

FLAX, J. (1990) *Thinking Fragments: Psychoanalysis, Feminism, and Postmodernism in the Contemporary West*, Berkeley, University of California Press.

FLAX, J. (1993) *Disputed Subjects: Essays on Psychoanalysis, Politics and Philosophy*, New York, Routledge.

FOUCAULT, M. (1972) 'The discourse on language', in *The Archaeology of Knowledge*, New York, Harper and Row, (pp. 215–38).

GADAMER, H.G. (1975) *Truth and Method*, New York, Continuum.

GROSZ, E.A. (1987) 'Feminist Theory and the Challenge to Knowledges', *Women's Studies International Forum*, **101**, 5, pp. 475–80.

GROSZ, E.A. (1990) 'Philosophy', in GUNEW, S. (Ed) *Feminist Knowledge: Critique and Construct*, London, Routledge, (pp. 147–74).

HARDING, S. (Ed) (1987) 'Introduction: Is There a Feminist Method?', *Feminism and Methodology*, pp. 1–14.

HEKMAN, S.J. (1990) *Gender and Knowledge: Elements of a Postmodern Feminism*, Oxford, Polity Press.

KUHN, T.S. (1962) *The Structure of Scientific Revolutions*, Chicago, University of Chicago Press.

REINHARZ, S. (1992) *Feminist Methods in Social Research*, New York, Oxford University Press.

SCOTT, J.W. (1988) 'Deconstructing Equality — versus — Difference: or the uses of poststructuralist theory for feminism', *Feminist Studies*, **14**, 1, pp. 33–50.

YEATMAN, A. (1990) 'A Feminist Theory of Social Differentiation', NICHOLSON, L.J. (Ed) *Feminism, Postmodernism*, London, Routledge, (pp. 281–99).

5   Being Economical with Politics

Alan Hamlin

Introduction

Like many of those who are drawn to study economics, my major initial motivation was an interest in economic policy — not so much the macro-policy issues of inflation or the exchange rate that seem to many to be the essence of economics, but the micro-policy issues of taxation and welfare benefits, of regional or training policy, of policy towards the nationalized industries (as they then were) and so on. In short, the myriad ways in which government economic policy decisions impact on the everyday lives of individuals. As an undergraduate, I took options in courses concerned with taxation and public finance, industrial economics, the economics of the nationalized industries and so on. On graduating, I decided to pursue these interests further by taking a post graduate degree at the United Kingdom department which (at that time) specialized most strongly in the analysis of the public sector and its policies — the University of York. My first year at York was spent in the relatively standard pursuit of taught courses at the Masters level, but once I was admitted to study for a DPhil, I began to think seriously of research for the first time.

My initial research topic was the relationship between local and central government policies, and the possibility of policy improvements in specific areas from closer integration between government agencies. But I wrote no thesis on this topic. Like many research students before and since, I found that my original topic was simply a point of departure.

The analysis of government policy that I had studied up to that date was almost entirely normative in character. That is, it attempted to answer questions of the form 'What should government do in situation X, on the assumption that the overall aim of government policy is to maximize some particular notion of social welfare'. Thus the concern was with deriving ideal or optimal policies from a specific moral criterion. This approach begs two obvious questions: (1) how do we analyze how governments actually decide what to do; and (2) what particular moral criterion is relevant to the evaluation of government policy. These questions, which we may label the political question and the ethical question, came to dominate my research interests to the extent that I never returned to the particular questions of the relationships between local and central government policy — although I did work out some of my ideas in relation to the questions raised by a federal structure of government.

The political question, the one I want to pursue here, concerns the construction of a way of thinking about government as a policy making (and law making) process made up of institutions and procedures operated by individuals in their roles as citizens, voters, politicians, civil servants and so on. The relative lack of interest in the mechanics of policy making shown by most economists of the previous period related directly to the conception of economics as a 'positive science' that was very influential in economics in mid-century. On that account, economics was seen as a largely technical exercise which could offer unbiased, value-free advice on the policy means to any particular desired end. This view led many economists to be relatively uninterested in the wider political and ethical questions, since these questions were felt to be separate (or, at least, separable) from technical economic questions and to lie wholly in the domain of politics and philosophy — it was relatively common to hear and read statements to the effect that politics was concerned with the determination of the desired social ends, and economics concerned with providing the means to those politically determined ends. As a result, economists typically engaged in policy analysis in a manner that was independent of any social, political or institutional structure — as if the economist were giving policy advice to an appropriately motivated benign despot.

Fortunately, there were two developing literatures which broke with this tradition (albeit in very different ways) and took social and political institutions and their problems seriously within an economic framework. One (social choice theory, associated with Kenneth Arrow and Amartya Sen) concerned the formal analysis of the aggregation from individual preferences and values to social choices and social values; the other (public choice theory, associated with James Buchanan) concerned the conceptualization of government in institutional terms and the analysis of the process of government in a manner which paralleled the economic analysis of the process of market exchange in the context of market institutions. I was drawn to these two literatures and was fortunate in being able to arrange for Jack Wiseman (who was perhaps the first UK economist to embrace the ideas of public choice theory) to act as my supervisor, and for Amartya Sen (both a distinguished social choice theorist and a leader of the movement to re-integrate economics and ethics) to act as my external adviser and examiner.[1]

These various elements came together to influence my DPhil research which analyzed the political institution of federalism from an economic perspective, drawing on both public choice and social choice theory. But perhaps more importantly, they also provided a developing framework for research in the longer term. After completing my DPhil, I took the first available opportunity to spend an extended visit with James Buchanan at the Centre for Study of Public Choice in Virginia where I met a number of others, with backgrounds in economics, politics and philosophy, with similar interests. Frequent contacts with other researchers who share basic perspectives — however different their particular research projects — are vital to maintaining active research commitments, and I have been fortunate in developing and maintaining a number of connections which have made such regular contacts possible.

As I have already suggested, the basic theme of public choice theory as a response to the political question of how we analyze how governments actually decide what to do involves the application of an essentially economic mode of analysis to questions which are normally considered to be in the domain of politics. Even making this statement raises a number of interesting questions: do we (and should we) identify individual social sciences with particular domains of study (economics with the economy, politics with the polity etc.) or with particular styles of theorizing; what is the difference, if any, between cross-disciplinary and inter-disciplinary research; what exactly is 'an essentially economic mode of analysis'; and what virtue might there be in applying it in the domain of politics? In this brief essay, I hope to tackle at least some of these questions, and one or two related topics.

In addressing these questions I have two major objectives in mind — first the explication of some aspects of the economic mode of analysis, particularly those associated with individualism and rationality; and second a suggestion to the effect that this mode of analysis is of value across the domain of social science. While my discussion is presented in terms of the application of economic methods to politics, I hope to suggest some further generalization. Questions of individualism and rationality are of relevance in many areas of social research, whether they are embedded in the economic method or not, and I hope that the discussion of these topics may be of interest to those who are neither economists nor political scientists.

In approaching my objectives I shall be operating at a level of discussion which fluctuates from methodology to method — at times the discussion will link back to the grand themes of epistemology and the philosophy of social science, while at other times I will be concerned with the more detailed and practical methods involved in economic analysis. The reader should be aware of these different levels of debate, and I will try to make the appropriate level explicit where confusion might arise.

I should also be explicit about what I am not attempting in this essay. In particular I will not discuss the general question of approaches to empirical work. I will be concerned to characterize aspects of the economic mode of analysis seen as a style of theorizing which might contribute to our understanding of the topics under study. Some might argue that the economic approach to social science involves not only a distinctive style of theorizing but also a particular approach to empirical work and the vexed questions of theory appraisal. I doubt this but, in any case, I will not be concerned with questions of empirical method or methodology here.

The final point that I would stress in laying out my intentions is that I will not be arguing that the economic mode of theorizing is in any way uniquely privileged relative to other modes of thought. My aim is much more modest: all I seek to argue is that the economic mode of theorizing is of value outside (as well as inside) the traditional domain of economics, providing a coherent and defensible project in the broad area of social theory. In short, that there is at least some merit in being economical with politics.

The remainder of this essay is presented in four further sections. The next section provides a thumbnail sketch of public choice theory and so provides an overview of the economistic approach to politics. Sections 3 and 4 then look in slightly more detail at two significant aspects of the economistic method which are often criticized. In section 3 I focus on the individualistic nature of the method, while in section 4 I focus on questions of rationality. Section 5 contains some final comments.

Public Choice Theory

To provide a caricature of public choice theory — or constitutional political economy as it is now sometimes called — one can simply reverse the view attributed to the traditional economist above. Rather than assuming that policy making is free of all institutional constraint and depends only on the technical ability to derive optimal policy conclusions from given (or assumed) moral criteria, the public choice theorist views policy as the emergent outcome of a complex institutional procedure. Once the institutional structure is established, individuals act rationally to achieve their own ends (whatever they may be) within that institutional structure, and policy is whatever emerges from that process. Policy can be evaluated relative to any moral criteria you like to specify, but policies derive from individual and rational actions within institutional contexts.

A common analogy is with a simple parlour game. Once the rules of the game are set, the outcome of the game (the result, score or whatever) is determined by those rules, together with the actions of the individual players. But the actions of the players are themselves influenced by their understanding of the rules of the game. Change the rules and you will change both the behaviour of players and the outcome of the game. Consider the game of chess, for example. The rules of chess define the strategies available to players, and the players then face the task of selecting the 'best' strategy given those rules and whatever they can learn about their opponent's strategy, where 'best' is normally understood as meaning 'most likely to win'. The game is complex and strategic and although we do not have any analytic solution to the question of the choice of the best strategy (as we do with some simpler games such as tic-tac-toe), the game may be understood and analyzed in terms of players attempting to find better strategies given their understanding of the rules. Change the rules (by introducing time limits, for example) and you will change the players' behaviour and the pattern of the game.

This allows us to identify the sense in which the approach taken by public choice theory (and economics more generally) is individualistic in nature. Complex social processes are analyzed in terms of the actions of individuals (just as chess games are analyzed in terms of the moves made by individual players). This is not to say that institutions are irrelevant, indeed the whole point is to view the impact of institutions, but simply to say that institutions are important precisely because of the influence they have on individuals (just as the institutional rules of chess are important in influencing the strategies of players). This basic idea of individualistic analysis will be taken up in more detail in section 3 below.

On this view of politics offering policy advice of the traditional type is largely irrelevant. Of course, some economic advice can be expected as political players attempt to ensure that they are reasonably well informed — but this suggests that political players will employ specialist advisers in order to work out their best political strategies (rather as chess players employ specialist advisers to help them construct their strategies), so that the role of advice is very different from that envisaged when thinking about a disinterested policy advisor to a benign government on the more traditional model. In short, each political actor will find an economic adviser who offers 'appropriate' advice.

Public choice theory has as its basic structural theme the idea of comparative institutional analysis. That is the idea that the appropriate focus of attention is the institutional structure or rules of the game. Thus, for example, the public choice theorist would argue that the questions of institutional and constitutional design and reform are the key questions in the political sphere, rather than the questions of policy design and reform. This means that the primary emphasis in public choice theory is on the study of the operating characteristics of alternative institutional structures. What are the properties of different voting rules or committee procedures? How do pressure groups interact with members of the legislature? What is the role of a system of parliamentary committees, or of a second chamber of parliament? How do political parties with this or that structure contribute to political outcomes? These are the basic questions addressed by public choice theory.

Once answers to questions of this general form can be sketched, the next step is to evaluate alternative institutional structures. That is to compare alternative arrangements not with some ideal but with each other. Clearly this step brings the ethical question back in to play, since the evaluative criteria must be made explicit. I shall say relatively little here about the ethical question beyond a brief discussion in section 3 below of the distinction between ethical individualism and methodological individualism.

In following this general strategy of analyzing and evaluating alternative institutional structures, the researcher must clearly say something about the way in which individuals might be expected to operate within the relevant institutions. Without some maintained hypothesis concerning the behaviour of individuals, it would not be possible to analyze the properties of alternative institutional structures (just as we would not be able to analyze chess without assuming some particular motivation on the part of the players — normally that each player is playing to win). In this context the typical behavioural hypothesis maintained by public choice theorists is again drawn from the more general economic method: The hypothesis of economic rationality. In fact, this hypothesis can be broken into parts including the idea that individuals act from the same basic motivations regardless of the institutional setting (I shall term this the hypothesis of single-mindedness), and the idea of a substantively egoistic motivation — the idea that individuals act to promote their own interests. I shall discuss each of these in section 4 below.

To recap, public choice theory involves the application of economic methods to the analysis of social and political institutions and this involves breaking with some traditions in economics in order to focus on comparative institutional analysis, but key aspects of the economic method are maintained. Some of the criticisms of the application of economic ideas in the political arena focus on the alleged limitations of the economic method, particularly in relation to individualism and rationality, so it is appropriate to view these commitments in slightly more detail.

Individualism

The economic method is often criticized for its individualism, the argument being that the reduction from society to individual obscures or eliminates many issues of interest and blinds the analyst to social forces and constraints which lie outside of the individual. A similar criticism is often aimed at psychology by sociologists. The point here is that economics and psychology share a commitment to the micro level of explanation, while politics and sociology operate predominantly at the macro level.

I believe this criticism to be ill founded, partly because it conflates several different senses of individualism and partly because it ascribes to the economic method a form of individualism that is much more extreme than is required. In this section I intend to simply distinguish between strands of individualism in order to suggest a defence of the type of individualism that I believe appropriate to the economic method. This section will, then, operate largely at the level of methodological debate.

Individualism must be distinguished into at least two major strands: methodological and ethical. My major concern here is with methodological individualism, although I shall say a little about ethical individualism at the end of this section. But even methodological individualism comes in a variety of forms — I shall distinguish three. At its most severe methodological individualism holds that no non-individual social entities are real. A less virulent strain maintains that, even if social entities are real, they are fully reducible to the individualistic, in the sense that any sentence containing reference to a social entity can be rewritten in purely individualistic terms — so that social entities are simply a sort of convenient short-hand notation. The mildest form of methodological individualism says that, even if social entities are real and irreducible, still they do not compromise individual autonomy: they do not undermine or pre-empt individual agency.

The economic method may appear to be individualistic because it depicts government (or any other social entity: a firm, a trade union, the European Community etc.) as secondary to the individuals who act in its name. Recall that my sketch of public choice theory involved viewing government as the actions of individuals within the institutional and procedural structures of government, rather than as some supra-individualistic agency. Nevertheless, I would argue that this does not involve any commitment to methodological individualism beyond the mildest strain, and that this mildest strain is readily defensible.

The economic method certainly does not entail the strongest version of methodological individualism which would require government and any other social entity to be unreal — which might be one reading of Margaret Thatcher's (in)famous remark that 'there is no such thing as society'. The only sense to the idea that government is unreal can be captured by an analogy. Peter Geach once introduced an entity which he named a 'surman'. Surman are men, and no doubt women, who share the same surname; two people named Jones may be different and unrelated, but they are (parts of) the same surman. It is clear that surmen are unreal, and it is also clear why. The concept of the surman plays no part in explicating the experiential or explanatory order of the world.

Does the economic method put the government and other such social entities in the same category as Geach's surmen? Obviously not, the approach allows us to acknowledge that our experience of the social world and our explanations of at least some of its patterns make considerable use of the concept of the government (and other social entities). We can recognize that government is no artifice created for purely theoretical purposes, but a reality that is salient in the world; indeed, we must recognize this since the object of our study is the impact of alternative institutional structures on the world. The reality of social entities is not denied by the economic approach (indeed, it is affirmed), so there can be no commitment to the strongest form of methodological individualism.

But what of the reducibility of social entities and the second sort of methodological individualism? Social entities, on the economic approach, are a certain sort of system of rules and rights — institutional and procedural rules and rights granted to office holders defined by those rules. In one sense that makes the entity reducible — it means that we can define the property of being a government in other terms. But that sense of reducibility is not relevant to methodological individualism, since the other terms, those involving rules and rights, are not themselves individualistic. The relevant question of reducibility turns on whether the property of being a social entity can be redefined strictly in individualistic terms, that is, terms which make no reference to society or any entities other than individuals. But there is nothing in the economic approach which requires this type of reducibility. What is true of the economic approach is that social entities are supervenient on individuals — in the sense that if two worlds were identical in respect of all individualistic properties, then they would also be identical in respect of their social properties — but this is a much weaker claim than the claim of reducibility.

The final question is whether the economic approach requires methodological individualism of the third and weakest type. Does it rule out the view that social entities such as government have an intrinsic power that undermines or pre-empts individual autonomy? Even here the answer is less than a full yes. The approach certainly rules out the wholesale undermining of individual autonomy, for it assumes that individuals act in a proper intentional manner when they act within social entities. But this is scarcely a burdensome conclusion. It simply rules out the view that individuals are pawns in the hands of non-personal entities. But there is nothing in the approach that rules out more limited pre-emption of individual agency. Indeed, it is precisely intended that individual agents should be seen as being influenced in their action by the institutional structures that they recognize.

In this way, the methodological individualism of the economic method may be seen to be both minimal and defensible. The commitment is to a form of analysis which takes institutions, rules, rights and other such social entities as important, but as important precisely because of their impact on individual behaviour and the outcomes generated by that behaviour. Methodological individualism of this mild form provides a basis for the study of the impact of social entities, and comparisons across differing institutional structures. I would suggest that many of the critics of the economic method — particularly when it is applied in areas of political and social institutions — make the mistake of taking the legitimate criticisms of more virulent doctrines of methodological individualism as being effective against the milder methodological individualism which characterizes the economic method.

A further potential confusion arises between methodological and ethical individualism. As I have indicated, the form of methodological individualism required by the economic approach is merely that social entities are seen as supervenient on individuals and that individual agency is not entirely eroded. Ethical individualism, by contrast, is a view concerning the basis for ethical evaluation. Loosely speaking, ethical individualism simply requires that if something is to be evaluated as good, it must evaluated as good as a result of some impact on individuals, in short if something is good it must be good for at least someone. This rules out the possibility that something be declared good even though no one actually benefits from it. Of course some people might wish to argue against ethical individualism. For example, some might with to argue that the preservation of an area of wilderness is good even if no one (either now or in the future) thinks it good or derives any benefit. It is in some way intrinsically good.

Whatever the merits of the arguments for and against ethical individualism, the point here is that the debate is logically distinct from the debate on methodological individualism. One could adopt the limited methodological individualism associated with the economic method and still go either way on the issue of ethical individualism. As a matter of fact, most who adopt the economic method also adopt one or other form of ethical individualism (as do many who work in other traditions), but the important point here is that they are distinct commitments.

Rationality

The first task of this section is to establish the appropriate level of debate. The debate on rationality and rationalism operates at many levels and some confusion can be generated if these levels are not distinguished. In particular it is important to distinguish between what I shall term epistemic rationalism and what I shall term practical rationality. Epistemic rationalism may be caricatured as the idea that the application of pure reason is the only route to truth. Put less glibly, the epistemic rationalist in the tradition of Descartes and Spinoza will emphasize the power of deductive logic in knowledge acquisition, and will de-emphasize attempts to gain knowledge from inductive or empirical investigation. There are many criticisms of extreme epistemic rationalism — not least the problem of an infinite regress if truth is to be found only by the application of the (true) rules of logic to true premises. Consideration of these criticisms gave support to empiricism in its variety of forms and to the attempts to combine elements of rationalism and empiricism by writers such as Popper.

By contrast to epistemic rationalism, practical rationality is the much more modest view that human action can be analyzed in terms of the idea that the actions to be explained/understood/predicted can be seen as the outcome of a reasoned choice. That is, that individual human action is reasonable in the sense that it fits into a specific pattern, a pattern which involves the individual's desires and beliefs. More specifically, an action is said to be rational in this sense if it is the action most likely to achieve the individual's desires given the individual's beliefs. A rational act is one which, all things considered, you have most reason to perform.

Whatever the relationship between epistemic rationalism and practical rationality, I should be clear in saying that my concern here is with practical rationality — the idea that individual human action can be modelled as the outcome of reasonable/rational decision making on the basis of given (but perhaps unobservable) desires and beliefs. It is this notion of rationality that is important to the economic method. Indeed, while opinions differ widely on the extent to which economics as a discipline is committed to a rationalist or an empiricist epistemology (or some combination of the two, or some alternative), there can be little doubt that economics routinely employs the construction of practical rationality and that this distinguishes it quite sharply from other disciplines within social science.

In its strongest form this commitment to practical rationality becomes a commitment to the assumptions which, taken together, define *homo economicus* as an extreme calculative egoist. Correspondingly, a major line of criticism of applying economic methods in the political domain focuses on the claim that these assumptions are inappropriate. Kelman speaks for many when he writes of economic models of politics:

> They all start with the assumption that there is no difference between economic man and romantic man or political man. People act everywhere as they do in the marketplace. They are out only for themselves, and typically in relatively gross, money-seeking ways like . . . 'pigs at the trough'. My own view is that this . . . is a terrible caricature of reality. It ignores the ability of ideas to defeat interests, and the role that public spirit plays in motivating the behaviour of participants in the political process.[2]

The first step in responding to this line of criticism is to distinguish between two points: one relating to the substantive motivational psychology to be adopted, and the second relating to the contrast between singular and plural motivational structures. The Kelman quotation relates to both points, and his first two sentences indicate that a singular model of motivation is in play in economic models, so that the motivational structure of the individual is identical whatever the institutional context; the third sentence then identifies that singular motivational structure as being narrowly self-interested. Clearly Kelman objects to both aspects of the economic approach. I will discuss the singular/plural issue, and then return to the question of the substantive motivational psychology.

If we are primarily interested in the comparison between alternative institutional and constitutional structures we will wish to focus on how the switch from one institutional regime to another will impact on outcomes. There are two possible routes for such effects. First the shift in institutional environment will reconfigure the external world as perceived by any individual. This effect will change the structure of incentives and opportunities facing the individual, or change the distribution of particular individuals across alternative roles, and so change individual behaviour and social outcomes. The second route by which a shift in institutional regime may influence outcomes is via a reconfiguration of the internal world of the individual; by changing preferences, attitudes and dispositions in such a way that, even if the feasible set of alternative actions is unaltered, different choices will be made.

If individuals are single-minded (whatever the nature of that single mind) only the first route is available, while if individuals are plural-minded, institutions may act via either the first or second route. In arguing that individuals be modelled as single-minded I am arguing for the study of the first route of institutional influence in isolation from the second. This argument does not necessarily deny that the second route may be of some significance in practice, and indeed it is possible to imagine an economistic account of this process at a suitably abstract level, the claim is simply that the two routes are best studied in isolation.

A second essentially methodological argument in favour of the assumption of single-mindedness is that if individuals are taken as plural-minded we lose the ability to make comparisons across institutions with respect to a consistent and individualistic criterion. Put simply, if individuals are plural-minded, which mind is to be used for purposes of comparing institutions? Note that if some ordering over the plural minds is invoked in order to answer this question, this will amount to an admission of single-mindedness, since the meta-ranking given by the ordering over the plural minds can be viewed as a single mind.

A third argument is that the plural-minded model might be thought to be dangerously close to assuming what needs to be argued. If we simply assume that, for example, agents in political roles act in the public interest (as they perceive it) then there is little to be said about alternative institutional structures and their impact. At the very least, we would need to have some account of the process by which individuals adopt different motivational dispositions in different spheres of activity. Such an account would be tantamount to a model of endogenous dispositions — a very demanding task.

What then is the appeal of the plural-minded assumption? I believe that much of this appeal is explained by the obvious fact that behaviour differs systematically as between different institutional settings, so that it may be tempting to think that the motivations of individuals have changed. For example, individuals who donate very little of their own income to the relief of poverty may vote for major poverty relief programmes, even in the knowledge that they will contribute via taxation. But such changes in behaviour do not imply plural-mindedness, and may be explained by appeal to the changed incentive structures operating under the alternative institutions of private charity and public poverty relief (for example, in the case of voting I am voting for everyone — including me — to contribute, while in making a voluntary contribution I am acting alone). More generally, I believe that it is more powerful to explain changes in behaviour by appeal to changes in the institutional structure with all psychological factors held constant, than it is to invoke additional *ad hoc* psychological shifts.

On the maintained hypothesis of single-mindedness, I now turn to the question of the substantive motivational psychology; that is, the nature of the single mind. Four possibilities seem particularly salient here. First, we might assume that individuals are themselves moral, so that we focus on the possibility that institutional failings might subvert the morality of society. Second, we might assume that individuals are immoral, so that we focus on the possibility of institutions rescuing society from immorality. Third, we might assume that individuals are amoral, so that we focus on the moral properties induced by institutions against a morally neutral background. Fourth, we might attempt to model individuals as they actually are, a complex and heterogeneous mix of morality, amorality and immorality, so as to focus on predicting the actual outcomes of any particular institutional arrangement.

Each of these approaches has its merits, and it might be particularly interesting to view institutions under a variety of assumptions about individual moral character, but to the economist the two major alternatives must be the third and fourth, the first might be dismissed on the grounds that in a world of saints no major problems will arise and hence institutional remedies are unnecessary, while the second might be dismissed on the grounds that there is unlikely to be any unique specification of what constitutes immorality even if we can agree on a unique specification of morality. The assumption that each individual is a prudent but essentially amoral maximizer of his or her own utility is not descriptively accurate, but neither is self-interest the most pessimistic assumption. The choice between descriptive accuracy and the moderate pessimism and moral neutrality of assuming individuals to be amoral must be made on methodological grounds.

Some argue that, even if we had available to us a descriptively accurate model of the moral character of individuals, we should use the more pessimistic, amoral, model when analyzing alternative institutional frameworks with a view to institutional or constitutional reform. The argument is essentially that institutions form a sort of insurance, that they should be robust against variations in the character of individuals and should perform reasonably even when individuals do not. This is the basic insight contained in the frequently quoted remark of David Hume's that: 'in constraining any system of government, and fixing the several checks and controls of the constitution, every man ought to be supposed a knave, and to have no other end, in all his actions, than private interest'.[3]

A second point concerns the moral neutrality of the assumption of self-interest. This relates to the basic structure of 'invisible hand' arguments in which desired outcomes are generated by the institutional structure — that is the pattern and form of relationships between agents — rather than by direct appeal to the motivations of the agents themselves. The choice of the assumption of amoral agents then focuses attention on the search for invisible hand mechanisms — mechanisms which economize on virtue in the sense that they do not require virtuous agents.

This is important both because of the special power of invisible hand arguments and because of the limitations of such arguments. For example, one type of social institution which will not appear to be effective under the assumption of amoral agents, but which may work in practice, is the type of institution which seeks to screen in the more moral members of a society, or socialize certain individuals to particular moral standards, in order to place them in certain significant roles. The 'public service tradition' so evident in the British civil service in the late nineteenth and early twentieth century might be an example of an attempt to socialize individuals into a particular outlook, while the method of selecting and rewarding judges in Britain (usually involving a significant reduction in salary) might provide an example of a screening process. Such institutions are not invisible hand mechanisms since they depend on the existence of 'more moral members' of society. The aim with this type of institution is to 'amplify' the social effects of existing moral character, and if this is the type of institution of interest, it would be more appropriate to base analysis on a plausibly realistic view of moral character.

In short, there is a role for both the amoral assumption and for greater descriptive realism. Each approach focuses on a different type of institutional effect — the incentive based invisible hand case and the selection based 'amplification' case. Excessive reliance on either approach may divert attention from the variety of ways in which institutions may operate to influence outcomes for better or worse.

Public choice theory has typically taken the line of modelling individuals as single-minded and amoral. I believe that an essentially methodological defense of this line is possible, but I do not see these methodological arguments as necessarily compelling. Moreover, the possibility of modelling individuals as more morally heterogeneous, so as to view screening and socializing institutions as well as invisible hand institutions, seems to me to be both exciting and well within the general scope of the economistic approach to politics.[4] In this sense the assumption of single-mindedness can be seen as being much more basic to the economistic enterprise than any more detailed assumption of prudent amorality.

Too often, critics of public choice theory (and of economics in general) focus on motivational questions: they understand economics as defined by the assumption that all agents act to maximize the satisfaction of their own interests, fairly narrowly conceived, and seek to discard the whole enterprise on the basis that that motivational assumption is empirically wrong or ethically objectionable or both. I do not dispute that *de facto* the *homo economicus* construction plays an important role in much public choice related literature, or that there is clear evidence that some significant practitioners do take *homo economicus* to be central. The truth of the matter is, however, that most of the core results of public choice theory are such that the assumption of wholly or even predominantly egoistic motivation is neither necessary nor sufficient.

Consider 'necessity' first. In public choice theory, as in the parent discipline of economics, most of the central results are comparative static results concerning the effects of changes in relative prices or other relevant variables or institutional structures. All that is required for such results is the assumption that agents are concerned about their own interests among other things. That is, *homo economicus* can be regarded as embodying a partial specification of agents motivational structures, rather than a complete description. This more modest assumption is all that is required, for example, to show that particular institutional arrangements encourage particular (desirable) modes of behaviour. There is no need to show that, in the absence of those institutional arrangements no-one would undertake the desirable behaviour. We do not need to assume that all drivers would routinely break the rules of the road in the absence of detection and penalty devices in order to argue that detection and penalty devices may have a positive impact on compliance. We do not need to assume that all candidates elected to life-line political office would break campaign promises, in order to point out that the the incentive mechanism provided by future elections may improve the rate of promise keeping. We do not need to assume that all political agents will always exploit all genuinely discretionary power assigned to them in order to believe that institutional devices that reduce or monitor discretion (or select political agents with care) may reduce exploitation overall.

What this means is that those exponents of public choice theory who believe that it is importantly constituted by the introduction of *homo economicus* in its strong form into politics (and those critics who take the same view) are mistaken — at least for a very wide range of relevant propositions. Occam's razor (a principle much beloved by economists) would require us not to make a strong motivational assumption when a weaker one will do. Even more important, however, is the 'sufficiency' aspect. Motivational assumptions in and of themselves are a matter of psychology, not of social analysis. The irony of the debate about motivational assumptions in public choice theory is that those assumptions are only an input into the real analytical game which is the analysis of institutional structures as such. The way in which institutional arrangements operate to determine social outcomes, and the differential operation of alternative institutions, form the central agenda items. Indeed, the economic approach goes to some lengths to finesse psychological questions of motivation (which is one reason why the behaviourist element embodied in revealed preference theory has such appeal to economists). What economics, and public choice theory, needs is the weakest possible set of motivational postulates, because the main quarry lies elsewhere, in the discussion of how different institutions work to produce different social outcomes from the interactions among a group of agents with no change in their motivations. Issues of institutional performance are obscure, and analysis often leads to results that are somewhat counterintuitive. It is this latter intellectual enterprise that the economic approach to politics is engaged in, and to be distracted by psychological questions involves a sacrifice of comparative advantage.

In my view, the economic approach to politics can be readily detached from any assumption of radical egoism as the central motivation, notwithstanding the practice (and sometimes the explicit claims) of some public choice scholars. The central interest in political institutions as possible remedies for principal-agent problems, the attention to the incentive effects embodied in particular institutional arrangements, a focus on the extent to which social outcomes emergent under particular institutional arrangements reflect the preferences of the individuals who act within these arrangements — none of these issues requires an assumption of unrelieved egoism on the part of agents to be interesting. Some analytic convenience may be bought by the strict homo economicus construction, but the price paid in terms of unnecessary antagonism may well be too high.

Finale

Economistic models of politics offer a distinctive approach to questions of the design and reform of political and social institutions. But the approach carries with it a certain amount of methodological baggage. This baggage is often seen by critics of the economic approach as being altogether too heavy, precluding useful analysis or discussion. I have tried to suggest that in two key areas — the areas of methodological individualism and rationality — this baggage is considerably lighter and more defensible than many critics claim. Public choice scholars and others interested in the economistic approach to politics are not tied to the implausible denial of the importance of social entities, and nor are they tied to the empirical claim that all actions are grounded in narrow self interest. It is relatively easy to sketch a caricature of the economic approach and to dismiss that caricature as untenable; but that is in the nature of caricatures rather than in the nature of the economic approach.

However, it is clear that the methodological baggage of the economic approach, even on a more subtle and sympathetic reading, is not empty. If it were there could be no purpose to carrying it. My claim is simply that this baggage can provide some insight into the operation of social systems, that being economical with politics is a worthwhile activity. But, as with any method, it is likely that social scientists will be lead astray if they adopt a method unreflectively and uncritically.

Notes

1 A bibliographic note at the end of this essay contains references which will enable the interested reader to pursue these and other ideas in more detail.
2 Kelman, S. 'Public Choice and the Public Spirit', *Public Interest*, 1987, pp. 80–94. Quoted from pages pp. 80–1.
3 Hume, D. (1985) *Essays Moral, Political and Literary*. Edited by E.F. Miller, Indianapolis, Liberty Classics. Quoted from page 42.
4 A beginning is made in Brennan and Hamlin (1995b).

Bibliographical note

This note is intended to provide some points of entry to the literature relating to the issues sketched here and to provide references to some of my own work in which these themes are developed or discussed in more detail. The literature on social choice theory tends to be technical in nature. Arrow (1963) initiated much of the literature; Sen (1970) is a classic text in which the technique is largely separated from the discussion; many of the seminal contributions are collected in Rowley (1993) which also includes a useful introductory essay. Public Choice theory is surveyed in Mueller (1989); Buchanan and Tullock (1962) is a locus classicus for the public choice approach to politics. Some relevant work by Jack Wiseman is collected in Wiseman (1989). Sen (1987) provides an introduction to the links between economics and ethics. For alternative interpretations of individualism see Lukes (1973) and O'Neill (1973). On rationalism and rationality see Brown (1988), and Elster (1986).

As for my own work, Hamlin (1986) contains a more detailed account of rationality and links to the analysis of the state, Hamlin and Pettit (1989) discuss individualism and other commitments of normative political analysis, Brennan and Hamlin (1992, 1993, 1994) provide examples of the economic analysis of political institutions, Brennan and Hamlin (1995a) offers a detailed discussion of the political philosophy of constitutional political economy.

References

ARROW, K. (1963) *Social Choice and Individual Values*, (Revised Edition) New Haven, Yale University Press.

BRENNAN, G. and HAMLIN, A.P. (1992) 'Bicameralism and Majoritarian Equilibrium', *Public Choice*, **74**, pp. 169–79.

BRENNAN, G. and HAMLIN, A.P. (1993) 'Rationalizing Parliamentary Systems', *Australian Journal of Political Science*, **28**, pp. 443–57.

BRENNAN, G. and HAMLIN, A.P. (1994) 'A Revisionist View of the Separation of Powers', *Journal of Theoretical Politics*, **6**, pp. 345–68.

BRENNAN, G. and HAMLIN, A.P. (1995a) 'Constitutional Political Economy: The Political Philosophy of Homo Economicus?', *Journal of Political Philosophy*, **3**, pp. 280–303.

BRENNAN, G. and HAMLIN, A.P. (1995b) 'Economizing on virtue', *Constitutional Political Economy*, **6**, pp. 35–56.

BROWN, H. (1988) *Rationality*, London, Routledge.

BUCHANAN, J.M. and TULLOCK, G. (1962) *The Calculus of Consent*, Ann Arbor, University of Michigan Press.

HAMLIN, A.P. (1986) *Ethics, Economics and the State*, Hemel Hempstead, Wheatsheaf Books.

HAMLIN, A.P. and PETTIT, P. (1989) 'The Normative Analysis of the State' in HAMLIN, A.P. and PETTIT, P. (Eds) *The Good Polity*, Oxford, Blackwell.

LUKES, S. (1973) *Individualism*, Oxford, Blackwell.

MUELLER, D.C. (1989) *Public Choice II*, Cambridge, Cambridge University Press.

O'NEILL, J. (Ed) (1973) *Modes of Individualism and Collectivism*, London, Heinemann.

ROWLEY, C. (Ed) (1993) *Social Choice Theory*, (3 Volumes), Cheltenham, Edward Elgar.

SEN, A.K. (1970) *Collective Choice and Social Welfare*, San Francisco, Holden-Day.

SEN, A.K. (1987) *On Ethics and Economics*, Oxford Blackwell.

WISEMAN, J. (1989) *Cost, Choice and Political Economy*, Cheltenham, Edward Elgar.

6 Family Behaviour and the Economic Method

George McKenzie

A Challenge

The aim of this book and of this chapter is to enhance the reader's awareness of the different traditions that characterize social and economic research, the historical basis of these traditions and their impact upon the actual process of research. It is our view that such awareness can be enhanced by reading about how researchers approach their work. Hence the implicit autobiographical nature of the several chapters in this book. However, a deeper understanding of a particular tradition can only be attained through immersion in the discourse of that tradition. That is, an actual involvement in the methodology and practice of other, alternative perhaps competing approaches is required. Such involvement not only enhances an appreciation of what others are up to but also enhances a process of self-reflexivity which can only serve to improve our individual critical insight.

This is the nature of the challenge which this chapter seeks to set explicitly — it asks readers to place themselves within the tradition of rational, deductive reasoning such as Descartes advocated as the basis for human enquiry. In this chapter, as an example, we shall explore the application of the *Economic Method* to an analysis of the decisions and problems of the family. It has long been my view that it is not possible to be critical of a particular approach to social and economic research or of the practice associated with that tradition without submerging oneself in the discourse of that tradition. This will not be an easy task and, in any case, we can only scratch the surface.

Readers will be asked for the moment to suppress their prejudices. This will be an impossible task. We have all developed our own approach to research and teaching that will have evolved from our individual personal experiences, including our educational experience. The latter, in turn, will have been influenced by ideas generated over the preceding centuries. Thus our prejudices, explicit or implicit, are bound to be deeply rooted. It will not be surprising if the initial reaction of many readers to what follows is one of deep anxiety if not anger. But there is some consolation. For the committed positivists reading this chapter the task will be even more difficult. They will be asked to reflect upon how the other traditions discussed in this volume would seek to understand the specific issues discussed here. But for all readers, the theme that I am seeking to draw out is that are many valid research methodologies and that the one discussed here is only one.

Our focus will be Gary Becker's analysis of the family (1987, 1991). Becker was awarded the 1992 Nobel Prize in Economics. This distinction was not gained through the discovery of some new technique or research method but rather through the extension of the discourse of deductive economic theory to a wider range of social issues such as discrimination, marriage, divorce and fertility. His approach to these topics is outlined in his Nobel Lecture (1993). This work illustrates the use of the central concept of economic analysis, the *doctrine of opportunity cost*. Basically, this states that 'there is no such thing as a free lunch'. In order to achieve a certain want, something must be given up. For example, for an individual with a limited income, purchasing a house might mean foregoing an automobile. Becker argues that this principle is relevant for all of life's decisions, not just those that are explicitly economic. This can be very frustrating for non-economists engaging in discussion with an economist. By utilizing the concept of opportunity cost, the economist can appear to be an expert on virtually every topic!

Blau (1987) notes that Becker has laid the foundations for what has come to be called the 'new home economics'. From a purely historical perspective, the words 'home' and 'economics' are redundant since the word 'economics' is derived from the Greek words $o\acute{\iota}\chi o\varsigma$ meaning 'house' and $\upsilon\acute{o}\mu o\varsigma$ meaning 'law' or 'rule'. Thus for the Ancient Greeks, economics referred to the practice of household management. It is in this spirit that we shall examine the application of the method of the economist to the analysis of family structure. For those who are not economists, the method will represent a challenge to the entire concept of interdisciplinary research. For everyone, Becker's work illustrates the difficulty and trauma frequently experienced in the process of research. In his speech accepting the Nobel prize, he admits to breaking publisher's deadlines and then feeling so exhausted after completion of the work that his research programme was interrupted for two years.

Following in the tradition of Max Weber, economic analysis distinguishes between normative or subjective statements and positive or objective statements. The latter, it is argued, are capable of analysis by rigorous, scientific analysis. Indeed the individuals that make up society are themselves thought to act in a scientific way, rational and capable of undertaking extremely complex decisions. Thus in Becker's analysis, each individual seeks to rationally maximize his or her level of satisfaction subject to constraints imposed by income, wealth, social practice and institutions. In the traditional model of consumer behaviour, such as studied by first-year students in economics, the individual is assumed to choose her or his consumption of goods subject to a given level of income. However, Becker has sought to 'pry economists away from narrow assumptions about self-interest' (1993, p. 385). He seeks to extend this mode of analysis to allow a wider range of behaviour to be incorporated in individual preferences and hence to enable an examination of the determinants of family size, marriage, divorce and the participation of women in the labour force.

In this way of thinking, individuals maximize their satisfaction 'as they conceive it, whether they be selfish, altruistic, loyal, spiteful or masochistic'. (p. 386, 1993). Such behaviour is taken as given. Rational behaviour admits to any set of preferences. No attempt is made to enquire whether markets and actual decision making processes have an influence upon behaviour. In the spirit of Weber, the subjective may influence objective and observable behaviour. However, it is a one way street and no attempt is made to examine the influence of markets, institutions or policies upon preferences themselves. This is a theme to which I shall return in the conclusion to this chapter.

To illustrate Becker's method, I will consider the interrelationship between four topics that figure prominently in his *A Treatise on the Family*: human fertility, the division of labour between genders, marriage and divorce. A complete exposition of his framework would require the extensive use of mathematics, something which is beyond the scope of this paper. Consequently, I will seek to develop the main elements of his approach in a very partial way, illuminated with the aid of diagrams.

To Have or Not to Have — A Family, That Is

Let us suppose that the preferences of male and female partners depend only upon the quantity of goods consumed, denoted by Z, and the number of children in the family, denoted by N. The preferences of the two as a group are represented in Figure 6.1 by a set of indifference curves, of which the curves labelled U1, U2 and U3 are examples. Along any curve such as U1, the couple derives equal satisfaction from the several patterns of goods consumed and family size. That is, the couple is indifferent between the combinations represented by the points I and II in the diagram. This reflects the assumption that in order to obtain more goods for consumption the couple is prepared to have a smaller family. The diagram also reflects two additional assumptions. The couple obtains more satisfaction from consuming more goods and from a larger family. This assumption is not necessary for the analysis which can be complicated by allowing for satiation. However, a second assumption is crucial. The indifference curves cannot cross. If they did, as in Figure 6.2, the couple would be considered to be irrational. That is, they would appear to prefer situation I to II, to be indifferent between II and III and by implication indifferent between I and III. However, this is not possible since they prefer IV to III and are indifferent between I and IV. In other words, indifference curves that cross are logically inconsistent. This is the positivist economist's concept of irrationality. One cannot both prefer and be indifferent between two situations. A fuller understanding of these concepts can be obtained by reference to a good economics textbook, such as that written by Begg, Dornbusch and Fischer (1993).

In Figure 6.3, the curve AB represents the constraints faced by the couple. Available choice may constrained by many factors but especially household income and the cost of rearing children. Thus at one extreme, if the couple decide to have no children, they could consume OA. However, if children are to be reared, the couple are able to devote less of their time to income generating work. At the other extreme, all family resources could be devoted to rearing OB children with no consumption at all, not a feasible outcome. Neither extreme is optimal for the

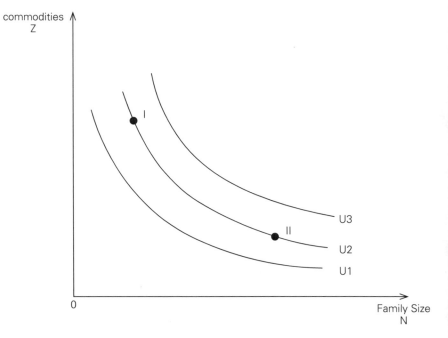

Figure 6.1

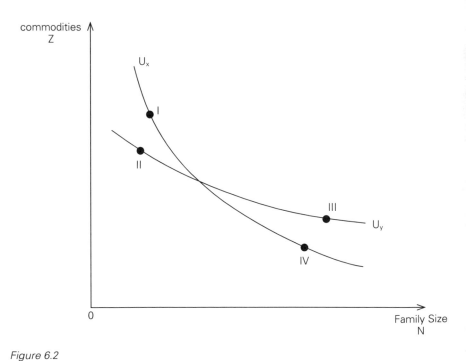

Figure 6.2

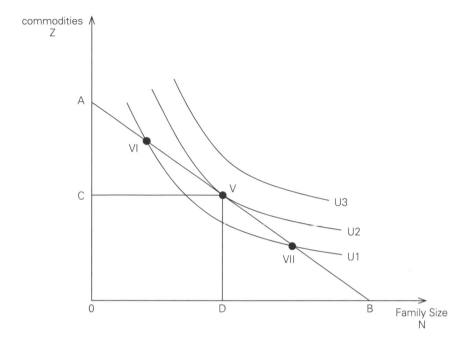

Figure 6.3

couple under consideration. Instead, they rationally choose to consume OC goods and to maintain a family of size OD. This yields the highest feasible level of satisfaction at V. A decision to operate at VI or VII would yield a lower level of satisfaction U1. Any pattern of family size and consumption along the indifference curve U3 is not feasible.

If the costs of rearing children were higher, then the couple would choose a smaller family size as in Figures 6.4a and 6.4b. If family size and consumption were viewed by the couple as being complementary, they would also choose to consume less (Figure 6.4a). However, if they were substitutes (Figure 6.4b), consumption would actually increase. This mode of analysis can be extended in a number of directions. For example, if employment opportunities exist for children, a larger family size will generate greater levels of satisfaction since it would also be a source of income.

At this point it is worthwhile taking a brief, methodological digression. Becker's theory as outlined so far places great emphasis on measurability. Income is earned, goods are consumed, children are produced. In addition, we have also spoken of individual satisfaction as if it were a measurable quantity. In fact, this is a fiction designed to simplify the exposition. However, this fiction is a holdover from an important debate in the discourse of economics. In the nineteenth century, the Utilitarians explicitly spoke of individual satisfaction as measurable in objective units of utility. However, as shown by Paul Samuelson and John Hicks, like Becker Nobel Prize winners, this assumption was unnecessary. All that was required was

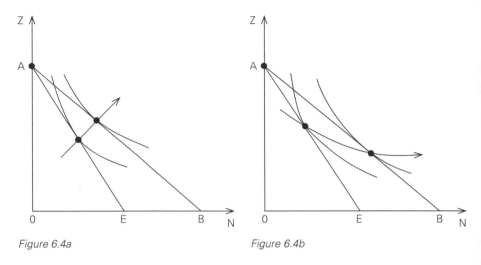

Figure 6.4a   Figure 6.4b

for individuals to be able to *rank* all feasible opportunities. Measurement was not required for rational decision making.

The Sexual Division of Labour

The previous discussion has implicitly assumed that the male and female partners have identical characteristics. However, this assumption is dropped when Becker turns his attention to the analysis of labour force participation by women and decisions concerning marriage and divorce. Although he takes care to give recognition to the role of cultural factors in these activities, he places a very strong emphasis on the *biological* differences between men and women. Two issues are involved: 1) the economies of scale emanating from the division of labour and 2) the preferences of women towards income generating employment versus child rearing.

The concept of the division of labour is one the most important in economics and was highlighted by Adam Smith in his *Wealth of Nations* (1776). He illustrated the idea with his classic example of the production of a pin. He argued that it was less efficient for a individual to undertake all the tasks involved. Rather, one individual could produce the shaft, another would sharpen the head and yet another would create the top. By specializing in this way, the group of workers would be able to produce more pins than if each tried to carry out the entire job. Economies of scale would arise in the sense that if each individual doubled their time on a particular task, their output would more than double.

By specializing in a particular task, each individual worker is able to exploit gains in efficiency from the scale of activity undertaken. Today the division of labour also provides the foundation for modern industrial production, for example, the assembly line of automobile production. Gary Becker proposes that it can also be used as a basis for understanding family life, which he views as analogous to

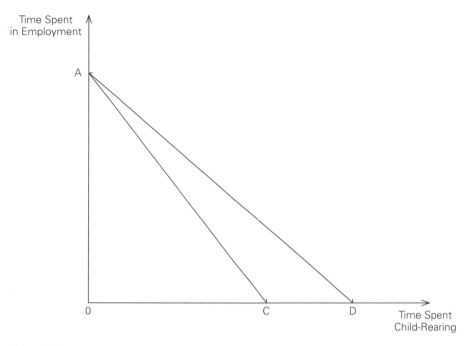

Figure 6.5

a factory. He argues that substantial division of labour is to be expected in families because of 'increasing returns from investments in specific human capital, such as skills that are especially useful in child rearing or in market activities' (1987, p. 283). This comparative advantage is illustrated in Figure 6.5. Here I assume that both men and women are equally efficient in carrying out market-oriented activities. That is, if neither spent any time in child-rearing, they would each be able to produce OA. However, the woman has a comparative advantage in child-rearing. For each hour less that is worked, she is able to increase her child-rearing activities by a greater amount than her male partner. Becker supports this analysis in the following manner:

> A man completes his biological contribution to the production of children when his sperm fertilises a woman's egg, after which she controls the reproductive process: she biologically houses and feeds the fetus, delivers the baby, and often feeds the infant with her own milk. . . . Women not only have a heavy biological commitment to the production and feeding of children, but they also are biologically committed to the care of children in other, more subtle ways. Moreover, women have been willing to spend much time and energy caring for their children because they want their heavy biological investment in production to be worthwhile. In addition, a mother can more readily feed and watch her older children while she produces additional children than while she engages in most other activities.

In other words, because of the basic biological difference between men and women, the argument is that the opportunity cost of child-rearing to women is less than it

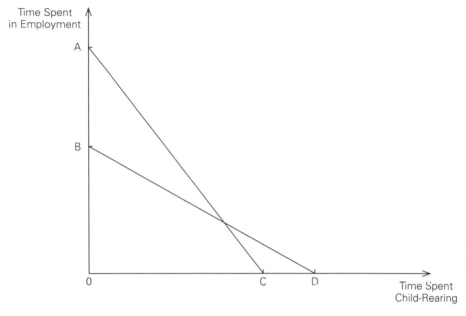

Figure 6.6

is for men. That is, if a woman spends more of her time in child rearing activities, she will be foregoing less income than a man who undertook these tasks instead. This case does not, however, establish a *prima facie* case that women should remain at home to look after the children. On the basis of biological difference, Becker is simply concluding that women have a comparative advantage in child rearing. What women actually choose to do depends upon their preferences, as will be argued in the next section.

The Working Woman

Becker utilizes the analysis of the preceding two sections to explain the simultaneous decline in fertility rates and the increase in labour force participation by women. First, it is necessary to note that the assumptions of Figure 6.5 will not hold exactly in Becker's analysis. Because women have a biological comparative advantage in child rearing, they will not have time to undertake the training for market related employment. Hence their income from such activities will be less than for men (Figure 6.6). However, increased potential earnings and educational opportunities for women have, over the past century, increased the opportunity costs of having a family and will have shifted the constraint more closely to OD as depicted in Figure 6.5. In addition, the costs of child-rearing in terms of education and health care have also increased over the past century.

Changes in wages and costs are only part of the picture. They alter the opportunities available to women. The actual outcome will also depend upon the

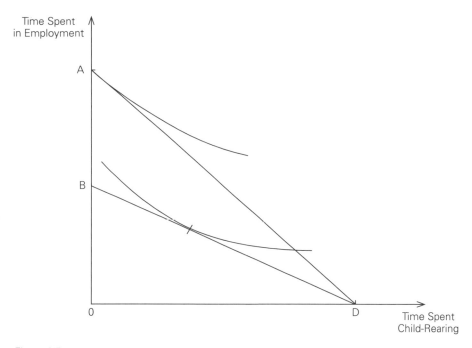

Figure 6.7a

preferences of women towards remunerative employment, on the one hand, and child-rearing on the other. In its simplest form, the economist's model of the supply of labour to any market assumes that the goal of work is not the work itself but the income to purchase goods from which satisfaction is obtained. However, behavioural theorists will argue that individuals obtain satisfaction from the job itself. Work may involve companionship, the pleasure from working as part of a successful group or enjoyment of the power involved in controlling other people (e.g. Lane (1991)). Thus if a woman's preferences are as shown in Figure 6.7a, she would decide to forego child-rearing entirely in order to enjoy the benefits accruing from remunerative employment. On the other hand, if her preferences are as shown in Figure 6.7b, the higher income from employment will enable her to reduce time spent on the job and to devote more of her time towards child-rearing. As a former teacher of mine once said: 'the answer to all questions in economics is: it all depends'.

In order to avoid the use of mathematical analysis, I have simplified the analysis considerably. The method of exposition is designed to be pedagogic. In reality, of course, the choice for men and women is not simply between work and child-rearing. There is also the choice of leisure time. To extend the analysis in this direction would require a three dimensional diagram. Hence a verbal presentation will have to suffice. The ultimate constraint on all of us is time. There are only twenty-four hours in each day. Hence, if a woman is to pursue a career and raise a family, it is because she values these activities more highly than her leisure time.

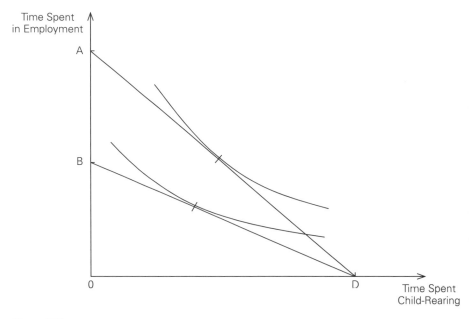

Figure 6.7b

However, if the preferences of the couple are complementary, the term which Becker uses to describe love, then the male partner will desire to forgo some of his leisure time and devote it to child-rearing in order that his partner may enjoy more leisure.

Marriage and Divorce, Economics Style

Becker extends the concepts of opportunity cost to an analysis of marriage and divorce. Here the idea of Pareto efficiency plays a crucial role. Consider the following example. A Pareto efficient situation is said to be one in which it is impossible to reallocate production and consumption so as to make any one individual better off without making others worse off. Similarly, a Pareto inefficient situation is one where at least one individual can be made better off without anyone else becoming worse off. For Becker, this way of thinking explains the institution of marriage:

> Marriage can be said to take place in a 'market' that 'assigns' men and women to each other or to remain single until better opportunities come along. An optimal assignment in an efficient market with utility-maximizing participants has the property that persons not assigned to each other could not be made better off by marrying each other. (1987, p. 284)

Important to this 'calculation' will be the extent of dowries, bride prices, leisure and the exercise of power that one or both parties may enjoy from the marriage.

The analysis of divorce follows on: a rational person will want a divorce if the satisfaction expected from remaining married is less than that which follows a divorce, especially if this involves a new liaison. The link between this situation and Pareto efficiency is as follows. If men and women were always Pareto efficient, then there would be no incentive for divorce. However, as Becker argues, new information becomes available. Chosen partners may turn out to be less desirable than anticipated, or an alternative partner is identified who appears to be more desirable. For Becker, this possibility explains the basis of the marriage contract. Since women tend to specialise in child care, for the reasons explained previously, they become economically vulnerable to separation and divorce. Hence a divorce will usually involve legally enforceable compensation to the woman.

Becker emphasizes that new information about a mate or a prospective mate is not the only cause of divorce. He argues:

> The rise in labour force participation of married women also lowered the gain from remaining married because the sexual division of labour was reduced, and women became more independent financially. (1987, p. 284)

Becker suggests that the liberalization of divorce laws has not had any permanent impact on the rate of divorce. Rather, he suggests that the decision to remain married or not depends upon whether family income is greater in a state of marriage than in a state of divorce:

> Assume that the husband appears to gain from divorce, but the apparent loss to the wife is greater. . . . If divorce were unilateral, he might be tempted to seek a divorce even when she would be greatly harmed. However, she could change his mind by offering a bribe that would make them both better off by staying married.

This passage illustrates another important concept of economic analysis, the *compensation principle*. It states that for efficiency to be improved by some action, gainers should be able to compensate the losers. This is simply another way of restating the concept of Pareto efficiency.

Reflections

My own research has built heavily upon many of the same foundation stones that Becker has utilized in his research on the family. This will be apparent, for example, from *Measuring Economic Welfare*. There I made most of the same assumptions made by Becker: rationality on the part of individuals, measurability, the representative person, certainty. The tools of mathematics that were utilized were identical. In the concluding chapter of my book I sought to identify limits as to the nature of the understandings that I thought that I had achieved. It seems reasonable that these same thoughts should be directed at Becker's work as well. Before doing that, however, it is important to note a significant difference between the two volumes. Becker is trying to extend the methodology of the economist to a wider range of social issues. He is advocating a particular approach towards interdisciplinary research. In my work, I was trying to undermine some of the dogma involved in a particular discourse about how to identify changes in individual and social well-being. This involved two objectives. The first was technical and involved pointing out that there were logical errors involved in traditional cost/benefit measurements of gains and losses. That is, conventional measurement techniques might show a gain in satisfaction whereas in fact there had been a loss. Rather than simply criticize the perceived status quo, I proposed an alternative method which was not radical but based upon the same methodological foundations as the flawed analysis. My second aim was to provide an antidote to those who would seek to construct measures of individual and social well-being that are 'objective'. Such measures may mask changes in the distribution of income that might be undesirable even if there were gains in efficiency.

But there are limits to all this. In order to understand these limits it is worthwhile saying a few words about the continuing debate over whether or not it is possible to construct a social science along the same lines as the physical sciences. There are many elements to this debate but I propose to concentrate on only one which I believe has been relatively neglected. Physical scientists, in very many cases, can undertake experiments. They can create situations in which certain variables are held constant and the relationship between those variables of interest is then studied. Undertaking experiments in a vacuum is a case in point. The molecules and atoms which form air are eliminated and hence have no influence upon the results.

In contrast, social scientists are generally not in a position to undertake such controlled experiments on individuals or groups of individuals. There are two reasons for this. First, the values of Western society suggest that the undertaking of such experiments is undesirable. It would impinge upon individual liberties. Second, once people knew that they were part of an experiment they might change their behaviour and hence bias the results. Indeed, it would be impossible to forecast the direction of any bias. In one experiment, individuals might seek to reinforce the preconceived notions of the investigators, whereas in another experiment, they might seek to undermine the investigators.

For these reasons, economists and many other social scientists resort to intellectual experiments. Using mathematics, geometry or verbal logic, the economist creates a structure in which all variables are assumed to remain constant except those which are of interest. These are the famous *ceteris paribus* assumptions. Very many of these experiments are clearly identified for what they are. They are not designed to be approximations in any way to the real world. Their aim is simply to enhance the understanding of the investigator. The investigator then passes on his insights, as Becker has done, in the form of articles and books. These are valid exercises in the sense that they are designed to raise questions and to enhance awareness and understanding. They are undertaken for their own sake.

Readers are then free to give their interpretation to the work in a variety of ways. I will consider two possible outcomes. First, some readers may disagree with the basic assumptions of the analysis. Modern critics of positivism have attacked the assumption of rationality, the representative person, the nature of certainty and the emphasis on Cartesian measurement. Alternative assumptions would need to be made. For example, psychoanalytic theorists might suggest that marriage arises from the desire to eliminate a lacking or rejection that followed childhood rejection by mother. Lane (1991) argues that markets are cockpits of emotion and that this undermines the economist's concept of rationality. We have noted above, Becker's view that the marriage contract protects the vulnerable woman from the costs of divorce. However, many women (cf. Viner (1994)) believe that marriage is institutionalized rape. Becker explicitly assumes away the possibility of rape (1991, p. 313). These thoughts suggest that research into family behaviour needs to extend beyond the discourse of the *economic method.*

If theories are simply intellectual experiments, then it does not matter whether its assumptions are unrealistic or not. Problems arise, however, when researchers seek to misuse theory. Even though the analysis is conceived as an intellectual experiment, this has not prevented investigators from attempting to see how well the theories approximate reality. In a sense, they see the theories as analogues to Newton's Law. But inevitably none of these theories will stand the test of time because they have not been constructed to reflect reality in its totality. They are what they are: intellectual experiments undertaken by complex but limited human minds. The construction of theories and their use in seeking to understand the world in which we live is, in my opinion an uncertain, conditional, open-ended activity. The methodology of the positivist or any research tradition provides a language whereby individuals with similar approaches to research can communicate with each other. A very great danger, of course, is that the methodology and its language become the end, rather than a means for understanding.

References

BECKER, G. (1991) *A Treatise on the Family*, Cambridge Massachusetts, Harvard University Press.

BECKER, G. (1993) 'Nobel Lecture: The Economic Way of Looking at Behaviour', *Journal of Political Economy*, 101, June, pp. 385–409.

BECKER, G. (1987) 'The Family', *The New Palgrave Dictionary of Economics*, London, Macmillan, pp. 281–86.

BEGG, D., DORNBUSCH, R. and FISCHER, S. (1993) *Economics*, London, McGraw-Hill.

BLAU, F. (1987) 'Gender', *The New Palgrave Dictionary of Economics*, London, Macmillan, 402–97.

LANE, R. (1991) *The Market Experience*, Cambridge, Cambridge University Press.

McKENZIE, G. (1983) *Measuring Economic Welfare: New Methods*, Cambridge, Cambridge University Press.

SMITH, A. (1950) *The Wealth of Nations*, London, J.M. Dent.

VINER, K. (1994) 'Sisters with Soft Centers', *The Guardian Tabloid*, 15 June.

Part 2

The Nature of Disciplines

The word *discipline* implies order and control. Thus those individuals who form themselves into the traditional or classical research communities such as economics, politics, sociology, psychology or statistics are implicitly seeking the order and control that will enable them to pursue their particular conception of systematic research. But for such disciplines to exist there must be a consensus which forms a common basis in the search for knowledge. The chapters in this second part address the question of 'what enables a particular community to call itself a discipline?'. The question is dealt with in an oblique manner, not directly but indirectly. The first three chapters seek to identify the unifying elements underlying new and emerging disciplines: information systems, nursing and social work studies. However, each of the authors focuses on different attributes of their particular discipline. Avison views Information Systems as interdisciplinary and multi-faceted, drawing on 'computer science, sociology, semiology, economics, mathematics, management, applied psychology, linguistics, politics, ethics, ergonomics and cultural studies'. Is it possible to define a discipline which encompasses virtually all the disciplines comprising social sciences? Or are historical labels irrelevant? Is a discipline defined by its community according to the functions that they seek to perform?

In seeking to define nursing as a discipline, Payne focuses not on its overlap with other, established disciplines but on research methods. She identifies three phases in the development of nursing research, the first based on natural science, the second involving the use of social science paradigms and the third reflecting contemporary controversies over the processes characterizing knowledge creation. She discusses the application of grounded theory, ethnography, phenomenology, feminist strategies and action research to the field of nursing. She also notes that in an attempt to reconcile the differences between qualitative and quantitative methodologies, some researchers have suggested the use of triangulation, the application of multiple methods with the niew that no single method is adequate. Like Avison, she is suggesting that the process of research is open-ended.

Joan Orme takes a somewhat different tack in identifying the central theme of social work research as practice, that is, the need to inform the practitioner. This is in contrast to the approach of the more traditional disciplines which adopt Weber's position in arguing that the research process must be objective and independent of those being researched. In this sense, some would argue that practitioners are a link between the research and the researched and hence capable of introducing bias. Hence, they conclude that practitioners should also be independent of the research process. Orme discusses these tensions and suggests that feminist writing on epistemology and methodology provides a clarification of the above dichotomy and of knowledge creation not only in social work but in all research practice.

Philosophers of science such as Thomas Kuhn note that science disciplines are less orderly and systematic than they claim to be. In the fourth chapter of this section, David Hand provides concrete examples of this by focusing on the use of statistical methods in the social sciences. This involves two steps. The first involves the specification of the question in the language of the particular discipline. The second involves ensuring that the statistical method used actually addresses the same question. His general conclusion is that before we can make progress in understanding our social and economic environment, we must focus our attention on carefully specifying the question being researched.

7   The Search for the 'Discipline' of Information Systems

David E. Avison

Background

This chapter is about some of the issues relating to establishing an academic discipline. It discusses this in the context of information systems, but many of the concerns are found in other subjects which are trying to establish themselves. Indeed there were similar growing pains relating to disciplines which are now well established in universities. In the Faculty of Social Sciences at Southampton, there are groups such as social work and accounting which are also not well established in many universities, as well as politics and economics which are well established. However, some of the concerns expressed here are also relevant to established disciplines. For example, there are debates in English and anthropology departments about the nature of their disciplines. Perhaps such debates are a healthy part of any lively discipline and an indication that the discipline is relevant and will remain relevant.

Some may argue that these concerns are merely 'academic'. However, the concerns discussed in this chapter are important in practice. The outcome of such debates will influence what we teach and research under the umbrella of the discipline. They will also influence how we research, that is, what research methods we might use. In some disciplines there are well-established research methods. Here, few question the research method used, and question only whether it was used according to the tenets of the discipline. However, some university groups might establish a reputation through their use of a particular approach which goes against the trend. In other disciplines, of which information systems is one, there seems to be a very wide range of topics taught in universities, in areas researched and in research methods used.

There are other reasons why this topic is important. Many are 'political' and 'financial'. For example, on the financial side, it is essential for those working in the discipline that the subject achieves recognition in order to gain funding from universities and funding bodies, such as the research councils. It is also important to have good representation in the political decision-making process. A young discipline may not be represented in research assessment exercises. This will have a direct financial implication.

As a 'founding professor' in information systems (IS) at the University of Southampton, I decided to introduce the discipline of information systems to the university in my inaugural lecture 'What is IS?' (Avison, 1995). As a new discipline, few people in the university had knowledge of what the subject was about, what impact it had made and could make, what was researched and how it was researched. Indeed, there was the widespread view that IS was Information Technology (IT) under a different name, and much of the talk was about the comparison of IS with IT as a subject (the latter expressed in popular books called 'What is IT?').

This chapter concerns itself most with the inter-disciplinary nature of information systems. There are many source disciplines which are relevant. However, this does not invalidate it as a discipline and many of the social sciences are similar in this respect. Further, well-established disciplines such as medicine are also inter-disciplinary. We look at research methods that are relevant to information systems. Again, their plurality is evident. We then consider one area of information systems teaching and research, that of information systems development. By showing how many different approaches to information systems development might be used, we return to our theme. Because of the nature of this text, the differences in research methods used in information systems are highlighted.

No attempt is made to suggest that those within the academic discipline should 'get their act together' and agree a very limited set of research methods and teaching topics. Such an exercise would restrict the potential of this young discipline as well as being divisive in the community. However, there is a discussion of the potential difficulties that this richness imposes.

The Domain of Information Systems

In recent years there has been much debate about the actual state and possible future of information systems as an academic discipline (Banville and Landry, 1989). While there is, as yet, no consensus as to what should be included or excluded from the field, it is generally accepted that information systems is an essentially pluralistic field, founded on knowledge from many other well-established source disciplines. This is true of many of the social sciences. The insights from the source disciplines have proved of relevance to researchers, teachers and practitioners alike.

The multi-faceted nature of the field is seen if we consider a definition of the central object of the discipline. Buckingham *et al.* (1987) define an information system as follows:

> A system which assembles, stores, processes and delivers information relevant to an organization (or to society) in such a way that the information is accessible and useful to those who wish to use it, including managers, staff, clients and citizens. An information system is a human activity (social) system which may or may not involve computer systems. (p. 18)

Thus, information systems is not simply about information technology. Indeed, it may not involve computers at all. The definition would seem to encompass a wide range of areas, for example, information theory (information), semiology (delivers information), organization theory and sociology (organization and society) and computer science and engineering (computer systems). However, information systems is not sociology, computer science, management or other related disciplines because it is a particular combination of these that is its essence. At present, there are relatively few university departments of information systems, academics teaching and researching information systems are to be found in management, computer science, psychology departments and elsewhere, and in faculties of business, science, engineering and social science.

Information Systems Research

We see a very broad area for topics of information systems research. Keen (1987), in an overview of research in information systems, critically examines particular areas of research. He argues that the mission of information systems research is to study 'the effective design, delivery, use and impact of information technologies in organizations and society'. He points out that there has been a high proportion of hard information systems research (that is, relating to the technology, for example, design methodologies, computers, implementation, productivity tools, office technology and telecommunications); research looking for particular gains for businesses in an economically competitive environment (for example, economic and competitive implications of computing); and also research looking for 'solutions' to perennial problems (for example, productivity tools, database management, personal computing and expert systems).

It is claimed (Galliers and Land, 1987; Orlikowski and Baroudi, 1991) that the positivist research approach, which has its roots in the natural sciences, is the most commonly adopted because of a technological view of information systems. For example, Orlikowski and Baroudi (1991) found that 97 per cent of the information systems literature they examined fell under positivist epistemology. These studies assume an objective reality, reducing information systems phenomena to their simplest elements whilst looking for causality and fundamental laws. These are seen as forming the basis for generalizable knowledge, often represented in mathematical models that can predict patterns of behaviour, independent of time and context (Foster and Flynn, 1984).

In recent years however social and organizational issues concerning information systems have been increasingly recognized. The work of IFIP Working Group 8.2 in particular reflects this (see, for example, Avison *et al.*, 1993). This view is reflected in the use of non-positivist research approaches to the study of information systems. There are various strands among the non-positivist studies, depending on their views of the nature of information systems and the approach to inquiry. For example, interpretive approaches aim to understand how members of a social group, through their participation in social processes, enact their particular realities and endow them with meaning (Walsham, 1993). Interpretive studies therefore view information systems as social constructions, focusing on a shared interpretation around information systems and how meanings arise and are sustained (Boland and Day, 1989). Within the interpretive studies, the role of theory in research also varies. For example, studies using a 'grounded theory' approach seek to develop new theory to explain information systems phenomena from the researchers' own interpretations (Orlikowski, 1993). In these studies, theories are seen as emerging from the data. Other studies illustrate the potential of a theory to explain an information systems phenomenon (Orlikowski and Robey, 1991; Walsham and Han, 1993; Jones and Nandhakumar, 1993). Another non-positivist approach to information systems research is critical epistemology (Klein and Hirschheim, 1993), which takes account of structural contradiction within the social system.

There is also a range of research methods which are generally associated with the positivist and non-positivist approaches to IS research. For example, much of the information systems research within the positivist traditions are primarily surveys investigating phenomena within a single slice of time. This method is normally associated with a scientific discipline and quantitative data. Interpretive studies on the other hand tend to employ longitudinal field studies, seeking to obtain in-depth understanding on information systems phenomena. Most widely used of these techniques in information systems research are interviews which are generally associated with qualitative data. Many other techniques are used in conjunction with interviews in the field such as observation (Orlikowski, 1992) and participant observation (Jones and Nandhakumar, 1993). Interpretive studies tend to present detailed case studies from the field data to describe a version of events from which alternative interpretations can be made. Many of these techniques are commonly used in other disciplines such as sociology and anthropology. For example, participant observation has its root in ethnographic research studies, where the researcher would live in tribal villages attempting to understand cultures (Easterby-Smith *et al.*, 1991).

Other field methods used in IS research are action research (Avison and Wood-Harper, 1991). In this method, the researcher seeks deliberately to intervene in the situation, often by employing specific techniques, in order to achieve a particular outcome. Action research is most frequently adopted in organizational development (Easterby-Smith *et al.*, 1991).

The strength of the positivist research approach lies in its ability to provide a wide coverage of various situations and to be fast and economical, as well as in its rigour and replicability in the conduct of scientific research. Orlikowski and Baroudi (1991) claim that the existing dominance of positivism in information systems research provides a partial view and has implications on the understanding of information systems phenomena, theory building and thus for the practice of information systems work. The strengths and weaknesses of the non-positivist approach are fairly complementary. Thus the main strength of interpretive approach is its ability to look at change processes over time, to understand actor's meanings, to adjust to new issues and theories as they emerge, and to contribute to the evolution of new theories (Easterby-Smith *et al.*, 1991).

In researching information systems development, surveys, case studies, and action research are particularly well used, but there are advocates of all the following approaches (Van Horn (1973), Dickson *et al.* (1977) Ein-Dor and Segev (1981), Galliers (1985 and 1991) and Benbasat *et al.* (1987)):

- Conceptual study,
- Mathematical modelling,
- Laboratory experiment,
- Field experiment,
- Surveys,
- Case studies,
- Futures research,
- Phenomenological research/hermeneutics,
- Ethnography,
- Grounded theory,
- Longitudinal study,
- Action research.

I will attempt to give the briefest of overviews of these research methods. Conceptual study is frequently referred to as armchair research. No actual on-site experimentation is carried out. It may precede other research. In mathematical modelling the degree of control is absolute: all variables are known, no human subjects are required and no context exists to affect the results. Objectivity is high. Phenomenology is concerned with meanings that give sense and significance to our experience and attempts to find out what things are. The context is important (as it might be in any study of social action). Hermeneutics refutes the idea of an objective world alone, 'reality' is flavoured by our subjective perception. In laboratory experiments, one of the independent variables is manipulated by the researcher. Compared to action research, more control can be exercised by the researcher.

Action research is often confused with case study research, but whereas case study research examines phenomena in its natural setting with the researcher as independent outsider, in action research the researcher is participant. Grounded research might proceed through a series of interviews or observations to hypothesis formation. No hypothesis is assumed before the interviews in this case, thus attempting to avoid prejudging the issues — it generates rather than tests theory. This is discussed in Chapter 13. In participant observation (see Chapter 15), a research approach frequently associated with ethnography, although there is active involvement by the observer, that person does not seek to influence the situation more than would be expected from other participants. Action research (see Chapter 14) is notable for the deliberate intervention of the researcher. Field experiments include field studies, field tests, adaptive experiment and group feedback analysis and demonstrate mixes of subjective and objective elements with a moderate degree of control. Survey, or opinion research, concerns the gathering of data from human subjects on attitudes, opinions and beliefs as well as responses which are more 'objective'.

I wish to make some observations about research methods in the context of information systems. First, I have purposely 'mixed up' the list. They are often described as being listed in a sequence that represents some continuum, say, from quantitative to qualitative; positivist to anti-positivist (Burrell and Morgan, 1979). Three observations are relevant here. The first is that there might be other series of continua (for example, degree of involvement) and also that the research methods do not sit easily in their positions on the continuum (some aspects might be 'positivist' and other aspects 'qualitative' — survey research provides an example). Second, in any research project, several research methods can be used (and not only the same mix). As we shall see in Chapter 14, the research in information systems discussed is described as action research, and indeed the cycle of theory, action, reflection and theory modification is a cycle of action research. But this whole research included 'conceptual research' carried out when considering the various research in the literature, 'case study' research when looking at the application of the alternative methodologies in context, and so on. Third, much research in information systems does not fit easily into a research category. The neat categories are the realm of texts and courses in research methods. To give one example, some research does not fit in easily to either case study or action research: the role of the researcher may have aspects in the project of 'observer' and 'decision maker'.

Information Systems Development

In order to illustrate the multi-disciplinary nature of information systems further, we look at one aspect of information systems research, teaching and practice: that of information systems development.

There is a wide variety of approaches to information systems development. Longworth (1985) identifies over 300 information systems development methodologies. Wood-Harper and Fitzgerald (1982) discuss two basic differences of approaches as lying either within a systems paradigm or scientific paradigm, illustrated by soft systems method (Checkland, 1981) and structured analysis and design (DeMarco, 1979) respectively.

Avison and Fitzgerald (1995) widen the basis for comparison and suggest that information systems development methodologies can be compared on the basis of philosophy, model, techniques, tools, scope, outputs, practice and product, and they classify approaches within a number of broad themes including:

- Systems,
- Strategic,
- Participative,
- Prototyping,
- Structured,
- Data,
- Object-oriented.

General systems theory attempts to understand the nature of systems which are large and complex. Organizations are open systems, and the relationship between the organization and its environment is important. Systems approaches attempt to capture this 'holistic' view, following Aristotle's dictum that 'the whole is greater than the sum of the parts'. By simplifying a complex situation, we may be reductionist, and thereby distort our understanding of the overall system.

Strategic approaches stress the pre-planning involved in developing information systems and the need for an overall strategy. This involves top management in the analysis of the objectives of their organization. Planning approaches counteract the possibility of developing information systems in a piecemeal fashion.

In participative approaches, the role of all users is stressed, and the role of the technologist may be subsumed by other stakeholders of the information system. If the users are involved in the analysis, design and implementation of information systems relevant to their own work, particularly if this takes the form of genuine decision-making (as against lip-service consultation at the other extreme), these users are likely to give the new information system their full commitment when it is implemented, and thereby increase the likelihood of its success.

A prototype is an approximation of a type that exhibits the essential features of the final version of that type. By implementing a prototype first, the analyst can show the users' inputs, intermediary stages, and outputs from the system. These are not diagrammatic approximations, which tend to be looked at as abstract things, or technically-oriented documentation, which may not be understood by the user, but the actual figures on computer paper or on terminal or workstation screens. Data dictionaries, fourth generation systems, CASE tools and workbenches of various kinds can all enable prototyping. These have become more and more powerful over the last few years.

Structured methodologies are based on functional decomposition, that is, the breaking down of a complex problem into manageable units in a disciplined way. The development of structured methodologies in systems analysis and design stemmed from the perceived benefits of software engineering. These approaches tend to stress techniques such as decision trees, decision tables, data flow diagrams, data structure diagrams, and structured English, and tools such as data dictionaries. Most of the techniques enable complex structures to be communicated using functional decomposition as the basic technique. Most of the documentation aids are graphic representations of the subject matter. This is usually much easier to follow than text or computer-oriented documentation.

Whereas structured analysis and design emphasizes processes, data analysis concentrates on understanding and documenting data. It involves the collection, validation and classification of the entities, attributes and relationships that exist in the area investigated. Even if applications change, the data already collected may still be relevant to the new or revised systems and therefore need not be collected and validated again.

Object-oriented information systems development has become the latest 'silver bullet'. The approach is more natural than data or process based alternatives, (the concepts of objects and attributes, wholes and parts and classes and parts are familiar to children) and also unifies the information systems development process.

In this brief tour around the various approaches to developing information systems, I hope I have at least communicated the potentially diverse nature of the information systems development process. None of these approaches is 'the answer'. Each of the above themes can be criticized as the basis of an information systems development methodology. For example:

- Systems approaches may not seem relevant to the practitioner who wants a quick answer to particular problems.
- Planning approaches frequently lead to priorities according to the power of managers and not organizational need.
- Participation may lead to inefficient systems designed by good managers, clerks or salespeople, who are poor and unwilling analysts.
- Prototyping often concentrates on the user interface but does not necessarily address the fundamental problems of the situation.
- In breaking down a complex system into manageable units, structured analysis offers a simplistic view and fails to capture all the meaning in the links between modules.
- Data analysis may not solve the underlying problems that the organization may have — it may have captured existing problems in the model.
- The messy world of complex organizations, people problems and the like may not be easily represented as objects.

None of these approaches can be described as different flavours to well accepted approach. They represent radically different approaches to information systems development and ways to perceive the information systems development process. They require different expertise: some emphasize people and stress the need for inter-personal skills; others require engineering skills and stress skills in the use of techniques; and yet others stress organizational issues. They represent different 'philosophies'.

It is true that different information systems development approaches can be blended, as in Multiview (Avison and Wood-Harper, 1990). In Multiview, which is a holistic or systems approach, differences in information systems development approaches are considered as different approaches to a common goal. However, some argue that information systems development approaches cannot be blended in any satisfactory way precisely because they emanate from different philosophies (Mingers, 1992).

If we consider the themes identified above as approaches to information systems development, disciplines relevant would seem to include, for example, computer science (prototyping tools), sociology (participation) and business and management (planning). We may add applied psychology, economics, linguistics, politics, semiology, mathematics, ethics, ergonomics, culture studies and probably others to the list of foundation disciplines. Information systems has a multi-disciplinary nature, and technology and computing are by no means dominant.

Potential Difficulties from this Multi-disciplinary Nature of Information Systems

We have seen that there are a number of source disciplines relevant to information systems. Within these disciplines, different theories and philosophies exist and they may be mutually inconsistent. Consider, for example, systems theory, information theory, the theory of science and scientific method. They represent only some of the foundation theories of the disciplines listed.

All this leads to a perceived lack of coherence in the discipline (see also Avison and Myers (1995). A particular fear is that the knowledge and understanding of work in the source disciplines of researchers working in information systems may be out of date or superficial. They are information systems specialists, not specialists in the source discipline.

It is true that many other disciplines (including medicine, French, management and geography) do not have a simple and single disciplinary status and can further be described as a collection of social practices. However, such disciplines can be seen by other academics as confused and lacking in coherence and academic rigour: information systems is often seen in the same light. In short, the 'discipline' of information systems lacks credibility. Indeed, Backhouse, Liebenau and Land (1991) state that 'Coming as it does out of computer science, management studies, and a variety of social and technical fields, it is hardly surprising that [information systems] does not have any theoretical clarity'. I agree with them that information systems lies in the social sciences and not engineering nor science and the complexity is to be expected. On the other hand, others disagree. For example, a technological emphasis is found in Gray (1992). This can be seen as confusion by many outside the discipline (and some inside it!), and the lack of an agreed and consistent theory is *potentially* disabling.

The choice of research method should depend on the area of concern. But in practice it also depends on other factors such as what type of research is acceptable to funding bodies, to university departments, and to assessors of various kinds. However, non-quantitative research *can* be rigorous and this extends to 'stories' (see Silverman, 1993). Likewise, the choice of information systems development methodology should depend on its appropriateness for the particular domain, but is more likely to depend on other factors, such as, the dominant paradigm in the organization (which may, in reality, be rule-of-thumb and experience) or the actors' familiarity with the particular methods.

The emphasis and influence of practice on the 'discipline' — seen in the curricula and research methods — is also a potential weakness. The reverse impact, that of academics on practice, is less strong. Practitioners do not read (nor contribute) to information systems journals as much as in many other applied disciplines. Academics in other disciplines regard information systems lecturers as able to bring in students who see university as a training ground for the few jobs available. This may be only a temporary phenomenon. Information systems academics are also seen as able to teach fundamentals in data processing and computing (work that they do not necessarily find stimulating), and information systems is often not perceived as an 'academic' discipline in its own right.

This has meant that there are few stand-alone university departments in information systems, especially in countries outside of North America. And even in the United States and Canada, less than half of the 1,889 IS faculty are found in stand-alone information systems departments (DeGross *et al.*, 1992). Most information systems faculty are found in computer science, mathematics, business and management, social science, commerce and other departments. Sometimes, groups of information systems teachers can be seen as 'islands' off the main influential 'mainland' departments, and in other cases information systems faculty are split between two separate departments. This makes communications between information systems people difficult. Thus information systems faculty as well as research students may find themselves isolated.

The lack of stand-alone university departments in information systems results in departments having a particular bias, such as a technology bias of most information systems academics in computer science departments, or the practitioner bias of those in business schools. This means that the eclectic nature of information systems is not always reflected in academic information systems communities in any individual department. Worse, neither group seems particularly interested in theory: their concerns are with practical issues. Most respected disciplines are built firmly on the rock of established theory. The potential gains of exploiting the source disciplines are not being made.

However, it is not the purpose of this chapter to suggest that such a discipline should give up our higher ideals for academic respectability, or that they should artificially restrict the scope of the discipline to fit in with an inapproapriate monistic view of science (Banville and Landry, 1989). The interdisciplinary nature of the subject provides richness and is a main reason for the interest shown by students on courses and researches. Witness the exciting debates in conferences which are inter-disciplinary! Different research methods *are* relevant and add to the potential for progress and discovery. The emphasis on practice provides an exciting and relevant environment to try out ideas in their natural setting. Indeed, it is this that shows us that different situations *do* demand different approaches. In other words, I would argue for the 'let many flowers bloom' philosophy. The 'potential weaknesses' are also 'potential strengths' and we need to address the issue so that their potential as strengths are realized. It may be unrealistic to expect an agreed and consistent theory to emerge, but it is important that more researchers work in areas that may establish the theoretical underpinnings of information systems. The inter-disciplinary nature of the subject is no excuse for a lack of rigour.

Borrowing Concepts and Methods — Advantages and Problems

Although different intellectual traditions can lead to a patchwork of unrelated theories, practices and beliefs, there is a possibility that it exposes common ground. As Orlikowski and Baroudi (1991) point out, there is much that can be gained if a plurality of research perspectives is effectively employed to investigate information systems phenomena. They argue that any one perspective is always only a partial view, and unnecessarily restrictive. The fact that the theme for the International Conference on Information Systems in 1993 was 'Valuing Diversity through Information Systems' would seem to suggest that Orlikowsi and Baroudi's valuing of a plurality of research perspectives is widely shared within the information systems research community.

One of the problems with the use of concepts from another discipline is that they may be used uncritically. Researchers in information systems may be unaware of their historical development within the source discipline, and may gloss over the fact that there may be a range of perspectives that operate concurrently. The social sciences 'are marked by a plethora of "schools of thought", each with its own metatheoretic assumptions, research methodologies, and adherents.' (Orlikowski and Baroudi, 1991; p. 2).

An example of the uncritical use of a concept can be seen with the use of the term 'culture' within information systems (Avison and Myers, 1995). Not only is the source discipline (anthropology) from which the concept comes itself usually unacknowledged, but the word is often used in a common-sense way, which might be at odds with the way the term is used in anthropology. As Schein (1984) says, 'Many definitions simply settle for the notion that culture is a set of shared meanings that make it possible for members of a group to interpret and act upon their environment' (p. 3). But as Alexander (1990) points out, there is extraordinary disagreement today over what culture actually is. There is also disagreement about the relationship between culture and social structure (see, for example, Carrithers, 1992). This last point can be seen most clearly if we look at the differences between American cultural anthropology and British social anthropology. As a general rule it can be said that American cultural anthropology privileges the concept of culture (Lewis, 1985; p. 380). The focus is on enculturation, socialization, culture-and-personality, and child-rearing practices (Caulfield, 1972; Lewis, 1985; Watson, 1984). Historically, 'culture was the important concept that held American anthropology together' (Yengoyan, 1986; p. 368). By contrast, British social anthropology privileges the concept of society (Lewis, 1985; p. 380). The primary emphasis of social anthropologists is on social relations, and culture is treated as the vehicle or medium for social interaction rather than an end in itself. In this view, social anthropology is more a kind of sociology than it is a branch of general anthropology (Watson, 1984; p. 353). The risk in using a concept such a culture, therefore, is that informa-tion systems researchers may use a 'textbook' definition of culture, and this usage may end up being a gross simplification.

Observations and Conclusions

It seems unlikely that there will be a merging of minds as to what discipline or set of disciplines is the most relevant to information systems and also as to which research methods are most appropriate. The first division of disagreements (or, perhaps, clashes of dogmas) occurs between those taking a technical and technological view and those taking a social and human view; this division can again be subdivided as much as the deepest functional decomposition diagram and can be as complex as the most complex spider's web! In fact, such a consensus may be unhelpful as well as unrealistic because information systems *is* multi-disciplinary and the different contributions enrich the discipline. Different research methods *are* appropriate to the academic study of information systems.

In this chapter we have also addressed the multidisciplinary status of information systems as a discipline. We have suggested that there are both advantages and disadvantages in trying to use insights from other disciplines to inform the information systems research enterprise, and that the advantages outweigh the disadvantages. The particular combination of relevant source disciplines and research methods define the discipline. Given this increasing recognition within information systems in recent years of the value of a plurality of approaches and relevant source disciplines, however, we do need to ensure that information systems researchers avoid becoming a 'Jack of all trades but master of none' and further that some coherence to the discipline can be established.

Acknowledgments

I am grateful to Guy Fitzgerald, Joe Nandhakumar, Michael Myers and Trevor Wood-Harper for help in the research that led to some of the ideas expressed in this chapter.

References

ALEXANDER, J.C. (1990) *Analytic debates: Understanding the relative autonomy of culture*, in ALEXANDER, J.C. and SEIDMAN, S. (Eds.), *Culture and Society: Contemporary Debates*, Cambridge University Press, Cambridge.

AVISON, D.E. and FITZGERALD, G. (1995) *Information Systems Development: Methodologies, Techniques and Tools*, McGraw-Hill, Maidenhead.

AVISON, D.E. and MYERS, M. (1995) 'Information Systems and Anthropology: An Anthropological Perspective on IT and Organizational Culture', *Information Technology and People*, **8**, 3.

AVISON, D.E. and WOOD-HARPER, A.T. (1990) *Multiview: An Exploration in Information Systems Development*, McGraw-Hill, Maidenhead.

AVISON, D.E. and WOOD-HARPER, A.T. (1991) 'Information Systems Development Research: An Exploration of Ideas in Practice', *Computer Journal*, **34**, 2.

AVISON, D.E. (1995) *What is IS?*, Inaugural Lecture Series, University of Southampton.

AVISON, D.E., KENDALL, J.E. and DEGROSS, J.I. (Eds.) (1993) *Human, Organizational, and Social Dimensions of Information Systems Development*, North-Holland, Amsterdam.

BACKHOUSE, J., LIEBENAU, J. and LAND, F. (1991) 'The Discipline of Information Systems', *Journal of Information Systems*, **1**, 1.

BANVILLE, C. and LANDRY, M. (1989) 'Can the Field of MIS be Disciplined?', *Communications of the ACM*, **32**, 1.

BENBASAT, I., GOLDSTEIN, D. and MEAD, M. (1987) 'The Case Research Strategy in Studies of Information Systems', *MIS Quarterly*, February, 1987.

BOLAND, R.J. and DAY, W.F. (1989) 'The Experience of System Design: A Hermeneutic of Organizational Action', *Scandinavian Journal of Management*, **5**, 2, pp. 87–104.

BUCKINGHAM, R.A., HIRSCHHEIM, R.A., LAND, F.F. and TULLY, C.J. (Eds.) (1987) *Information Systems Education: Recommendations and Implementation*, CUP, Cambridge.

BURRELL, G. and MORGAN, G. (1979) *Sociological Paradigms and Organizational Analysis*. Heinemann, London.

CARRITHERS, M. (1992) *Why Humans Have Cultures*, Oxford University Press, Oxford.

CAULFIELD, M.D. (1972) 'Culture and Imperialism: Proposing a New Dialectic', in HYMES, D. (Ed.), *Reinventing Anthropology*, Random House Inc., New York.

CHECKLAND P.B. (1981) *Systems Thinking, Systems Practice*, Wiley, Chichester.

DEGROSS, J.I., DAVIS, G.B. and LITTLEFIELD, R.S. (1992) *1992 Directory of Management Information Systems Faculty*, McGraw-Hill, Minnesota.

DEMARCO, T. (1979) *Structured analysis: system specifications*, Prentice Hall, New York.

DICKSON, G.S, SENN, J. and CHERVANY, N.L. (1977) 'Research in Management Information Systems: The Minnesota Experience', *Management Science*, **23**, 9.

EASTERBY-SMITH, M., THORPE, R. and LOWE, A. (1991) *Management Research: An Introduction*, Sage: London.

EIN-DOR, P. and SEGEV, E. (1981) *A Paradigm for Management Information Systems*, Prager, New York.

FOSTER, L.W. and FLYNN, D.W. (1984) 'Management Information Technology: Its Effects on Organizational Form and Function', *MIS Quarterly*, **8**, 4, pp. 229–35.

GALLIERS, R.D. (1985) 'In Search of a Paradigm for Information Systems Research', in Mumford *et al.* (1985), *Research Methods in Information Systems*, North-Holland, Amsterdam.

GALLIERS, R.D. (1991) 'Choosing Appropriate Information Systems Research Methods', in NISSEN, H-E., KLEIN, H.K. and HIRSCHHEIM, R. (1991) *Information Systems Research: Contemporary Approaches and Emergent Traditions*, North Holland, Amsterdam.

GALLIERS, R.D. and LAND, F.F. (1987) 'Choosing Appropriate Information Systems Research Methodologies', *Communications of the ACM*, **30**, 11, pp. 900–02.

GRAY, P. (1992) 'New Directions for Group Decision Support Systems', in KENDALL, K.E., LYYTINEN, K. and DEGROSS, J.I. (Eds.) *The Impact of Computer Supported Technologies on Information Systems Development*, North-Holland, Amsterdam.

JONES, M.R. and NANDHAKUMAR, J. (1993) 'Structured development? A Structurational analysis of the development of an Executive Information System', in AVISON, D. *et al. Human Organizational and Social Dimensions of Information Systems Development*, North-Holland Amsterdam.

KEEN, P.G.W. (1987) 'MIS Research: current status, trends and needs', in BUCKINGHAM, *et al., Information Systems Education: Recommendations and Implementation*, CUP, Cambridge.

KLEIN, H.K. and HIRSCHHEIM, R. (1993) 'The application of neohumanist principles in information systems development', in: Avison, D. *et al.* 1993.

LEWIS, I.M. (1985) *Social Anthropology in Perspective*. Cambridge University Press, Cambridge.

LONGWORTH, G. (1985) *Designing Systems for Change*, NCC, Manchester.

MINGERS, J. (1992) 'SSM and Information Systems: an Overview', *Systemist*, **14**, 3.

MUMFORD, E., HIRSCHHEIM, R.A., FITZGERALD, G. and WOOD-HARPER, A.T. (Eds.) (1985) *Research Methods in Information Systems*, North-Holland, Amsterdam.

ORLIKOWSKI, W.J. and BAROUDI, J.J. (1991) 'Studying Information Technology in Organizations: Research Appraoches and Assumptions', *Information Systems Research*, **2**, 1, March 1991, pp. 1–28.

ORLIKOWSKI, W.J. (1992) 'The Duality of Technology: Rethinking the Concept of Technology in Organizations', *Organization Science*, **3**, 3, pp. 299–326.

ORLIKOWSKI, W.J. (1993) 'CASE tools as organizational change: Investigating incremental and radical changes in systems development', *MIS Quarterly*, **17**, 3, pp. 309–40.

ORLIKOWSKI, W.J. and ROBEY, D. (1991) 'Information Technology and the Structuring of Organizations', *Information Systems Research*, **2**, 2, pp. 143–69.

SCHEIN, E.H. (1984) 'Coming to a New Awareness of Organizational Culture', *Sloan Management Review*, Volume 25, Number 2, Winter 1984, pp. 3–16.

SILVERMAN, D. (1993) *Interpreting Qualitative Data: Methods for Analysing Talk, Text and Interaction*, Sage, London.

VAN HORN, R.L. (1973) 'Empirical Studies of Management Information Studies', *Data Base*, 5, Winter.

WALSHAM, G. (1993) *Interpreting Information Systems in Organizations*, John-Wiley: Chichester.

WALSHAM, G. and HAN, C.K. (1993) 'Information Systems Strategy Formation and Implementation: The Case of a Central Government Agency', *Accounting, Management, and Information Technologies*, **3**, 3, pp. 1919–209.

WATSON, G. (1984) 'The Social Construction of Boundaries Between Social and Cultural Anthropology in Britain and North America', *Journal of Anthropological Research*, **40**, 3, pp. 351–66.

WOOD-HARPER, A.T. and FITZGERALD, G. (1982) 'A Taxonomy of Current Approaches to Systems Analysis', *Computer Journal*, **25**, 1.

YENGOYAN, A.A. (1986) 'Theory in Anthropology: On the Demise of the Concept of Culture', *Comparative Studies in Society and History*, 28, pp. 368–74.

8   Nursing Research: a Social Science?

Sheila Payne

Introduction

Research in the social sciences has a relatively short history in comparison to the natural sciences. Their relative 'immaturity' in theoretical and methodological terms has been emphasized by their critics. It is proposed that nursing research represents an interesting case example of an emergent academic discipline; one that may have similarities with other essentially professional groups such as education, social work and para-medical therapies. The development of nursing research over a relatively short period reflects in microcosm the more general development of social science research. This paper aims to explore the emergence and development of British nursing research as a separate academic entity. It will emphasize the historial, political and social context in which nursing research is embedded. It will describe a number of tensions in nursing research in its search to identify and legitimize a separate focus, theoretical basis and methodology which have parallels in other social sciences. Nursing research has drawn many of its theoretical foundations and methodological approaches from the natural and social sciences. It is proposed that broadly three phases can be identified; an early use of natural science methods which aimed to establish academic credibility, the subsequent influence of social scientific paradigms, and the current challenges presented to disciplinary integrity by health services research. This has culminated in a claim that there is 'no such thing' as nursing research (Stacey, 1994). I will argue that the research agenda and methodologies adopted by nurses are not situated in isolation or even in 'best practice' but in what is timely, trendy and funded.

The Context of Nursing Research

Early research which focused on nurses was conducted because of concerns about the role and functioning of the profession within the National Health Service. These early studies were conducted by non-nurses and addressed issues of concern to policy makers rather than practitioners of nursing. The slow development of a nursing generated research agenda has been attributed to medical dominance and gender inequalities (Hardey and Mulhall, 1994). It is important to recognize that nursing education was predominantly biomedical in content, and was largely delivered by, and examined by doctors until the early 1980s. Thus it is unsurprising that biomedical models of health and quantitative methodology were very influential in early research done by nurses. The Briggs Report (1972) emphasized the importance of nursing research to the development of the profession and was the first official document to suggest that nursing needed its own research base for practice.

During the 1980s, nursing research developed in the context of emerging nursing theories; a greater professionalization of nursing practice with pressure to increase the academic content and status of nurse education; an emergence of an academic nursing 'elite', and an increasing orientation to social science. It is difficult to disentangle these elements, although I shall attempt to highlight important issues.

Critical Issues

The practitioner-academic divide in nursing, along with other practice-based disciplines like social work, needs to generate knowledge which is useable or even useful for the majority of practitioners, in comparison with economics, political science or sociology, where the attainment of academic knowledge may be seen as an end in its self. According to Rolfe,

> there is a widening gap between nursing theorists and practitioners, such that the findings and recommendations from a great deal of research is never translated into practical nursing interventions. (1994, p. 969)

The debate about what constitutes relevant research to nursing is ongoing. It has been argued that the current model of academic research, which aims to develop knowledge but is largely unconcerned about its implementation in clinical practice, is elitist and does little to contribute to improvements in nursing care. This type of model of research may be appropriate for academic disciplines such as sociology or economics. However, the majority of clinical nurses have little understanding of research and perhaps, even less commitment to, or knowledge of how to implement research findings. There are similar complaints voiced by teachers who claim that educational theories have little relevance in actual classroom teaching.

Moreover, there is a tension within practice-based disciplines about the purpose of research. The clients or patients can be seen as direct 'consumers' of research findings. Thus on the one hand there appears to be an imperative to make all research applied and applicable to clinical contexts but such research may not be conducive to theoretical development. A more cynical view is that research in academic institutions is concerned with income generation and personal advancement. The location of nursing research units within universities or institutions of higher education potentially removes researchers from clinical contexts and daily involvement with patients or clients, which means that their efforts are often seen to be removed from the reality of hands-on-care.

Mulhall (1995) has argued that the exposure of many nurses to research has been as data collectors on projects led by other disciplines, usually doctors. This lowly status has served to alienate them from the research process and made them cynical of research findings. It has also failed to equip them with the necessary skills to generate research proposals and manage projects. It appears that nurses are often employed as 'manual' labourers on other people's research endeavours.

The Role of Theory

Specific nursing theories have largely originated from North American nurse academics. These theories have attempted to characterize definitions of nursing activity and human interactions. It is debatable whether theories which relate to such a culturally specific phenomena as health services, can be applied cross-culturally. There are similar difficulties in other social science disciplines in researching culturally defined practices such as parenting behaviours. The danger is that Western norms are imposed as the ideal. This ethnocentricism has also been found in psychological research in child development. Perhaps the most influential recent nursing theory, also proposed by North Americans, (Benner and Wrebel, 1989) is derived from Lazarus's cognitive psychological model of stress and coping combined with a phenomenological approach to understanding the 'lived' experience of health and illness. These models are largely descriptive rather than explanatory. They are frequently used, with more or less success, to guide the recognition of patient's problems and as a framework in planning nursing interventions within the nursing process. It is less clear that they have a useful function within nursing research, partly because their vagueness makes it difficult to derive testable hypotheses. A review of 428 nursing studies published between 1986 and 1990 in six leading academic nursing journals, revealed that only 7 per cent used nursing theories (Jaarsma and Dassen, 1993). Although overall, 21 per cent of the studies were guided by theoretical frameworks, these were predominantly derived from the social sciences. It seems safe to conclude that the use of nursing theory to guide research appears minimal.

Professionalization of Nursing

Throughout the last decade, there has been pressure from within nursing to increase its professional status. From a sociological viewpoint, nursing is often regarded as a semi-profession, in that it is an occupation which is predominantly female, with a non-graduate qualifying examination, and much of the work may be defined as manual. Mackay (1989) suggests that there are three patterns which characterize the way nurses perceive their occupation. The majority regard it as a job in which their commitment extends no further than functioning in a safe and appropriate manner whilst at work. A small minority regard nursing as a vocation, in which personal characteristics such as caring, patience, duty, devotion and unquestioning obedience are seen as important. For this group nursing is seen as a lifestyle. Thus nurses are born rather than educated into their role. It is derived from models of nursing provided by religious institutions and military nursing services. Although few nurses currently espouse this view of the occupation, the vocational model is still regarded as an ideal by the general public. A third minority group within nursing has a professional model of the occupation. Interestingly, this group, which includes nurse educationalists and managers, have been successful in reforming the status of basic nurse education, from an apprentice model of training to diploma at higher education level. This change was to a large extent resisted by the majority of practising nurses. At the same time, other health professional groups such as radiography, physiotherapy and occupational therapy have moved to an all graduate basic qualification to practice. Thus nursing has maintained its place as being the least well educated of the health professions.

However, nursing does have a small academic elite, some of whom have been based in universities for over two decades. By 1992, twenty-nine university nursing studies departments were identified in the Research Assessment Exercise, although the majority had been in existence for less than ten years (Tierney, 1994). One of the major contributions of university nursing departments has been in the generation of good quality scholarship and research. Yet, these departments are often geographically and intellectually distant from the practice of nursing and criticisms are made about the relevance of their work to both clinical nursing (Rolfe, 1994) and nursing education (Millar, 1993). These criticisms may also be made about academic psychology which may have little in common with applied psychology such as the practice of educational or clinical psychology. The model of 'scientist-practitioner' has been proposed for clinical psychologists, in that all members of the groups should be active in research and clinical work, while within nursing the commonly espoused position is that all nursing practice should be research based, but only certain nurses will be active researchers. The latter position is more typical of social work and teaching.

During the 1980s, the basic nursing curriculum moved away from an emphasis on biomedicine to incorporate social sciences. This has influenced clinical nursing by an increasing acknowledgment of the psychological and social needs of patients. Its influence on nursing research has been somewhat more profound and will be the focus of the next section.

Epistemological Pluralism

Nursing research appears to have a dilemma in its understanding of the nature of social reality. In the natural sciences the primary objective of research is to test theory to develop a body of knowledge, in an objective, verifiable manner. In this approach conventions adopted include the control of variables within experimental paradigms, the collection of predominantly numerical data (or data that may subsequently be treated numerically), the testing of data by statistical analyses to determine the probability of occurrence of a phenomenon within a given population, and finally the literary convention of using the third person in the research report. These conventions are often regarded as the hallmark of good research, and in some disciplines, such as psychology (until recently) may be taught to students as the only way to do research. The assumption is made that it is possible to obtain objective knowledge which is not influenced by the idiosyncrasies of the observer. This is called naive realism. Such a positivist approach emphasizes the need to develop or discover generalizable laws which enable human activities to be predicted. Widely used nursing research texts such as Polit and Húngler (1983) have emphasized such 'scientific' methods, in particular the use of experiments. An alternative social constructionist approach derived from the social sciences, especially symbolic interactionism and ethnomethodology, have emphasized a need for research to understand the social world. Proponents of this view argue that rather than subjecting the social world to distortion by experimentation, it should be examined in as natural a state as possible. Thus research using a naturalistic paradigm would not seek to change the object of study but rather observations or other data collected would be regarded as representations of reality. Typically, the researcher would do field studies to enable data to be collected in its social context. Moreover, as researchers are part of the social situation in which they seek to study, their accounts should be reflexive (Porter, 1993). The resulting data may well be non-numerical and the analysis qualitative. The aims of the research may include generation of theory.

Lincoln and Guba (1985) identified five different underlying assumptions in qualitative compared to quantitative research. It may be helpful to rehearse these assumptions here. The nature of reality within the quantitative paradigm is assumed to be single, tangible and fragmentable, while in qualitative research it is believed to be multiple and socially constructed. The role of researcher and researched is clearly defined and independent in quantitative studies rather than interactive. What is more, the researcher is more powerful than the respondent. Quantitative research aims to make generalizations at a population level which are temporally and contextually free, while qualitative researchers emphasize the embeddedness of their results. Quantitative research aims to discover causal mechanisms which are largely conceptualized as linear, while qualitative paradigms emphasize the interactive nature of causality. Finally, the ideal of 'scientific' research is that it is value free and that well planned, careful studies will enable the 'facts' to be discovered. An alternative proposal is that all research is inherently value bound, both in its design and execution, but that the values of the researcher should be presented to readers so that they may use this information in evaluating the study.

It is commonly stated that qualitative methods have come to dominate nursing research in the last decade (e.g. Rolfe, 1994). Nurses have been introduced to these research methods through such books as Field and Morse (1985). However, analysis of 428 published studies in six leading academic nursing journals between 1986–1990, indicate that only 6 per cent used a qualitative design (Jaarsma and Dassen, 1993), the rest using quantitative designs. This may of course, represent biases in the journal review process and a greater preference by editors for publishing quantitative research. It is interesting that within psychology, similar fears are expressed about the need to maintain a 'hard' science approach, and the denigration of alternative approaches. (For a critical discussion of the 'hardness' and 'softness' of data within a sociological study of social support in pregnancy see Oakley, 1992).

A Specific Qualitative Approach: Grounded Theory

The next section looks in more detail at one qualitative approach which has gained considerable popularity within nursing research, grounded theory analysis. Grounded theory was developed by Glaser and Strauss (1967) as an alternative to the at-that-time popular survey method within sociology and has gained considerable popularity as a method for nursing research. It was first used in a study of dying patients' awareness of their status in American hospitals (Glaser and Strauss, 1965). In the 1950s and 1960s, it was not common medical practice to inform patients of their prognosis, or to speak to them directly about dying, thus a questionnaire survey would have been entirely inappropriate. Since it was first described, grounded theory as a method has evolved over time (Strauss and Corbin, 1990). The method aims to generate rather than test theory. Transcripts of tape recorded interviews and conversations, field notes and other written material are used as raw data. The samples are selected on the basis of some defining characteristic rather than being representative of a particular population. Typically, sample sizes are smaller than those needed for statistical studies but it is often impossible to specify the number of participants required at the outset because analysis of the data, and the saturation of categories determines the completion of data collection. The analysis commences shortly after the researcher starts collecting data. It may be helpful to summarize briefly the five main stages of analysis.

1   Development of categories to describe the data: Close examination of the transcripts are used to identify categories which describe the data. These categories closely fit the data and are not imposed by previous theories.
2   Saturation of categories: The initial selection of categories is dependent upon the first interviews analyzed. However, as additional examples of the phenomenon are discovered in subsequent transcripts, the categories become saturated. The discovery of new categories in later analyses may necessitate re-analysis of previously processed transcripts.
3   Definition of categories: As sufficient instances of a particular category are developed, it is possible to define it. The definition is used to place limits and boundaries around a category, enabling it to be compared and contrasted with other categories. After definition, categories are integrated to form a grounded theory. To achieve integration, it is necessary to formulate a storyline around the central phenomenon of the study. This involves relating the central phenomenon or 'core category' to other categories. The categories are arranged and re-arranged until they seem to fit the story, and provide an analytical version.
4   Linkage with existing theory: After being immersed in the data for a number of months/years, one begins to recognize differences and emerging

patterns. At this stage, the emerging theory may be linked with existing theoretical constructs.

5   Testing of emerging theory: Finally the 'constant comparative method' is used to test the emerging theory. This involves an active search of the data to find examples which confirm or refute the new theory. Validating the theory against the data completes its grounding. It may also be necessary at this stage to re-interview participants to present the emerging theory for their confirmation or modification, thus enabling them to influence the final version. It may also be necessary to recruit new participants, especially if the phenomenon under investigation is a process where it may be anticipated that people's understandings change over time, to check out specific parts of the theory. A deliberate attempt may be made to recruit people who represent extremes on some continuum to challenge the theory.

Typically, grounded theories are mid-range theories. Further development may require more quantitative testing of hypotheses derived from the new theory. The method has been criticized because it is based on an assumption of the existence of categories and that data can be forced into them. It also relies heavily on the unseen and unverifiable cognitive processes of the researcher. Even though researchers are recommended to write analytic memos (Turner, 1981) during the process of analysis, it is often difficult for readers to understand how theoretical linkages are made. The use of a research diary as well as the writing of memos may provide an audit trail. Thus it may be possible to monitor the development of understanding and insight. From my own experience, I regard the writing of grounded theory account as an iterative process which contributes to the refinement of an emerging theory. These accounts should provide rich descriptions of the phenomena which are illustrated with verbatim quotes. Another source of criticism, is how these quotes are selected. It is desirable that material is used which both supports and refutes the emerging theory. It is naive to assume that one can 'tell it as it is', as was claimed by Melia (1982) in her account of the learning experiences of student nurses. This is problematic in at least two ways; firstly in what participants choose to tell a researcher may differ from what they tell to others, and secondly, how a researcher selects the final account to present in their written report will be influenced by explicit and implicit biases.

The grounded theory method has become very popular in nursing research, partly because it enables processes to be explored systematically and it does not require large sample sizes. However, less worthy explanations of its popularity include nursing student's dislike of statistics and the perception that it is easy to do a grounded theory analysis on just a few interviews. This has given rise to a large number of poor quality studies, with inadequate sample sizes to ensure adequate saturation of categories and a failure to develop conceptually an analytical version of the theory. At its worst, grounded theory analysis appears to be used as a type of poorly controlled content analysis. It may be helpful to mention a few examples of grounded theory studies. Hawker (1983) used this approach to investigate the interactions between nurses and patient's relatives on a number of hospital wards.

She used participant observation and interviews to identify how nurses controlled their interactions with relatives. Her observational data indicated the range of strategies they used to avoid contact; for example, the 'legitimate gait' involved walking quickly with minimal eye contact to give the impression that one was in a great hurry and thus could not be interrupted by relations. Another study examined how nurses dealt with the patient's body (Lawler, 1991). Lawler used observations (some of them covert observations) and interviews to understand how nurses coped with potentially embarrassing situations whilst providing intimate care. In my own research, I have used this method to understand the process of undergoing palliative chemotherapy for breast cancer (Payne, 1990) to explore elderly people's experience of residential care (Smith and Payne, 1993), and to identify palliative care patients' and staffs' perceptions of a 'good' death (Payne *et al.*, 1996). These studies have enabled 'insider' views of various processes to be articulated.

My own research strategies have been shaped by the tensions I feel at being located in an academic Psychology Department and my nursing imperative to do clinically relevant research. During my academic education in a traditional psychology degree programme, I was taught only about experimental and quasi-experimental methods which yielded data suitable for statistical analysis. These strategies were promoted as being rigorous, theoretically driven and 'scientific'; yet, I found them to be of little use in investigating processes such as undergoing chemotherapy in real-world contexts. I confronted these methodological dilemmas in my doctoral research which resulted in both a quantitative and qualitative analysis of the same data set (Payne, 1989). I would not necessarily advocate this strategy as one still has to resolve the dilemmas of how to integrate what may be two divergent representations of a phenomenon (see section on triangulation). However, I have subsequently employed the use of mixed methods and the combining of quantitative and qualitative methods, especially in health services research.

Triangulation

This chapter has highlighted the development of two very different approaches in nursing research, such that a clear dichotomy between quantitative and qualitative methodologies is evident. Confusion has arisen from epistemological differences (Taylor, 1993). The use of triangulation has been proposed to reconcile the opposing positions (Corner, 1991; Cowman, 1993). There are four types of triangulation: data, investigator, theory and methodological (Denzin, 1990). This technique involves the use of multiple methods in the investigation of a phenomenon, in the belief that no single method will provide a complete picture. However, it is unclear how basic epistemological differences can be resolved by this technique. If we take the interview as a common data source in nursing and social sciences generally, what is the status of this type of data? Within a positivist perspective, interview accounts represent real 'facts' about behaviour or attitudes to a topic. Thus the researcher may be concerned with ensuring that there is standardization in interview format (using structured interviews) and procedure, obtaining supporting evidence of the accounts (e.g. from observations), and typically selecting samples by random techniques. In comparison, within an interactionist perspective, interview data may be regarded as a moral account or narrative in which the interviewee attempts to present themselves to the interviewer. Typically such interviews are unstructured or semi-structured. The analysis aims to understand the discourses used by participants in presenting their account. There is little concern about the verification of actual events. Interviews are themselves problematic, and are markedly different in their structure and social functions from 'ordinary' conversations. Thus if triangulation is used to 'marry' qualitative and quantitative data sets, it appears to me that there are potential difficulties as it is often unclear what assumptions are made about the status of the data. By fudging these issues, we could get into a sticky mess!

Corner and Wilson-Barnett (1992) report on the use of triangulation in a longitudinal study of the educational experiences of newly qualified nurses working with cancer patients. They used it to resolve disputes between their funding body who required a quantitative design, and their wish to include qualitative assessment to identify the needs for education as perceived by their respondents. The authors concluded that triangulation contributed to a more detailed understanding of the nurses' needs but at the expense of a considerably increased work load for the researcher. The technique in its self can not resolve dilemmas in the relative 'weight' to be given to different data sources, especially if they are contradictory.

Where to from Here?

Whatever the theoretical positions or methodologies employed, British nursing research is not in a healthy state. In the most recent Universities' Funding Council research assessment exercise (in 1992), nursing was rated as the lowest of all the seventy-two subjects reviewed (Tierney, 1994). Although there was considerable variation between departments, none were awarded the maximum '5' rating and only two reached the '4' standard, with seventeen of the twenty-nine departments receiving the lowest rating possible. Within the specialist area of cancer nursing research, Payne (1993) has highlighted some of the important constraints on nursing research; namely, inadequate funding of both postgraduate level research training and postdoctoral research programmes, which results in few people with adequate experience to offer research supervision or initiate and conduct new research projects from a nursing perspective. A survey conducted in Britain in 1992, revealed only ten funded cancer nursing projects, of which eight were being undertaken by postgraduate students registered for PhDs (Corner, 1993). Overall, the majority (85 per cent) of nursing research in Britain is funded by the government and is policy related (Levine *et al.*, 1993). In the past, the Department of Health has been the main supporter of nursing research from earmarked money, especially in the funding of research training studentships, but a recent report (Report of the Taskforce on the Strategy for Research in Nursing, Midwifery and Health Visiting, 1993) indicates that they no longer perceive the need for a separate funding structure for nursing. In the future research funding will be made available via Regional Health Authority Research and Development Committees. They aim to sponsor health services research which is multidisciplinary and specifically addresses issues of relevance to the health and social services. However, the problems of this approach from a nursing perspective are that medical dominance on committees or in the way issues are conceptualized may lead to a disease-orientated model. In addition, a 'scientific' medical epistemology regards the Randomized Controlled Trial as the model of all good research. Thus studies with qualitative designs are unlikely to be funded as they fail to satisfy criteria such as generalizability. In collaborative research endeavours, there is a danger that nurses merely participate as data collectors. These changes in funding appear to be signalling the demise of nursing research as a separate entity. Research funded through this route is unlikely to be discipline specific or to address specific nursing concerns. Questions about how the research agenda is determined will be vitally important if nurses are to retain any influence. Moreover, it is unlikely that research funded from these sources will contribute to theoretical developments in nursing.

Is the future for nursing research bleak? Given its poor academic performance in the last University Assessment Exercise, does it matter? Should nursing research input be merely seen as a contributing discipline to a larger endeavour, that of health services research?

References

BENNER, P. and WREBEL, J. (1989) *The Primary of Caring*, Addison-Wesley, New York.

BRIGGS, A. (1972) *Report of the Committee on Nursing*, HMSO, London.

CORNER, J. (1991) 'In search of more complete answers to research questions. Quantitative versus qualitative research methods: is there a way forward?' *Journal of Advanced Nursing*, 16, pp. 718–27.

CORNER, J. and WILSON-BARNETT, J. (1992) 'The newly registered nurse and the cancer patient: an educational evaluation', *International Journal of Nursing Studies*, **29**, 2, pp. 177–90.

CORNER, J. (1993) 'Building a framework for nursing research in cancer care', *European Journal of Cancer Care*, 2, pp. 112–116.

COWMAN, S. (1993) 'Triangulation: a means of reconciliation in nursing research', *Journal of Advanced Nursing*, 18, pp. 788–92.

DENZIN, N. (1990) 'Strategies of multiple triangulation', in DENZIN, N. (Ed) *The Research Act in Sociology*, Aldine, Chicago.

FIELD, P.A. and MORSE, J.M. (1985) *Nursing Research*, Chapman and Hall, London.

GLASER, B.G. and STRAUSS, A.L. (1965) *Awareness of Dying*, Aldine, Chicago.

GLASER, B.G. and STRAUSS, A.L. (1967) *The Discovery of Grounded Theory: Strategies for Qualitative Research*, Aldine, New York.

HARDEY, M. and MULHALL, A. (1994) *Nursing Research: Theory and Practice*, Chapman and Hall, London.

HAWKER, R. (1983) *Interaction between nurses and relatives*, unpublished PhD thesis, University of Exeter.

JAARSMA, T. and DASSEN, T. (1993) 'The relationship of nursing theory and research: the state of the art', *Journal of Advanced Nursing*, 18, pp. 783–87.

LAWLER, J. (1991) *Behind the Screens: nursing, Somology and the Problem of the Body*, Churchill Livingstone, London.

LEVINE, E., LEATT, P. and POULTON, K. (1993) 'Nursing research in the UK', in LEVINE, E., LEATT, P. and POULTON, K. (Eds) *Nursing Practice in the UK and North America*, Chapman and Hall, London.

LINCOLN, Y.S. and GUBA, E.G. (1985) *Naturalistic Inquiry*, Sage, Beverley Hills.

MACKAY, L. (1989) *Nursing a Problem*, Open University Press, Milton Keynes.

MELIA, K.M. (1982) '"Tell it as it is" — Qualitative methodology and nursing research: understanding the student nurse's world', *Journal of Advanced Nursing*, 7, pp. 327–35.

MILLAR, M.A. (1993) 'The place of research and development in nurse education', *Journal of Advanced Nursing*, 18, pp. 1039–1042.

MULHALL, A. (1995) 'Nursing research: what difference does it make?', *Journal of Advanced Nursing*, 21, pp. 576–83.

OAKLEY, A. (1992) *Social Support and Motherhood*, Blackwell, Oxford.

PAYNE, S.A. (1989) *'Quality of Life in Women with Advanced Cancer'*, unpublished PhD thesis, University of Exeter.

PAYNE, S.A. (1990) 'Coping with palliative chemotherapy', *Journal of Advanced Nursing*, 15, pp. 652–58.

PAYNE, S. (1993) 'Constraints for nursing in developing a framework for cancer care research', *European Journal of Cancer Care*, 2, pp. 117–120.

PAYNE, S.A., HILLIER, R., LANGLEY-EVANS, A. and ROBERTS, T. (1996) 'Impact of witnessing death on hospice patients', *Social Science and Medicine*, **43**, 12, pp. 1785–94.

POLIT, D. and HUNGLER, B. (1983) *Nursing Research Principles and Methods*, (2nd. Edition) Lippincott, Philadelphia.

PORTER, S. (1993) 'Nursing research conventions: objectivity or obfuscation? *Journal of Advanced Nursing*', 18, pp. 137–43.

REPORT OF THE TASKFORCE ON THE STRATEGY FOR RESEARCH IN NURSING, MIDWIFERY AND HEALTH VISITING, 1993, Department of Health, Leeds.

ROLFE, G. (1994) 'Towards a new model of nursing research', *Journal of Advanced Nursing*, 19, pp. 969–75.

SMITH, L. and PAYNE, S. (1993) 'A qualitative study of elderly people's perceptions of residential care', *Elders*, **2**, 2, pp. 23–38.

STACEY, T. (1994) 'Achieving effective multi-disciplinary health services research and development', Conference on Nursing and Therapy Professions Contribution to Health Services Research and Development, Department of Health, London, 12th May.

STRAUSS, A.L. and CORBIN, J. (1990) *Basics of Qualitative Research: Grounded Theory Procedures and Techniques*, Sage, Newbury Park, CA.

TAYLOR, J.S. (1993) 'Resolving epistemological pluralism: a personal account of the research process', *Journal of Advanced Nursing*, 18, pp. 1073–1076.

TIERNEY, A.J. (1994) 'An analysis of nursing's performance in the 1992 assessment of research in British universities', *Journal of Advanced Nursing*, 19, pp. 593–602.

TURNER, B.A. (1981) 'Some practical aspects of qualitative data analysis: One way of organizing some of the cognitive processes associated with the generation of grounded theory', *Quality and Quantity*, 15, pp. 225–47.

9   The Case for Research into Practice

Joan Orme

Introduction

This paper is based on the proposition that a research base is necessary for the development and improvement of practice in social work, but that concerns about epistemology and methodology have influenced responses to research by practitioners. It argues that social work can benefit from the contribution that feminist writing has made to the research debate, and that the issues for social work might be pertinent to other areas of study, or disciplines. Therefore, it has to be read as complementary to a number of others in the reader, particularly the papers by David Avison, Jackie Powell and Pat Usher.

That the need for research into practice is particularly relevant to social work is postulated by Powell when she argues that evaluating social work practice leads to more fundamental questions about the nature of social work. As she rightly points out this only becomes significant for those who regard social work as more than a set of skills (or competencies, in current parlance) and perceive the need for a knowledge base for social work practice which is informed by research and reflection. Hence the practitioner moves away from routinization and technical expertise (Schon, 1987). Moreover, Avison's account of the search for a discipline in Information Systems echoes some of the challenges facing those theorizing and researching in social work.

In his other paper, Avison argues the case for action research, suggesting that the identification of a discrete methodological approach helps to establish the identity of a discipline. Action research does have its limitations. Mies (1983), points out that it may fail to integrate science and knowledge, and asserts that it is necessary to go beyond a particular method. The limitations of particular methodologies leads her to focus on the process of research, the engagement in the activity, and an exploration of how this contributes to the construction of the knowledge. Hence she argues for the integration of praxis and research claiming that 'the demand to link praxis and research consistently follows an historical, dialectical and materialist theory of knowledge. According to this concept the "truth" of a theory is not dependent upon certain methodological principles and rules, but on its potential to orient the processes of praxis towards progressive emancipation and humanization' (1983, p. 124). Such an approach has particular relevance to social work where a degree of resistance to the research process has arisen out of the value base of practice.

Social Work in the Academy

Powell implies that there are those in the profession of social work who deny the need for a theoretical base for social work. They resist attempts to legitimize social work's academic role in making a contribution to the theory base of practice and to knowledge formation, either as a discrete activity, or drawing on other disciplines. To develop an integration of knowledge and praxis is fraught for any subject area, raising questions of what constitutes knowledge, the criteria established for the recognition of knowledge and the processes of knowledge formation. However, for social work this is further confounded by a lack of consensus about the role and function of the activity within society, and in some cases what constitutes the activity of social work. There are some (Brewer and Lait, 1980) who have explicitly challenged the need for social work as a practice, thereby negating the need for an academic discipline. Others (Bailey and Brake, 1975; Wilson, 1977) have questioned the basis on which social workers intervene in the lives of individuals, and while not wanting to eliminate the practice of social work, would base it on different understandings of social problems, and therefore offer different responses to dealing with those problems. In the case of Bailey and Brake this was from a Marxist perspective, whilst Wilson was one of the earliest writers to present a feminist critique of social work practice. More recently, government committees have been established to identify what social workers do, to speculate about what they *might* do, and to consider whether the tasks need to be performed by social workers at all (Barclay, 1982; Griffiths, 1988; Audit Commission, 1989).

However, the purpose of this paper is not to document the current precarious state of social work and its educational base, but to explore the resistance to the creation of a research base, which is integral to the development of an academic discipline and a set of professional practices. The aim is to explore further how the inextricable link between the activity and the research (the practice and the theory), as documented by Powell, can influence the validation of epistemology and methodology. If research practice is alien to the principles of the subject being researched then there will be resistance. Alternatively, the conduct of the research and the application of its results can contribute to, and influence practice. As Goldberg and Fruin comment, the lack of definition of the social work task 'does not excuse social workers from becoming more explicit about the problems they are trying to tackle, with or on behalf of their clients, the specific goals they set themselves and the expertise and resources required to explain these objectives' (1976, p. 7).

The need to explain the aims of social work is precisely the stimulus for research, but the resistance to the use of research findings and consequent involvement in the research process has been identified as a particular drawback in social work. In plotting this resistance Everitt *et al.*, argue for 'research minded practice [which] is concerned with analytical assessment of social need and resources, and the development, implementation and evaluation of strategies to meet that need' (1992, p. 4). Hence the invocation from Goldberg and Fruin could be answered by the process of practice research, but also for research praxis which incorporates the dialectics of doing and knowing (Mies, 1983). Social work, with its emphasis on intervention and change should be attracted to the argument that 'the object of research is not something static and homogeneous but an historical, dynamic and contradictory entity' (Mies, 1983; p. 125).

The tension between theory, as represented in a research base, and practice is not a recent phenomenon in social work. The conflict which surrounded the introduction of the first social work course in the London School of Economics (for psychiatric social workers) in 1929 was seen to be between 'instilling of disciplined habits of thought' and 'the business of training, or imparting particular skills' (Brewer and Lait, 1980; p. 37). On the one hand, the academy became the site where ' "purists" fear the distortion of theory by pragmatists who seek to tailor it to meet the needs of practice' (Brewer and Lait, 1980; p. 38). On the other, there was a concern that practitioners and their practice, or more particularly their clients, might be used for research purposes but that this might not necessarily enhance practice (Everitt *et al.*, 1992). Hence the debate was about who takes preeminence, the theorist or the practitioner. In exploring the notion of praxis it can be argued that neither need to; the dialectic of doing and knowing can create a partnership between practitioner and researcher.

While the development of theory and praxis relating to the research process did not originate in feminist thinking, it has been feminist discussions of epistemology and methodology which have most fruitfully questioned the process of knowledge construction (Mies, 1983; Stanley and Wise, 1983; Stanley, 1990). The challenge to the established methodologies presented by feminism has been documented by Pat Usher, as are the alternative ways of knowledge formation, or at least the processes of seeking after knowledge. Just as Powell documents her commitment to evaluation as a methodological framework, so I hold firmly to the view that feminist approaches offer the means to move forward for a social work research tradition.

It is not suggested that social work has accepted the arguments of feminism, but that the concerns that are raised for social workers can be met by feminist approaches to research. There are many reasons why social work needs to attend to the position of women in society, not least because women constitute the majority of workers (Nottage, 1991) and clients (Hanmer and Statham, 1988). Moreover, the resonance between social work practice and feminism provides compelling reasons for a synthesis. Both are committed to social and personal change and both seek an understanding of private and public worlds. More significantly, both stress the dialectic relationship between theory and practice, but in doing so accept feelings as facts and value self knowledge (Dominelli & McCleod, 1989). It is because of this that the feminist exploration of praxis can allay some of the resistance of social workers to research.

Resistance

The nature of this resistance has been identified as coming from a number of sources, often contradictory. Hanvey (1990) has suggested that it was the immaturity of social work which has to 'come of age' as a profession. The implication being that in doing so it will encompass a research base. This fails to recognize the need for social work to establish its research base before it can reach maturity. The concept of the reflective practitioner, who can reflect on the practice (or action), and reflect on the reflection in action (Schon, 1987) is predicated on the need for research. What is contentious is the nature of the research practice which will facilitate this reflection.

Others suggest that the modernist managerialism of social work accountability (Parton, 1994) involves the collection of statistics and data which do not relate to the quality of practice and alienates the practitioner, making him or her resistant to the activity. This process is challenged in Stanley's account of the role of researchers in social services departments. Her case study method (1990), indicating the 'invisibility' of much of the data, highlights the manner in which official accounts, based on monitoring and statistical information, tell little about the work that is being done. This, she suggests, is because researchers are constrained to connect human relationships to numerical research. In undertaking this exercise they often fail to discover all the information, and as such produce findings of limited value. That the case study was of her own family which meant that she had a great deal of private/personal information further illustrated the limitations of the methodology. Such an approach challenges the orthodox understanding of objectivity. However, it amply demonstrates the feminist claim that the personal is the political, that one person's experience is as valid a piece of knowledge as the sum total of the experience of many. For social work this claim is echoed in Ungerson's work on the documented experiences of individuals who are involved in caring roles and relationships of the most intimate nature. Her title *Policy is Personal* (1987) reflects not only that each individual's experience is valid, but also that global policy decisions impact on these individuals in different ways.

The inefficiency of positivistic methods is therefore a shared concern of social work and feminism. A further resistance to research from social work practice is that the reductionism of research practices associated with positivism is alienating. Social sciences research is into the sensitive areas of people's lives. It makes public what is often kept private. This is much more pertinent in social work where the power to pathologize individuals because of perceived patterns of behaviour or problems can have significant effects on the outcomes of intervention, which in turn have implications for justice and liberty. To avoid such inappropriate uses of power and damaging interventionary processes it is necessary to acknowledge both the individual experience and the social circumstances which contribute to that experience. As Goldberg argues 'putting people into categories and quantifying phenomena, which in the last analysis are subjective experiences, cuts right across the social worker's belief in the uniqueness of individual experiences and the need to individualize problems in order to help people in their difficulties' (1972, p. 139).

Research Practice

Such concerns can of course be met by any challenge to positivist styles: for Everitt *et al.*, 'interpretive epistemologies reject the possibility of objective social facts.

Rather, social phenomena are given meaning by those who define and make them explicit. Thus different people will have different subjective understandings of social phenomena' (1992, p. 7). Such a standpoint is consistent with the definition of one of the core values of social work, individualization. The classic explanation, 'that clients are not regarded as fulfilling certain types and paradigms but as presenting a particular problem which needs to be considered against its own particular background' (Plant, 1970; p. 9) would seem to negate a research base for social work practice, if such a base is created from an amalgam of information about individuals, their problems and methods of intervention. While interpretive epistemologies might reflect the concept of individualization, it is feminist research which has drawn attention to the 'particular problems' of women and the 'particular background' of patriarchy which have provided some of the significant developments in practice in social work. These developments pertain not only to intervention in the lives of women, but have also facilitated analysis of the delivery of social work services to black and ethnic minority people. A more recent development has been the acknowledgment that feminist praxis, that is a specific dialectic between theory and practice, precipitates significant changes in service for men. Hence Carlen's (1989) work which originally focused on the treatment of women in the criminal justice system now proposes a feminist jurisprudence, capable of bringing about a more humane treatment of all who are dealt with within that system.

A further shared concern about research practice is the power differential which is reflected in the process of knowledge creation (Mies, 1983; Croft and Beresford, 1986). This is particularly pertinent to social work when the knowledge base is extrapolated from the experience of selected individuals. When notions of power and legitimacy are explored in relation to epistemology then the 'desire to know is a desire for power, but knowledge of itself does not give power. On the contrary it is those who are authorized "to know" and whose "knowledge" is afforded privilege' (Worrall, 1990; p. 7). Individuals or groups of clients of agencies who become the 'subjects' or 'objects' of research are not empowered to know. It is the researcher whose position is most validated, even though that position exists only because of the collection of data about the experiences of others. Those who are objects of knowledge are frequently described as the 'subjects' of research. Such a definition reflects the worst aspects of positivist practice. The extremes of such practices are summarized by Guba and Lincoln thus:

> In order to accomplish rendering the study as confounding or contamination-proof as possible it is thought sometimes appropriate or even necessary to deceive the 'subject' (*humans who are by that very term dehumanized and objectified, that is, made into objects*), to invade privacy without prior knowledge, to place them at physical or psychological risk, or otherwise exploit them for the researcher's or evaluator's own private and professional ends. (1989, p. 120)

Such practices, or even those which are less extreme, arise directly out of epistemological claims to be objective and value free, and the assumption that there is an external reality which can be identified and measured, independently of either the measurer or the individuals or groups being measured.

As Pat Usher has noted, feminist researchers make a direct challenge to such assumptions and it is this challenge which has resonance for social work. In acknowledging that the

> objects of social science research are also distinguished from those of natural sciences by being subjects in their own right, indeed by producing their own understanding and theories of their independent experiences, but also those which involve researchers and their activities. (Stanley, 1990; p. 9)

This reverses the standard perception of the relationship between the researcher and the persons researched and is consistent with another fundamental principle of social work practice, respect for persons. Such a principle requires that in the methods chosen for the collection of data, the conduct of the research, the interpretation and dissemination of the results the rights of individuals should be respected (Orme and Forbes, 1991).

A further feminist critique of the positivist approach which echoes the concerns of social work is that the process of research separates the knowledge constructed from the origin of that knowledge,

> by constructing 'what is known' at a conceptual and categorical level, even if reference is made to 'research findings', then how these are known are rendered invisible. Their indexical properties denied, their contextually specific meaning glossed in universalist terms. The result is *alienated knowledge*, a product apparently complete, bearing no apparent trace of the conditions of its production and the social relations that gave rise to this. (Stanley, 1990; p. 11)

For social work and feminism the construction of knowledge through research, and separation of that knowledge from its source, is a way of controlling those who are the very subjects of that knowledge creation (Croft and Beresford, 1986). The production of large data sets of, for example, abortion broken down into sub-categories of nationality, age and marital status have no connection with the personal and, in some cases, traumatic decision to terminate a pregnancy. To reduce such an experience to a statistic which is then used to speculate on the morality of women, and on which to argue future policy is part of the alienation to which Stanley refers.

This form of reductionism has precipitated concerns about the involvement of practitioners in the process of knowledge creation, and has, for social work, contributed to the resistance identified at the beginning of this paper. The concerns relate not only to the conditions in which the research is conducted, but also to the assumption that acquiring the knowledge contributes to the professionalization of social work. Power relations are evident in the professional relationship and 'professional ways of knowing in our society have served to objectify and control others. Professionals are regarded as knowledgeable: others are objects of this knowledge' (Everitt *et al.*, 1992; p. 18). Reactions to the striving for professionalism have been associated with the search for a knowledge base and the establishing of an academic discipline of social work. The concern is that a knowledge base, or theory, of social work intervention will dictate the outcomes of intervention, legitimating the performance of some tasks rather than others. Moreover, this legitimation is controlled by the environment in which the research is generated, and by factors such as who funds or commissions it. The role of the researcher and those who disseminate research thus becomes critical in influencing what is actually done under the name of social work. The validation of knowledge and its role in legitimizing certain kinds of activity also presents specific problems for social work in the academy and this leads to a questioning of the validity of the academic project. Within the current climate, for example, funded research into the criminal justice system is framed by the current ideology of 'just desserts', and the Home Secretary has been known to ignore outcomes which are counter to his own ideology. In such an environment, Carlen's work is unlikely to get support, or at least financial support, from official sources, and validation.

Feminism and social work therefore become subject to a debate about their place in the academy. For feminism, the validation of a knowledge base which is framed by men, or by women using masculinist techniques for its construction, legitimizes a particular way of seeing the world, which is further reinforced by the practitioner base (be that as teacher or researcher) being predominantly male, framing female experience (Bowles and Klein, 1983). However, one criticism of academic feminism is that the discourse generated by those involved has become too abstract (Segal, 1987). This is part of the conundrum for feminist researchers, and one which they share with social work researchers. To have their findings respected and legitimized they must abide by the rules and norms of the academy, even when the project is to challenge those same rules. In response, Mies claims that the potential of an approach which integrates praxis and research which 'is not acquired in the sheltered world of academic institutions' (1989, p. 124) is pertinent for feminists and social workers.

Dissonance

The argument that there is congruence between social work research and feminist research goes beyond the simplest definition of feminist research as being 'on women, by women, for women'. Such a position was a direct challenge to the process of universalizing results, drawn predominantly from studies of males. For Pat Usher, the post-modern challenge from feminism is much more complex. It is not just about who does the research, nor on whom the research is 'done', but about that very power balance which is inherent in the notion of research 'by' a researcher 'on' a subject. It simultaneously transcends discussion about methodologies, but is central to them.

This is important because a limited view of the feminist contribution to research, seeing it merely as a critique of positivist approaches, has led to assumptions that it merely involves a questioning of methodology, and that feminist methodologies equate with qualitative methodologies. However, Pat Usher's account questions the very dualities which have operated in the debates about methodologies. The important shift here is that feminist researchers do not just challenge the 'facts' they 'theorise the relationship between personal and the political, private and public, between subjective and objective' (Everitt *et al.*, p. 15), and demonstrate the false dichotomies between these.

It is therefore not enough to argue that feminist research has to eschew the old positivist, quantitative methodologies, replacing them with a new one (Mies, 1983). Identifying a single epistemology is in itself positivistic and deterministic (Halberg, 1989) and argues for a privileged position on the basis that it provides the correct version of how things really are. Halberg argues, in particular, that 'post modernism challenges, when taken seriously, undermine the feminist epistemological project, unless the idea of a new cognitively privileged position can be defended' (1989, p. 4). Her error is in assuming that there is a unifying feminism and a unified project which is merely to uphold women's experience as a legitimation of a grounding for knowledge, over and above men's rather than recognizing the difference.

The contribution that feminist research makes can be more radical than this. It involves the acknowledgment of 'unalienated knowledge' (Stanley, 1990), achieved by attention to the relationship between ontology and epistemology, the relationship between ways of knowing and ways of being. Access to such knowledge can be achieved by a variety of methodologies, but it is the very process of accessing which makes it a project with which social work researchers can identify. What makes it a *feminist* task, for Stanley (1990), is the identification of the social construction of women, and the acknowledgment of this construction as oppressive. Here is the challenge for the coupling of social work with feminism because social work itself has provided challenges for feminism, being seen as contributing to a particular construction of women and to their oppression (Brook and Davis, 1985; Wise, 1990).

Praxis

It is the notion of praxis which ensures that this challenge can be responded to positively. Praxis is relevant to social work in that it stems from an understanding that there are many ways of being, and many social conditions which lead to oppression. These have to be addressed both in the process of research, but also in the way that social work is performed.

Hence the counter argument to Halberg's criticisms is that the feminist project is not merely a perspective nor an epistemology, but an ontology, a way of being in the world. What emerges is a 'deconstructed and reconstructed feminist standpoint epistemology, one which rejects the "successor science" label and insists on the existence of feminist stand*points*, i.e. promoting academic feminist pluralism' (Stanley, 1990; p. 47).

Such a notion can be open to criticism for being subjective or politically motivated. This may be so, but being open about it may be more honest than falsely claiming neutrality and objectivity. As Guba and Lincoln point out,

> the value-free claim of positivism papers over the realization that science, like every human activity, is a *political* act. Science, by asking only certain questions maintains (or reinforces) the status quo; it asks those questions that have been formulated by its own theories, and never takes account of the emic formulations of its 'subjects'. We would argue that conventional science is, as a result, a force for disenfranchisement and disempowerment, for maintenance of the status quo (1989, p. 125).

Feminism outside the academic mode has insisted on the crucial need for useful knowledge, theory and research as practice. Social work makes similar demands of those engaged in its pursuit. The essence of praxis is that it is 'knowledge for' rather than any one static concept of knowledge production. The purpose of the knowledge is 'to change the world, not only to study it' (Stanley, 1990; p. 15). In undertaking this project the theory/research divide is erased, or rather united into a symbiotic activity in which the need for theory to have a research base is acknowledged. More powerfully, the 'how' and the 'what' of generating the theory are indissolubly interconnected and the shape and nature of the 'what' will be a product of the 'how' of its investigation. Hence praxis involves attention to every aspect of the process that undertaking research is based upon, and contributes to the theoretical understanding. For researchers on practice, and these predominate in social work, there is a much more specific connection because such research is to do with affecting change. There is an imperative that the change to be affected is beneficial, or at least not harmful.

Managerialism

There is a further set of concerns for both practitioner and researcher when considering the impact of research, whatever the methodological approach. The validation of knowledge can be used to legitimize certain activities, or alternatively to outlaw practices. The critique of feminist approaches that they are associated with political correctness implies rigidity and censorship. While this is rarely the intention of feminist methodologies, it illustrates how outcome does not necessarily accurately reflect intent. Similarly, the acceptance of research findings relating to professional practice can lead to the research becoming part of a regulatory discourse, whether or not that is the intention of the researcher. Having said that, there is no doubt that some researchers consider it their responsibility to provide the template, or the yard stick, for professional practice. Hence MacDonald (1994), reporting on the results of research into the use of behavioural methods, questions why all managers in the probation service are not requiring staff to use such methods. Such a stance contributes to the resistance of practitioners discussed earlier in this chapter; it also raises questions about the appropriateness of privileging certain findings. If there is an explicit assumption that research findings, however they are generated, should automatically contribute to the regulation or management of professional practice, then the concerns about access to publishing outlets and the constitution of the gatekeeping bodies have to be addressed. Women and black and ethnic minority writers have challenged the control exercised over publishing by white male academics.

More significantly for practitioners who are intervening in the lives of others, the assumption is that there is a linear progression in terms of causal factor, intervention and outcome and that there is absolute certainty about the effects of interventions. So, for example, the development of risk scales in certain areas of social work draw upon the accumulated findings of certain research to attempt to determine who might offend against the law, commit an act of child abuse or be prone to a depressive illness. That such research might draw social workers' attention to situations is perhaps no bad thing, but if the outcome of such scales is that resources are targeted only on those individuals, or that punitive intervention or surveillance is imposed upon individuals, before they have committed an antisocial act, or an act which puts themselves or others at risk, then the role of research in the process of social control becomes open to question.

The dilemma, therefore, is between the need for practitioners to be aware of, and open to, social sciences research, while remaining alert to the limitations of both the findings and the process. To ensure this, it is necessary for practitioners to receive appropriate level education which prepares them to critically evaluate knowledge which is generated. It also requires that they become involved themselves in the process of research and contributing to the analysis and evaluation of their own practice, and that of their fellow professionals. Moreover, there is a parallel imperative on the part of those undertaking research. It is not enough to assume that the presentation of detail about methodology, findings and analysis allows for the replication of findings which, in themselves validate and legitimize the findings. Just as there is a need for practitioners and educators to be reflective, so too the researcher needs to acknowledge that the conclusions reached are indeed only one perspective, arrived at at a certain moment in time when a certain set of circumstances prevail, and that there is the potential for refutation or development of the findings by others. This dialectical approach is a continuation of the research process, which ensures that the knowledge generated is not assumed to be absolute and alienated, but part of a wider canvas or, in a metaphor used elsewhere in this text, a different way of telling a story.

Conclusion

Plotting the course of feminist research highlights the perils which are inherent in challenging any orthodoxy. Similar perils exist for social work researchers. The unintended and harmful consequences of intervention or analysis, or indeed of the interpretation of research findings which are constructed as 'alienated' knowledge, without attention to the process of knowledge construction, can have significant impact on the understanding of the individual within their environment. It can lead to research being undertaken in a vacuum, with the results being challenged, or even worse, ignored. Alternatively, political agendas may lead to some research findings being privileged and incorporated into regulatory discourses.

The contribution that properly conducted research makes to social work is that it can empower those who participate in the research, both workers and service-users. It can make individuals and groups visible and it ensures the evaluation of practice which leads to more effective interventions and outcomes. In order to satisfy the criticisms and overcome resistance the research process must reflect good practice and be congruent with the value base of social work.

This paper has sought to demonstrate that feminist writings on epistemology and methodology, have provided a clarification and rationale for the ways that research practice can be congruent with a value base which respects and validates those who become the subjects of, or more accurately the sources of knowledge creation. It is for these reasons that feminist approaches are relevant, not only to social work but to all research practice.

References

AUDIT COMMISSION (1989) *Making a Reality of Community Care*, HMSO, London.

BAILEY, R. and BRAKE, M. (1975) *Radical Social Work*, London, Edward Arnold.

BARCLAY, P. (1982) *Social Workers: their role and tasks*, Bedford Square Press, London.

BOWLES, G. and DUELLI KLEIN, R. (1983) 'Introduction: theories of women's studies and the autonomy/integration debate', in BOWLES, G. and DUELLI KLEIN (Eds) *Theories of Women's Studies*, R., RKP, London.

BREWER, C. and LAIT, J. (1980) *Can Social Work Survive?* Temple Smith, London.

BROOK, E. and DAVIS, A. (1985) *Women, the Family and Social Work*, Tavistock, London.

CARLEN, P. (1989) 'Feminist Jurisprudence or Women-Wise Penology?' *Probation Journal* **3**, 3, pp. 110–114.

CROFT, S. and BERESFORD, P. (1986) *Whose Welfare: Private Care of Public Services?*, Brighton, L. Cohen Urban Studies Centre.

DOMINELLI, L. and MCCLEOD, E. (1989) *Feminist Social Work*, Macmillan, Basingstoke.

EVERITT, A., HARDIKER, P., LITTLEWOOD, J. and MULLENDER, A. (1992) *Applied Research for Better Practice*, BASW/Macmillan, Basingstoke.

GOLDBERG, E.M. (1972) 'The Use of Research in Social Work Education', in *New Themes in Social Work Education*, International Association of Schools of Social Work, New York.

GOLDBERG, E.M. and FRUIN, D.J. (1976) 'Towards Accountability in Social Work', *British Journal of Social Work*, **6**, 1, pp. 4–22.

GRIFFITHS REPORT (1988) *Community Care: Agenda for Action*, London, HMSO.

GUBA, E. and LINCOLN, Y. (1989) *Fourth Generation Evaluation*, Sage, Newbury Park.

HALBERG, M. (1989) 'Feminist Epistemology — An Impossible Project?', *Radical Philosophy*, **53**, pp. 3–7.

HANMER, J. and STATHAM, D. (1988) *Women and Social Work: Towards a Women Centred Practice*, Macmillan, Basingstoke.

HANVEY, C. (1990) 'Through a glass clearly', *Community Care*, 24 March, pp. 23–4.

MACDONALD, G. (1994) 'Developing Empirically-based Practice in Probation', *British Journal of Social Work*, **24**, 4, pp. 405–27.

MIES, M. (1983) 'Towards a methodology for feminist research' in BOWLES, G. and DUELLI KLEIN, R. (Eds) *Theories of Women's Studies* RKP, London.

NOTTAGE, A. (1991) *Women in Social Services: a neglected resource*, HMSO, London.

ORME, J. and FORBES, I. (1991) 'Equal Opportunities in Higher Degree Research' in ALLAN, G. and SKINNER, C. (Eds) *Handbook for Research Students in Social Sciences*, Falmer Press, London.

PARTON, N. (1994) '"Problematics of Government", (Post) Modernity and Social Work', *British Journal of Social Work*, **24**, pp. 9–32.

PLANT, R. (1970) *Social and Moral Theory in Casework*, RKP, London.

SCHON, D. (1987) *Educating the Reflective Practitioner*, Josey Bassey, San Francisco.

SEGAL, L. (1987) *Is the Future Female? Troubled Thoughts on Contemporary Feminism*, London, Virago.

STANLEY, L. (Ed) (1990) *Feminist Praxis: Research, Theory and Epistemology in Feminist Sociology*, Routledge, London.

STANLEY, L. and WISE, S. (1983) *Breaking Out: Feminist Consciousness and Feminist Research*, RKP, London.

UNGERSON, C. (1987) *Policy is Personal*, London, Tavistock.

WILSON, E. (1977) *Women and the Welfare State*, London, Tavistock.

WISE, S. (1990) 'Becoming a feminist social worker' in STANLEY, L. (Ed) *Feminist Praxis: Research, Theory and Epistemology in Feminist Sociology*, Routledge, London.

WORRALL, A. (1990) *Offending Women: Female Lawbreakers and the Criminal Justice System*, London, Routledge.

10 Scientific and Statistical Hypotheses: Bridging the Gap

David J. Hand

Introduction

Mathematical statistics, if viewed as a branch of mathematics, is motivated partly by its own internal structures and aesthetics. Statistical science in general, however, is driven primarily by problems arising in applications. One might in fact define statistics in general as the science of answering questions formulated in other disciplines. New statistical tools are developed to answer new problems arising in the areas to which statistics is applied, as well as to answer old problems more accurately. The ability to give better answers to old problems occurs as restrictive and unrealistic assumptions are relaxed, so enabling more appropriate models to be constructed and fitted to the data. Such models arise as a result of progress in theoretical statistics and advances in computer technology.

The acronym GIGO, standing for 'Garbage In, Garbage Out', which is used in computer science, applies equally to statistical science. Normally it is taken to apply to the data to be analyzed: inaccurately measured data, biased samples, or incomplete data necessarily raise questions about the validity of any conclusions. However, the acronym applies equally to research questions themselves: poorly formulated research questions inevitably raise doubts about the validity of the conclusions. The aim of this article is to examine such issues of research question formulation in more detail.

It has often been said that the clear formulation of a question is half the battle of answering it. Ambiguity in a question raises the possibility of different answers, each one applying to a different interpretation of the question. The more precise a question statement, the more confidence one can have in the answer. For statistical questions, however, ambiguity can arise via two routes. The first is the initial scientific formulation of the question; the statement in terms of the underlying scientific language. And the second is via the mapping from the scientific question to the statistical version of it.

To illustrate, consider the question: 'Are the people in group A more intelligent than those in group B?'. This is really a pre-scientific statement of the question. Before we can answer it we need to define what we mean by 'intelligent', a notoriously difficult exercise. One strategy is to construct a measuring instrument, the value of which one believes varies (preferably monotonically!) with intelligence (for example, the number of correct scores in a mental test), and to adopt this as an *operational definition* of intelligence. People who score higher (say) on this instrument are (subject to measurement error and other sources of random variation) taken as more intelligent.

However, things do not stop there. Using the instrument, we can now reformulate our initial question in a 'scientific' form as 'Are the IQ scores of the people in group A larger than those of the people in group B?'. While superficially this is straightforward, problems arise as soon as one tries to answer it. In particular, people have IQ scores, groups do not. Somehow one has to introduce a definition by which the groups may be compared. Obviously, to be meaningful, this has to be based on the comparison between individuals. One might also require the definition to reduce to the between individuals comparison if the groups each have a single member.

One way to approach such a problem is to summarize the scores in each group and then compare the summaries. This is fine, but why should one summary (the mean, say) be adopted rather than another (the median, say)? Any such summary statistic represents a particular mapping of the scientific question to a statistical question. A strong justification is surely needed for adopting one rather than another, especially if different statistical versions lead to different conclusions.

A second way to approach such a problem is to compare individual scores between the groups (for example, to compute all the pairwise differences), and then summarize the comparisons. In many cases the two ways yield identical statistics but, as we shall see below, this is not always the case. This distinction between these two approaches turns out to be of fundamental importance, and yet quite often to be overlooked.

A slightly different class of problems arises with the question: 'Are the IQ scores of the people in group A more variable than those of the people in group B?'. Presumably 'variable' here refers to the magnitudes of the differences between the IQ scores, so that now we need to (a) say what we mean by a difference between IQ scores and (b) how a set of such differences is combined to yield a single measure of variability. The second of these questions clearly poses the same problems as saying whether one group of scores is 'larger' than another. The first introduces issues such as whether or not it is meaningful to speak of a 'difference' between scores — as well as how to define such a thing (as the simple arithmetic difference a−b, as the ratio a/b, as the difference between square roots, etc). In general, the scientific question reflects the nature of the data: it is arguable, for instance, whether it is meaningful to speak of the numerical size of the difference between two preference scores. It would almost always not be meaningful to speak of the arithmetic mean of numerically coded hair colours (red=1, blond=2, and so on). Scientific (and hence statistical) data are not merely numbers. They are the numbers and the context associated with those numbers: what the numbers mean. What the numbers mean imposes constraints on what numerical manipulations can be performed on them in scientifically meaningful ways.

This chapter illustrates the importance and difficulty of the mapping from the scientific hypothesis to the statistical one via two examples. In the first, in Section

2, we explore two group comparisons, briefly discussed above, in greater detail. In particular, we suppose that a researcher wishes to make an inference about the difference between the means of two populations based on samples from each and examine how this might be done. The second example explores in more depth the distinction, also noted above, between comparing summaries of observations and summarizing comparisons between observations. In fact this distinction turns out to be ubiquitous, arising in all sorts of unexpected guises, and in Section 3 we look at some of the situations where it occurs.

Two Group Comparisons

To illustrate the care which has to be taken in choosing the statistical technique so that it faithfully reflects the scientific hypothesis to be investigated, in this section we consider the apparently straightforward comparison of the means of two populations. We shall see that, unless great care is taken, one can end up testing a hypothesis other than the one that one really wants to test. We shall also see that there are secondary, *model*, assumptions which must be satisfied for valid conclusions to be drawn. Note that the scientific objective in this example already implicitly contains a great deal. In particular, it implies that it is sensible to speak of means. If the measurement scale was only ordinal, for example, then, many would argue, such a comparison would not be meaningful. However, so as to avoid such issues, which would take us into even deeper water, we shall assume that we have ratio scale data.

The data which are to be used to investigate the difference between the means will be two sets of independent observations. In such circumstances, most researchers would first turn to the two sample Student t-test. (see, for example, Daly, *et al.*, 1995) This, of course, requires one to make certain assumptions about the distributions of the populations from which the data arose. In particular, these are required to be normal with equal variances. That is, the *model* assumed by the t-test is that the two distributions are normally distributed with equal variances. If the data appear to satisfy these assumptions then one would proceed happily with the t-test. If they do not, then one has to consider questions of robustness, and decide whether it is wise to proceed or if some alternative test should be adopted. It is known, for example, that the t-test is fairly robust to unequal variances if the sample sizes are roughly equal and are not too small (Boneau, 1960; Baker, Hardyck, and Petrinovich, 1966; Labovitz, 1967).

One may, of course, be uneasy about testing higher order assumptions to justify the t-test. The hypothesis of interest is about means and it might seem to be presenting a hostage to fortune to risk rejection because of breakdown of a part of the model which is irrelevant to that hypothesis. In fact, let us assume that the data are skew (i.e. the distributions have a long tail, such as that in Figure 10.1(b), as opposed to the symmetry evident in Figure 10.1(a)) and that we are uneasy about relying on robustness arguments. In this case a common approach is to try to apply a monotonic increasing *transformation* to the data so that the result more closely matches the requirements of the test. (Often this is a data-driven activity — a

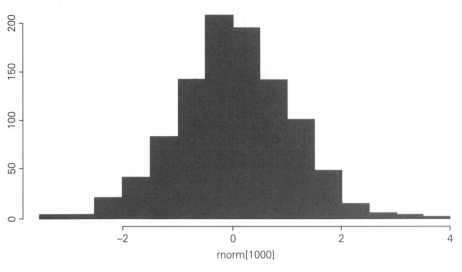

Figure 10.1(a): *The histogram of a random sample from a symmetric distribution*

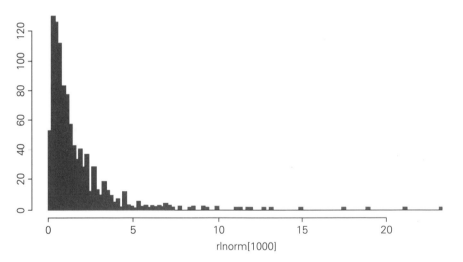

Figure 10.1(b): *The histogram of a random sample from a skew distribution*

transformation is selected on the basis of the empirical data distribution rather than a theoretical understanding of the observed data distributions.) Various transformations are used for this purpose. Box and Cox (1964), for example, develop a whole family of such transformations. For the purpose of this example, we shall adopt the logarithmic transformation, a transformation which is common and very important. We suppose here that such a transformation leads to distributions which do satisfy the assumptions made by the t-test. We can now legitimately proceed with the test.

At least, the statistician will now be satisfied that we can now proceed with the test. But what about the researcher? Recall that the researcher's original aim

David J. Hand

was to study the difference between the arithmetic means of the two groups, as measured on the original scale. This is what a t-test does. However, by carrying out a log transform and then calculating arithmetic means, one is no longer comparing the arithmetic means on the original scale. In fact, the comparison is now between log(geometric means). Moreover, instead of studying the difference between them, one is now studying their ratio. The *model* required for the student t-test has been satisfied by the transformation, but the *hypothesis* that is being tested has been altered.

Fortunately if, after the transformation, the two groups do satisfy the t-test assumption then equality of means on the transformed variable implies equality of means on the original variable (since it implies identical distributions). On the other hand, it might happen that no suitable transformation can be found which simultaneously normalizes the groups and yields equal variances. If such a transformation cannot be found, what should be done?

There are versions of the t-test which permit different variances (Welch, 1938; Best and Rayner, 1987). Unfortunately, however, these are inadequate for our purposes because, if the variances are different, then it is no longer true that equality of the expected values implies identity of the distributions and hence equality of all other parameters. In particular, it is no longer true that equality of the expected value of the transformed distribution (logically equivalent to equality of the geometric means of the original distribution) implies equality of the expected value of the original distribution. The *model* required for application of the Welch t-test is now satisfied, but the *hypothesis* in question is not tested by this test.

What remains? One common alternative is to apply the Mann-Whitney-Wilcoxon test. This tests the hypothesis that a randomly chosen score from one population will have a higher value than one randomly chosen from the other population. It says nothing about the *size* of the difference between the two scores, which is of the essence in the t-test, where means are involved. The problem here, as with the t-test on transformed data, is that although the *model* is satisfied (and for the Mann-Whitney-Wilcoxon test it is a much less restrictive model) the test is testing a *hypothesis* other than the one the experimenter really wished to test. We need to find some test which focuses on this hypothesis and which also has a model which uses appropriate population distributions.

We can devise a suitable test if we have background knowledge about the underlying distribution; if, for example, we assume that the skewness has arisen because the data come from exponential distributions. Nowadays, for a large class of models, fitting them and conducting tests is made simple by the existence of statistical software such as GLIM (Aitken, *et al.*, 1989). On the other hand, one may not be sufficiently confident in postulating some alternative form, simply noting from the available data that the normal models seem inappropriate.

One is in the position of having a highly specific hypothesis — the aim is to make a statement about the difference between two means — but a very loosely specified distributional model. We need a test which uses the difference of means as a test statistic but which requires no further distributional assumptions. There are various ways forward. The Fisher randomization test, for example, satisfies these requirements and thus is one possible solution. On the other hand, it is based on a fundamentally different underlying philosophy from that of drawing a random sample from a population. Another approach to such problems is based on *quasi-likelihood*, which focuses merely on the means and variances and the relationships between the two, without requiring knowledge of higher order aspects of the distributions. However, we shall not go into further details here.

The purpose of this, superficially straightforward, example was to focus attention on the fact that both the *model* assumptions — the things one was prepared to assume about the distributions underlying the data — and the *hypothesis* one wanted to study have each played crucial roles. It would be wrong to focus attention on only one of them. Ignoring the model means that the results may not be relied upon. Ignoring the hypothesis means that the researchers are studying something other than that which they want to study.

Individuals *vs* Populations

Suppose that the response of each individual to a stimulus of gradually increasing strength is zero up to a certain threshold, after which it is a constant, k say, the same for all individuals. That is, each individual's response is a step function, of the same height, but with possibly different values for the threshold. Suppose also that we collect data for these curves by measuring the responses at several values of the stimulus. Then there are two ways of analyzing such data, corresponding to two different questions.

The first is simply to look at the average of the responses at each of the stimulus values where measurements were taken. The results will be an average of n 0's and m k's, where n individuals have thresholds greater than the stimulus at which the measurement is taken and where m have thresholds less than the stimulus at which the measurement is taken. As the measurement stimulus is increased, so the proportion of k's will increase, so that the average score will increase monotonically. However, and this is the feature which is of particular interest here, the curve will be relatively smooth. Steps will be of size $1/(n+m)$, assuming that no two individuals' thresholds are exactly identical. Certainly, the curve will *not* be zero up to some value, and a constant non-zero value after that. That is, the curve will not have the same form as the individual constituent curves. What we have here is *the pattern of average responses*.

Figure 10.2 illustrates this kind of situation, but where the step functions have been replaced by smooth curves, so that it is clearer what is going on. Each of the curves has the same shape, but they are positioned at different points. This corresponds to step functions with different thresholds. The dotted line shows the mean curve, the curve which results by taking the average of the curves at each value of x. We see that it is flatter than the individual constituent curves.

In contrast, the second way of analyzing such data studies the shape of each individual's curve — perhaps using measurements on each individual at several stimulus levels to provide an estimate of the thresholds for each individual. These

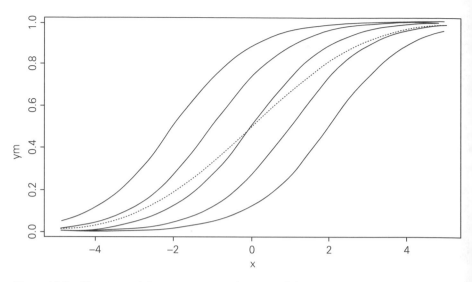

Figure 10.2:   The curve of the means versus the mean of the curves

individual curves are then combined to produce an average curve. For example, having established that the curves have the same shape, although with different thresholds, the average curve is defined as that which also has the common shape, and with threshold value equal to the average of the individuals' thresholds. We can describe this as *the average pattern of responses*.

In terms of Figure 10.2 and the smooth curves, the middle one of the five similar curves shows where the mean curve, according to the definition, will lie. This mean curve has the same shape as each of the constituent curves, and is positioned in the midst of them. Of course, in order to undertake the second kind of analysis we need to be able to model the shape of each individual's curve and to do that we need to have measurements on each individual taken at several stimulus values. This is not always possible. The obvious example is bioassay, in which the stimulus level is amount of toxic substance — above the animal's threshold it dies — but less extreme examples can also be found.

We thus have two distinct kinds of question relating to pattern of response, and we have seen that they can lead to quite different kinds of answer. Above we termed them 'pattern of averages' versus 'average of patterns'. Other terms are also used. For example, in the context of repeated measures data the terms 'population averaged' and 'subject specific' are used respectively. More generally, we might characterize the questions as relating to *unconditioned* questions and *conditioned* questions. Unconditioned questions summarize the data as if it were a single set. Conditioned questions partition it up according to the value of covariates (we might, for example, divide *age* up into five year bands and model each age group separately, assuming that the models have the same basic shape, but with different values of some parameter). We shall see examples of this below. Another way of describing the distinction that is sometimes used is to describe the questions as referring to, respectively, the between and within aspects of variation. Clearly it is vital that any investigation should sort out precisely which of the two questions is intended.

That the distinction can have far reaching consequences can be seen from the following simple example. Suppose that, in place of the step function response above, we assume that each individual has a linear response to the stimulus, $y = a_i + b_i X$, with intercept and slope which vary independently from individual to individual. (This is a *random effects* model, where the parameters defining each response curve are randomly sampled from a distribution. The step function example, in which the position of the threshold varied randomly from individual to individual, was also a random effects model.) Then, for a fixed value of x, we see that $V(y) = \sigma_a^2 + \sigma_b^2 x^2$, where σ_a^2 and σ_b^2 are, respectively, the variance of the a and b distributions. It is immediately obvious that this variance changes with x. The assumption of homoscedasticity, so common in introductory accounts of simple regression, does not hold. In contrast, if one assumed that all individuals had the same response pattern (apart from random measurement error) then constant variance would not be an unreasonable assumption. The difference depends on whether one postulates a model for the average of the response patterns or for the response pattern of the average. The above example also illustrates how the difference can be described in terms of *conditioning*. Formulating a model for individuals and averaging these to produce an overall model is, in essence, formulating a model conditioning on individuals.

Here is another example showing how confusion can arise unless the conditioning is made quite explicit. In a study of the effectiveness of trimmed means (variants of the ordinary mean which ignore extreme values) Efron (1992) used jackknife-after-bootstrap approaches (jackknife and bootstrap methods are sophisticated modern statistical tools for squeezing information from data. They are based on re-examination of multiple subsets of the available data and so are very computationally intensive). He applied the ideas to the following problem. A subatomic particle, called the tau particle, decays soon after production into various collections of other particles. Some of the time the decay produces just one charged particle, and this can happen in four major and various minor ways. The proportion of time that a single charged particle is produced can be estimated and similarly the proportion of time that each of the four major types is produced can be estimated. The primary aim of the study is to estimate and find a confidence interval for $d = d_0 - d_1 - d_2 - d_3 - d_4$ where d_0 denotes the proportion of experiments producing a single charged particle (of whatever kind) and d_i denotes the proportion of experiments producing a particle of type i, $i = 1, \ldots, 4$. Efron wanted to use trimmed means $T(x)$ to estimate d and the associated confidence interval.

However, things are not as straightforward as the above suggests. As Efron (1992, p. 95–6) says: 'because of certain physical constraints, any one experiment provides only one estimate . . . , either an estimate for the composite rate decay [d_0 above], or for one of the four modes [d_1 to d_4]'. Because of this, instead of using $T(d)$, Efron used $T(d_0) - T(d_1) - T(d_2) - T(d_3) - T(d_4)$. That is, instead of computing the trimmed mean of individual statistics of interest (the d values for individuals) he computed the statistic of interest for the trimmed means. These two things will generally not be equal. Again the distinction is one of conditioning: whether we condition on individuals, so finding the average individual response pattern, or do not, so finding the pattern of average response. This example also leads to another way of looking at things. In general, if f is a nonlinear function, then $E[f(x)]$ will not be equal to $f[E(x)]$. Here a trimmed mean is nonlinear.

Sometimes we want to study the average pattern of responses but are unable to do so. The bioassay situation mentioned above represents an example of this. Such a situation generally arises when it is impossible to take more than one measurement on each subject. For example, consider the case when we want to compare two treatments or conditions but where only one can be applied to each individual respondent. This would be the case, for example, if the 'treatment' was a method of teaching children to read or if it was a medicine for extending life. What we really want to do in such situations is study some summary statistic of the $(z_A - z_B)$ differences, where z_i represents the response the subject would give to 'treatment' i, but we cannot do this since for any given individual we will have only one of z_A and z_B. We might try to overcome the problem by matching subjects — but this can at best increase one's confidence and never completely remove doubts. After all, one can never be certain that the covariates used for the matching are really the important ones.

If the summary statistic one adopts is linear then no problem arises since $L(z_B - z_B) = L(z_A) - L(z_B)$, where $L(x)$ represents a linear summary statistic of components like x. Then one can estimate the two right-hand elements separately, from independent samples. In particular, this is true of the mean, E. (We return to this issue in the next section.) In fact, this strategy is often adopted for other, non-linear, summary statistics. That is, given that it is impossible to summarise the $(z_A - z_B)$ differences directly, researchers often summarize the z_A and z_B values separately (based on independent samples) and then subtract the summaries. This means that the researchers have shifted from the typical response pattern question to the pattern of typical responses question. However, as we have seen repeatedly above, these two approaches will not generally yield the same result: they are answering different questions.

One can ensure that the two questions are logically equivalent (the truth/falsity of one implies the truth/falsity of the other) by making extra assumptions. What these should be will depend on the summary statistic involved. However, they inevitably involve the unknown and unknowable relationship between the two measurements on each subject, one of which must remain latent. (Further discussion of this problem is given in Hand, 1992).

A similar example arises in *Simpson's paradox*, though here the conditioning is not taken as far as the level of individuals and simply arises by classifying cases into strata or subgroups. To take a hypothetical example, suppose we have two treatments, A and B, and that we are interested in both the total response and the response of two age groups, those under thirty and those thirty or over. Suppose the data are as given in Table 10.1, where x/y means that, of y people in the category, x lived and $(y-x)$ died. We see that for each of the two age groups separately

Table 10.1: *Hypothetical example of Simpson's paradox*

Treatment A		Treatment B
	Aged >30	
20/100	>	1/10
	Aged ≤30	
5/10	>	39/100
	All ages	
25/110	<	40/110

treatment A is superior, but for both age groups combined treatment B is superior. The apparent contradiction arises because of the weights used in combining the separate proportions (the weights are the denominators, so that the 20/100 and 39/100 have a greater influence on the combined result than the other two ratios). However, the important thing for us is not why the apparent contradiction arises, but the fact that the two questions, one relating to overall ratios and one to ratios categorized into subgroups are different. It is hardly surprising that different questions yield different answers. The issue which the researcher must address is which of the two questions is really the object of the study. A real example of Simpson's paradox, with a more detailed explanation of why it arises, is given in Hand (1994, Section 3.5).

All of the above examples illustrate the difference between the two questions by contrasting the results obtained by summarizing the individual response patterns with the pattern of the summary responses. A less obvious example, but one which nevertheless falls into the same class, is as follows.

Diagnosis describes the problem of classifying a person into one of two or more disease classes, according to the values of a number of variables such as symptoms (which may simply be binary). For our purposes we shall suppose that there are only two disease classes: sick and healthy. In contrast, *screening* is the problem of identifying those people within a population who are most likely to be suffering from the disease in question. Again we shall suppose that interest lies in a single disease, contrasted with 'healthy'.

Superficially these two problems are identical: in both a classification of an individual into class 1 (sick) or class 2 (healthy) is achieved on the basis of a vector of scores for that individual. However, suppose that it is known that the disease prevalence is about 1/10, so that about 1/10 are ill and 9/10 healthy. Suppose also that, no matter what further covariates we split the population on, there is a majority of healthy people in each subgroup. For example, categorizing the population by age may lead to fewer ill people at younger ages and more at older ages, but in every age group there are more healthy people than ill people. Then the most probable class for any individual, whatever their values on other variables, is healthy. That is, if our aim is to diagnose, to classify an individual into the group from which they have the highest probability of coming, we should classify everyone as healthy.

This is fine from the individual's perspective. It is clearly the right thing to do since each such individual is much more likely to be healthy than sick. But what

Table 10.2: Risk of Down's syndrome by age of mother

Maternal age	Risk of Down's syndrome per 100 births	Total births (%) in age group	% of total Down's syndrome occurring in age group
<30	0.7	78	51
30–34	1.3	16	20
35–39	3.7	5	16
40–44	13.1	0.95	11
>=45	34.6	0.05	2

about from the overall population perspective? From this perspective it is absurd: we *know* that about 1/10 are ill, so how can we possible justify concluding that none of them are ill? From the population perspective, surely what we want to do is find that 1/10 who are most likely to be ill. This is the objective of screening. The way to achieve this is not simply to classify each individual into the class from which they have the highest probability of coming, but to rank people according to their probability of being ill and classify the top scoring 1/10 as sick. Entirely different results have emerged from two superficially identical but in fact quite distinct objectives. One relates to properties of individuals and the other to properties of populations.

A similar example, in which the interests of the individual differs from the interests of someone concerned with overall population properties arises in Rose (1985). The data are reproduced in Table 10.2. Mothers aged less than 40 have a much lower chance of having a Down's syndrome child. Therefore, to reduce an individual's probability of giving birth to a Down's syndrome child we should encourage her to have the birth under the age of 40. However, we also see that 87 per cent (51+20+16 per cent) of such births occur in mothers aged less than 40. Therefore, to reduce the number of Down's syndrome births *in the population* we should focus research effort on ways of reducing the risks for mothers aged less than 40. Again there is an apparent paradox: an individual should be encouraged to have children at a younger age, but research aimed at reducing the number of Down's syndrome children should be focused in the low risk groups!

Diagnosis and screening involve multivariate statistical ideas (or, at the very least, bivariate: a predictor and the disease class) and multivariate statistics in general is susceptible to problems of the kind described in this section. Multivariate statistics deals with properties of multivariate distributions: their correlation structure in factor analysis, their grouping structure in cluster analysis, and so on. However, often the questions of interest relate not to the population structure but to the behaviour of individuals. In one of the earliest papers on these sorts of issues, Robinson (1950), who introduced the term *ecological correlation* to describe correlations between (rather than within) groups, said: 'ecological correlations are used simply because correlations between the properties of individuals are not available'. The risk, however, is that, in answering different questions, they may lead to incorrect conclusions. Robinson gave a now classic example of the correlation between colour and illiteracy for the American Census Bureau's nine geographical divisions of the United States in 1930. This was 0.946, apparently showing a very strong relationship. However, the correlation coefficient computed at the level of individuals turned out to be only 0.203, giving quite a different story.

A more modern example is Quality of Life assessment, where factor analysis of groups of individuals is used to develop scoring instruments. In fact this merely tells us about the structure of the population and not about how individuals are likely to behave under different conditions. We may, as noted above, make additional assumptions relating the two, but they are assumptions.

Conclusions

Precise specification of the research question is fundamental to scientific progress. To the extent that the question is ill-defined, so the answer will be ambiguous. In the above, we have looked at two examples of this. Further examples may be found in Hand (1994).

Whatever one's philosophical school of statistics, all will surely agree that the most fundamental component is data. Moreover, although there are statistical schools emphasizing model-free interpretative styles (such as exploratory data analysis (Tukey, 1977)), optimal scaling methods (Gifi, 1990), and biplots (Gower and Hand, 1996)), modern statistics places a heavy emphasis on formal models (see for example, McCullagh and Nelder, 1989, and Bernardo and Smith, 1994). In view of this, a suitable way to end this article is to cite two passages from key researchers in statistical science, the first contrasting the role of question formulation with that of the data, and the second contrasting it with that of models.

> The most beneficial result that I can hope for as a consequence of this work is that more attention will be paid to the precise statement of the alternatives involved in the questions asked. It is sometimes considered a paradox that the answer depends not only on the observations but on the question; it should be a platitude. (Jeffreys, 1961, preface to the first edition)

> A major point, on which I cannot yet hope for universal agreement, is that our focus must be on questions, not models. . . . Models can — and will — get us in deep trouble if we expect them to tell us what the unique proper questions are. (Tukey in discussion of Nelder, 1977)

References

AITKEN, M., ANDERSON, D., FRANCIS, B., and HINDE, J. (1989) *Statistical Modelling in GLIM*, Clarendon Press, Oxford.

BAKER, B.O., HARDYCK, C.D., and PETRINOVICH, L.F. (1966) 'Weak measurements vs strong measurements: an empirical critique of S.S. Stevens' prescriptions on statistics', *Educational and Psychological Measurement*, **26**, pp. 291–309.

David J. Hand

BERNARDO, J.M. and SMITH, A.F.M. (1994) *Bayesian theory*, Chichester, John Wiley and Sons.

BEST, D.J. and RAYNER, J.C.W. (1987) 'Welch's approximate solution for the Behrens-Fisher problem', *Technometrics*, **29**, pp. 205–10.

BONEAU, C.A. (1960) 'The effects of violations of assumptions underlying the t-test', *Psychological Bulletin*, **57**, pp. 49–64.

BOX, G.E.P. and COX, D.R. (1964) 'An analysis of transformations (with discussion)', *Journal of the Royal Statistical Society, Series B*, **26**, pp. 211–46.

DALY, F., HAND, D.J., JONES, M.C., LUNN, A.D. and MCCONWAY, K.J. (1995) *Elements of Statistics*, Wokingham, Addison-Wesley.

DAVISON, M.L. and SHARMA, A.R. (1988) 'Parametric statistics and levels of measurement', *Psychological Bulletin*, **87**, pp. 564–67.

EFRON, B. (1992) 'Jackknife-after-bootstrap standard errors and influence functions (with discussion)', *Journal of the Royal Statistical Society, Series B*, **54**, pp. 83–127.

GIFI, A. (1990) *Nonlinear multivariate analysis*, Chichester, John Wiley and Sons.

GOWER, J.C. and HAND, D.J. (1996) *Biplots*, London, Chapman and Hall.

HAND, D.J. (1992) On comparing two treatments, *American Statistician*, **46**, pp. 190–92.

HAND, D.J. (1994) 'Deconstructing statistical questions (with discussion)', *Journal of the Royal Statistical Society, Series A*, **157**, pp. 317–56.

JEFFREYS, H. (1961, 1983) *Theory of probability*, Oxford, Clarendon Press.

LABOVITZ, S. (1967) 'Some observations on measurement and statistics', *Social Forces*, **46**, pp. 151–60.

MCCULLAGH, P. and NELDER, J.A. (1989) *Generalized linear models*, London, Chapman and Hall.

NELDER, J.A. (1977) 'A reformulation of linear models', *Journal of the Royal Statistical Society, Series A*, **140**, pp. 48–76.

ROBINSON, W.S. (1950) 'Ecological correlations and the behaviour of individuals', *American Sociological Review*, **15**, pp. 351–57.

ROSE, G. (1985) 'Sick individuals and sick populations', *International Journal of Epidemiology*, **14**, pp. 32–8.

TUKEY, J.W. (1977) *Exploratory data analysis*, Reading, Addison-Wesley.

WELCH, B.L. (1938) 'The significance of the difference between two measures when the population variances are unequal', *Biometrika*, **34**, pp. 28–35.

Part 3

Research Practice

This final section, with its focus on practice, builds upon many of the philosophical questions posed in the previous chapters. The emphasis is upon interpretative and qualitative research methods. Only the last chapter deals with some of the practical problems associated with quantitative methods. This was not a conscious decision taken by the contributors or by the editors. This imbalance has occurred because no one researching within a positivist tradition felt able to contribute to a volume which was largely reflexive in nature. However, all the chapters in one way or another adopt the empiricist tradition advocated by Francis Bacon in the seventeenth century. The research studies discussed in Part 3 involve the collection of information about particular individuals whether in the context of the school, the office or a hospital and then the drawing of inferences from that information. Bacon felt that such investigations could be objective. However, all of the chapters in this section are sensitive to the subject/object dichotomy, namely that it is impossible for the investigator (the subject) to be independent of the investigated (the objects). The process of data collection cannot be independent of those collecting the data. Each of these chapters investigates the implications of breaking down the subject/object dichotomy and transforming it into a complementary *and* interactive relationship between the researcher and the researched.

Powell's personal account of research practice emphasizes the importance and relevance of the researcher's biography in the research process. In exploring approaches that enable a closer association between research, theory and social work practice, she raises issues around different conceptions of knowledge and the need for critical reflection and openness to uncertainty in undertaking research. This theme is also explored in Scott's chapter, which describes how qualitative methods can be used to examine school practices. By focusing on the processes of data collection and analysis, he illustrates the ways in which the researcher's knowledge and experience are brought to bear in a context where change, realignment and modification is an integral part of the research process. In setting out the rationale and historical development of grounded theory and detailing many of the procedures adopted, Bartlett and Payne also refer to the need 'to maintain an attitude of scepticism' as a means of examining their own assumptions and expectations. Grounded theory, they argue is a powerful and robust method for generating theory and, as an approach in the post-positivist tradition, makes a significant contribution to the search for justified belief in knowledge claims.

Both Chapters 14 and 15 examine the use of particular research methods in the context of information systems. Avison argues that the value of action research lies in its ability to engage both the researcher and the researched in a joint enterprise which is ultimately directed at solving real-world problems. Drawing on his personal experience as a participant observer in a large manufacturing company, Nandhakumar presents a critique of this method. He concludes that despite the many practical difficulties associated with this role, the direct access to participants' own interpretations of events and the understanding gained through immersion in the research context provide valuable insights into the social and organizational practices associated with information systems.

In the concluding chapter, McKenzie discusses the conditionality of statistical enquiry highlighting well known problems which are usually neglected in the reporting of quantitative data. It seems appropriate that this chapter, as the final one in the overall text, should end with a series of questions aimed at promoting inter-disciplinary research. It takes us back to the origins of this enterprise and usefully reminds us that our endeavours to stimulate dialogue and debate amongst social researchers must remain on-going.

11 Researching Social Work and Social Care Practices

Jackie Powell

Setting the Scene

Having graduated in the natural sciences, I undertook a 'conversion' course — a Diploma in Social Administration — as a necessary pre-requisite to professional social work training. My early experience as a social work practitioner was in a variety of mental health settings. Following a brief career break (or a transition period into a dual career role), I held a series of temporary research and teaching posts in the health/social care field for over a decade. My appointment as a full-time academic in the faculty was made six years ago.

What underlies this brief autobiographical note and why have I chosen to present it in this way? One response might be that I have taken this opportunity to be self-indulgent and to present or emphasize certain aspects of my life in ways which seem meaningful for me and enable me to make sense of where I find myself at this point in time. All this is true. In arguing the importance of biography Rees (1991) makes three points.

> The first concerns the struggle to make sense of individual circumstances in rela-
> tion to the dominant constraints and opportunities of a specific issue and time,
> a matter of struggle in context. The second point is an acknowledgment of the
> continuous and ongoing process of trying to comprehend and influence the world
> around one. The third point concerns the growth of freedom and the exercising of
> power in a spontaneous and creative way. (p. 11)

By adopting this style I am also seeking to emphasize the importance and relevance of a researcher's biography to the research process and the centrality of critical reflection in the practice of both social work and social research. Whilst remaining uneasy about categorizing my thinking and doing within a particular methodological approach, as this suggests an oppositional way of viewing the world, in this paper I seek to make explicit my own perceptions and assumptions and how these influence my approach to social scientific research in the field of social work and social care.

Becoming involved in 'academic research' was largely an accident as, at the time, it provided a way of utilizing my experience of interviewing people about sensitive and potentially distressing areas of their lives. Adopting a qualitiative approach based on empathic interviewing in order to understand more about a person's experience, in this case the experience of social work intervention in response to an attempted suicide (Gibbons *et al.*, 1979), was very similar to my involvement with clients, where an understanding of experience and feelings was an important part of the social work process.

However, on finding myself a researcher, concerns about the nature of the social sciences, first experienced when I moved from the world of the natural sciences to that of the social sciences in order to pursue a career in social work, were reawakened and explored again in the context of research and its relationship to professional practice.

There appeared to be differences between the two activities. These centred around the perceived role of the researcher as the gatherer of data and primarily engaged in finding out about the world, which contrasted sharply with my previous role as practitioner, where the emphasis was on action and change. Furthermore, the involvement of the researcher in the interviewee's social world challenged my naive assumption of the detached and neutral role of the researcher, who in this context at least, has to be seen as no mere medium through which knowledge is discovered, but can also be involved in the construction of knowledge. Thus the role of research in relation to action, and the role of researcher in relation to the researched, became issues of interest and concern in my research practice.

Presently, as a social work academic with a 'history' in social work practice and social work related research, I have a keen interest in understanding the nature of social work as both a theoretically informed area of study and a practice based activity. What is the role of research (and the researcher) in making a contribution to both? How can research be seen to be sufficiently relevant to be useful to those engaged in practice on a day-to-day basis? Are there particular approaches to research within the social sciences that enable a closer association between research, theory and social work practice to be forged? These questions, together with the issues raised in the previous paragraph are the themes addressed in this paper.

The Role of Research

The nature of the relationship between social work and research has been and continues to be a much disputed issue. For many practitioners, research often seems irrelevant and unconnected to their day-to-day engagement with ordinary people, albeit that such engagement takes place 'in situations of conflicting values, ambivalent motivations and ambiguous social demands' (Sainsbury, 1985). For others, research which categorizes people and attempts to quantify their experience is resisted in the belief that the essence of social work is its emphasis on the uniqueness of individual experience, in terms of achieving either an understanding of the individual's situation or any resolution of their difficulties.

However, social work in its early years as a formally recognized activity had a very close relationship with social research through the work of many of the great reformers of the late nineteenth and early twentieth century (Finch, 1986). This early research tradition in social work was lost, or at least obscured, as social work and social administration took different routes in their development of ideas and practices.

The history of social work as an emerging profession has been intimately bound up with both the development of other caring professions, most notably those allied to medicine, and the organizational contexts in which it has been located (Hugman, 1991). These several strands have, over time, influenced both the nature of social work as a practice and the type and range of research undertaken. A strong empirical tradition in social work research reflects its long association with health, and the influence of medical research, where positivistic approaches are more evident. For example, the use of experimental and quasi-experimental designs to examine the effectiveness of social work practice has been well documented, most notably by Sheldon (1986). A strong advocate of this approach, Sheldon (1986) argues that 'experiments remain the strictest test of therapeutic intent' (p. 239).

This approach to evaluating social work practice raises wider questions related to the very nature of social work itself, as well as about the most appropriate ways of studying it; both in terms of its effectiveness in practice and as to means of generating knowledge and understanding. Evidence of these wider debates can be found from time to time in the academic journals (see Sheldon, 1978; Jordan, 1978; and Sheldon, 1984; Raynor, 1984; Smith, 1987). For example, Smith's (1987) paper, entitled 'The Limits of Positivism in Social Work Research', argues that such an approach is inadequate on epistemological grounds, and that the procedures characteristic of positivism, particularly the experimental method, are unlikely to prove generally feasible or useful.

A more recent debate about the nature of social work, and in particular the concept of anti-oppressive practice (Webb, 1991a; 1991b; Dominelli, 1991; Smith, 1992) raises similar issues, not least about the relevance of the social sciences to the study of social work. The different theoretical traditions and their alternative methodological approaches within the social sciences are evident in this discussion, or rather dispute, along with the possibility and appropriateness of detachment, or, put another way, the inevitability of commitment (conscious or by default).

For those who regard social work practice as essentially a set of skills and competencies, the relationship between theory, research and practice is relatively unproblematic. Both theory and research are given the status of real or universally applicable knowledge, based on facts which are gathered independently of how people interpret them. Practice is the application or translation of this knowledge into skills. This differential status is also evident in other areas of professional practice, most notably nursing and education. Theory and research are held in high esteem by practitioners, although frequently criticized for being irrelevant and not located in the 'real world'. In response, greater attention is given to ways of disseminating knowledge in order to bridge this 'gap' (see Paley, 1987).

The view of theory as objective knowledge of the external world, i.e. a world independent of the knower, somehow separate from practice has been challenged by a number of writers, most notably Schon (1983; 1987). He argues that in many kinds of practice, nursing and education as well as social work, it is not a straight-forward matter of using acquired skills to undertake routine tasks. Given the complexity of task and context, and the frequent uncertainty of outcome, professional practice is invariably a messy business. In responding to such situations the practitioner engages in thought and action or what Schon describes as 'reflection in action'. Thus, the more traditional assumptions about the place of theory and research and their relationship to action are challenged.

Without this reflection, it is argued, the professional maintains the role of technical expert, attempting to fit the situation with pre-existing theory. As Schon (1983) writes:

> Many practitioners have adopted this response to the dilemma of rigour or relevance, cutting the practice to fit professional knowledge. . . . When people are involved in the situation, the practitioner may preserve his sense of expertise at his clients' expense. (p. 45)

He goes on to contrast this approach with that of the reflective practitioner where:

> the practitioner allows himself to experience surprise, puzzlement, or confusion in a situation in which he finds himself uncertain and unique. He reflects on the phenomena before him, and on the prior understandings which have been implicit in his behaviour. He carries out an experiment which serves to generate both a new understanding of the phenomena and a change in the situation. When someone 'reflects in action', he becomes a researcher in the practice context. (p. 68)

For the practitioner to remain open and responsive to the particular situation in which she or he is engaged, a degree of uncertainty has to be accepted and worked with positively. Without this reflection, the professional maintains the role of technical expert and practice becomes a matter of routinization and ultimately very likely to be ineffective in responding to the situation presented.

This process of critical reflection on practice suggests the way in which practice can be used creatively to generate new understandings and ways of knowing the world, which in their turn can inform and generate new patterns of practice. Reflexivity, promoted as good practice in social care work, and especially in social work, also has relevance for those engaged in research. Research can also be seen as a practice, where the complexity of the task involves rather more than the relatively straightforward application of techniques of data collection. The continual process of reflexivity as an integral part of the researcher's practice is a topic further considered in the next section.

Social Work Practitioner as Researcher

The view of social work with which I align myself has been articulated most clearly and consistently over the years by Bill Jordan. He has recently restated it eloquently in relation to present discontents:

> Social work is crucially concerned with fairness, both in redistributing resources
> to people in need and in negotiations over problems in relationships in families,
> neighbourhoods and communities. (Jordan, 1990)

Social workers therefore, in their day-to-day practice, are concerned with the different ways in which people construe their social worlds. A person's account of their actions is seen as essential to developing an understanding of their particular situation, and to the tasks of mediation and negotiation in a wider social context. The importance that the practitioner attaches to the significance of meaning, to a person's lived experience, and to the social processes through which these are constructed, suggests the need for a research approach within the interpretative tradition. As Everitt *et al.* (1992) argue:

> ... epistemologies that take account of the processes and structures through which
> subjective understandings of the world are formed and ... methodologies that cre-
> ate and validate data through participatory processes are compatible with social
> welfare practice. These contrast with epistemologies and methodologies from which
> practitioners have become alienated: those which engage in a process of research
> that, in striving for objectivity, seek distance between the researcher and the re-
> searched and attempt to control for social variables, including the researcher, lest
> they contaminate the data collected. (p. 19)

Over a number of years my empirical research has been mostly in service evaluation at the health/social care interface. In collaboration with colleagues, an approach to evaluative research has developed in the context of a number of studies. This has more recently become characterized by its emphasis on pluralism, process and partnership (Powell and Lovelock, 1992). Such an approach makes explicit the need to acknowledge a plurality of views and interests in any social intervention and attaches importance to research as a practice, in terms of the research being conceived as a process in which the researcher and those being researched are actively engaged.

In seeking to illustrate this approach, the main piece of research drawn upon concerns the organizational and practice issues involved in implementing a policy of community care for people with mental health problems. The central focus of this case study was on describing the shift of hospital services into the community and analyzing the impact of this on the multidisciplinary team providing the day-to-day services and on the people using them. It was a piece of work commissioned by those generating policy at a local level in an attempt to inform themselves and others of the processes involved and the success or otherwise of the service (and within that context the effectiveness of professional practice). It was also conceived by the researchers as making a contribution to a wider understanding of the changing nature of professional practice operating within the framework of contemporary legislation.

With its emphasis on exploring the implementation process and a requirement to clarify and interpret this process for policy makers and practitioners, this study was itself conceived as a process, where description and interpretation were given pre-eminence over measurement and prediction. This 'illuminative' approach to research developed by some educational researchers (Parlett and Hamilton, 1977; Buist, 1988) recognizes the limitations of positivistic methods and adopts an interpretative perspective in studying the implementation of the innovation in context. The progressive focusing on key issues in the particular situation is central to 'illuminative evaluation'.

Such an approach is common to many qualitative approaches, including ethnography. The researcher engages in participant observation, meeting the research subjects in their everyday contexts, and observes these at first hand. As Hugman (1988) comments, when discussing the use of ethnography in the study of social care:

> . . . data are obtained through watching, listening and talking. However, this is not to imply that anything goes. Rather it requires that the researcher makes a conscious, deliberate and systematic use of ordinary skills in engaging with a chosen social context. (p. 12)

Data are generated by the researcher in the form of notes which record events and perceptions. As part of this activity the researcher includes herself or himself in the data gathering and analysis. Whilst this continual process of reflexivity is applicable to all forms of research, it is central to the conduct of this type of approach and the way in which data is generated and analyzed.

This principle of reflexivity, alternatively described as the acknowledgement of the human dynamic in the research process, is a much contested area in research (Hammersley and Atkinson, 1983), although strongly and persuasively argued by many researchers (Steier, 1991). Drawing on her own experience of research and practice, Munn-Giddings (1993) makes the following observation:

> Using a 'reflexive' framework to reflect on practice seems to me to be the most constructive way forward for practitioner researchers. Starting from the viewpoint of those being studied, knowledge is not conceived abstractly but is viewed as a dynamic process in which theory develops from practice. It is a perspective that facilitates the understanding, undertaking and use of research by practitioners. (p. 283)

In arguing the importance of attention to process and the centrality of reflexivity on the part of the researcher, an appropriate emphasis is placed on the use of qualitative data. However, the use of quantitative methods are not thereby excluded. The combining of several sorts and sources of data, often including qualitative and quantitative material, can yield a more informed understanding for some aspects of a social phenomenon, rather than relying on any single method or data source. This multi-method approach, commonly referred to as 'triangulation' (Denzin, 1970), is also discussed in relation to case studies by Bryman (1989). However, there are epistemological issues as well as technical considerations involved in bringing together qualitative and quantitative data, and these are more fully explored in

Brannen's (1992) edited collection of papers on 'Mixing Methods: Qualitative and Quantitative Research'. Also, the case studies described in the second part of this book usefully highlight the several ways in which qualitative and quantitative approaches can be brought together in a critically reflective manner.

Exploring Differences of View

In the inherently political context of policy research, (within which social care research is located,) there is considerable value in bringing together a variety of data, not least as an attempt to recognize the multiplicity of views and often competing interests of those involved in the process of policy implementation. In the specific context of evaluating services, exploring the various legitimate definitions of success and the means by which the various interested parties seek to sustain their definitions is a key area of focus in our work (Powell and Lovelock, 1992).

> Organizations, including those which provide social and health care services are not homogeneous entities with clear and unitary goals; rather they are made up of a variety of sub-groups with differing interests and concerns. In addition, social and health care services typically have a variety of users with differing needs: not only direct users and their families or other carers, but in a different sense professionals providing services complementary to that forming the focus of the evaluation concerned. (pp. 8–9)

Thus, the assumption of consensus and unity among all parties within an organization is discarded and a rather different understanding of the social world, based on acknowledging the complex nature of organizations is employed. This 'pluralistic' approach to evaluation (Smith and Cantley, 1985 and 1988) is founded on the view that organizations have a diverse range of goals and are made up of a diverse range of sub-groups with often competing concerns and interests, an understanding of which needs to be incorporated into the research methodology.

> Ambiguity and lack of agreement in perception between parties of the policy shaping community would then be a central feature of the research, rather than an embarrassment as is the case when the presumption of consensus prevails. (Smith and Cantley, 1985, p. 9)

Smith and Cantley's approach seeks to overcome the conceptual, methodological and political difficulties of the more traditional experimental strategies employed in programme evaluation. They argue that a research strategy which acknowledges an evolutionary process and a diversity of views, rather than one which seeks to minimize or circumvent these features, has wider applicability. Thus:

> . . . pluralistic evaluation offers an ethnography of the way the service develops and an explanation of this development (in terms of the pluralistic interests of participating groups) as well as (somewhat complex) conclusions about the success

of the service on a range of criteria interpreted in different ways. Our claim is that the attempt to link the problems of the organization as perceived by its constituents, to the performance of the institution's programme of service, constitutes evaluative material. (Smith and Cantley, 1988; p. 149)

What might be seen as both an advantage and a potential disadvantage of this approach lies in its ability to identify several different constituent groups and to attend to the ways in which they are able to marshal power and resources to pursue their interests, and at what cost to other groups. The revealing of the processes, frequently exposed as jockeying for power, opens up the way for change. Certain groups can be assisted or supported in pursuit of their interests, not least those whose interests have received, until relatively recently, insufficient attention in developing health and welfare programmes: especially users, front line practitioners and other less powerful groups.

For example, the central focus of our study of the implementation of a policy of community care for people with mental health problems was on exploring the impact of this process on the multidisciplinary team providing the day-to-day services and on the people using them. In seeking to explore the different perspectives of those involved in this process, we actively sought to put onto the agenda the views of those who may otherwise not have been heard, most notably those involved in front-line services as either providers or recipients of the evolving service.

Whilst attention can be broadened to include a wide range of interested parties, the risk of exclusion remains. There is always a danger of selecting key groups and justifying their inclusion on grounds which reflect a particular set of interests, not made explicit. For example, client or user views have become an integral part of many evaluative studies of social work and social care services. However, as Sainsbury (1985; 1987) has noted, an uncritical 'consumerist' approach may present problems. Service users frequently have very low expectations about both the availability and quality of services. It is important, therefore, to ensure that such evaluations are not simply used to ration services or preserve the status quo. The task of the researcher, like the social worker, is to negotiate the meanings of what the client says. As Howe (1990) argues:

Client study researchers have tended to be stronger on moral prescription than on sociological theorizing. Their wish to give the client a good hearing has had a healthy and welcome impact on social work research and practice. But without an equal measure of social theory there is always the danger that understanding is sacrificed to reforming zeal. Asking clients to speak remains a fundamentally important research task. Adding theory to the client's view not only tells us how practice is experienced but also helps us to understand something of the nature of social work itself and the times in which it was formed. (p. 76)

Wallace and Rees (1988) however, argue strongly for the highest priority being given to clients' evaluations.

Social work's major task is to respond to problems which have largely been thrown up by an economic and cultural system which operates for the considerable benefit of some and results in the exploitation and suffering of others. In response to these problems, social workers' responsibility is never to lose sight of the needs of the most powerless people . . . (Wallace and Rees, 1988; p. 58)

Making this view explicit does not in their view hinder the conduct of the research.

On the contrary, the pretence that values do not influence the choice of research interests and methods is more likely to produce bias than the explicitness that we have documented. (Wallace and Rees, 1988; p. 59)

This is a contentious topic which, once again, demonstrates the importance of reflexivity on the part of the researcher. It also raises issues about the purposes and use of research and the role of the researcher. These are further explored in discussing the possibility of collaborative partnerships between the researcher and those being 'researched'.

Research as Partnership

The work of Guba and Lincoln (1981; 1989) in the field of educational evaluation in the US, in several respects parallels the pluralistic approach of Smith and Cantley (1985) and our own work. However, it also explicitly addresses the issue of organizational change through working in partnership with the several stakeholders involved. This more active involvement in a process which seeks to contribute to improvements in service quality was adopted in our study of the development of community-based mental health service. We worked most closely with front-line workers and managers, offering structured feedback throughout the study period to those most closely concerned with providing the service (Powell and Lovelock, 1989). This contact provided an opportunity to report on work in progress and to offer a reflective account of the continuing process of moving out and its impact on some of the interested parties. It also enabled us to check out our understandings of developments with those of some of the direct participants, mainly those engaged in front-line service delivery (McKeganey and Bloor, 1981). The final report on the evaluation offered an assessment of the development of the service over a critical two-year period of transition; issues needing further attention were identified and discussed.

As indicated earlier, this piece of work was commissioned by those involved in policy planning and implementation at a local level as a means of informing themselves and others of the processes involved in developing a community based service. There have been many attempts in recent years to consider the potential contribution of social research to social policy and the various roles which researchers do or might play. Bulmer (1982) identified three models of the relationship between research and policy: the empiricist model, the engineering model and the enlightenment model. An alternative role, that of the advocate, where the research seeks to represent the perspectives of its subjects, has been proposed by Finch (1986). This opens up the possibility of a more participative partnership between the researcher and those being 'researched'; an approach we have sought to adopt in our own practice.

In a subsequent study of implementing a 'community care' policy for older people with mental health problems, a more explicit stakeholder approach was adopted through the setting up of a stakeholders' representative group in conjunction with the service managers (Powell and Goddard, 1996). Membership was drawn from all the principal interest groups. In examining the value of this group as a forum for debate we concluded:

> Both the setting up of the stakeholder representative group and the seeking of stakeholders' views via interviews contributed to the opening up of the decision-making processes within the service. Although these approaches had limitations, the use of both mechanisms together proved successful in ensuring a wide range of views were taken into consideration. (Powell and Goddard, 1996)

However, attention was also drawn to the way in which this approach can deny or accept some of the built-in inequalities of power among, for example, managers, different professional groups and service users.

This model of the researcher as actively engaged in the process of change is a well established research tradition in education, but is nowhere near so developed in social care research. The researcher is involved in the process of reflexivity and collaboration in bringing about change. However, many forms of participatory research, which seek the active involvement of research subjects in the research process, have been criticized for failing to confront social inequality at whatever level it occurs (Holman, 1987; Oliver, 1990). Rather, the researcher retains the role of expert, with overall control of the methodology. For example, in the field of poverty research, Holman (1987) argues:

> The researchers have established not only the extent and nature of poverty, but can claim some credit for bringing it to public notice. . . . [these] studies have done something to improve services for the socially deprived. May such efforts continue. But valuable as it is, it is largely research about, on or for the poor, not by or with the poor. (p. 670)

What is needed, Oliver (1992) and others argue, is a fundamentally new approach, 'changing the relations of research production', going beyond partnership and adopting an emancipatory stance. The importance of this lies:

> . . . in establishing a dialogue between research workers and the grass root people with whom they work, in order to discover and realize the practical and cultural needs of those people. (Reason, 1988, p. 2)

Once again, issues concerning the relationship between values and research practice are raised. As Ravn (1991) states, social research is not a neutral medium, it

is: 'an activity recognized by many not just as unveiling the facts but as constructing them, and the researcher plays a major role in this'. (p. 112)

Mies (1983) takes this further by arguing that:

> The postulate of *value free research*, of neutrality and indifference towards the
> research objects, has to be replaced by *conscious partiality*, which is achieved
> through partial identification with the research objects. (p. 122)

Conscious partiality recognizes the wider social context and the research participants' (including the researcher) place in it. This view has much in common with
those expressed by Wallace and Rees (see earlier), where the researcher's own
values are acknowledged as part of the research.

Theorizing Social Work Practice

In bringing this chapter to a conclusion — whilst the discussion continues — I
want briefly to return to the contribution that research into practice might make to
social work theory. Much of the research into social work and social care practices
has centred around studies of effectiveness. This ever-growing demand to evaluate
effectiveness comes from a long-standing professional commitment to improve and
enhance practice and from a more recent need to demonstrate a careful utilization
of public resources. Thyer (1993) identifies a growing body of empirical research
which demonstrates the value of social work services in a variety of settings. He
argues that these developments are largely due to the use of research methods
located within the positivistic tradition. However, he also acknowledges that this
approach has a number of limitations.

> For example, conventional scientific methods do not provide us with much in
> the way of guidance in developing new theories themselves, or in formulating
> original research questions to be investigated. Such activities may be guided by
> one's practice experience and clinical wisdom, serendipitous findings, curiosity,
> professionally-informed speculation, reasoning processes, intuition and sometimes
> (the history of science tells us) by our dreams! (p. 20)

Rather more contentiously, he continues:

> A number of so-called qualitative research methods may be useful for this purpose,
> investigatory strategies which in themselves do not produce 'facts' in a positivistic
> sense, but certainly may be valuable to generate hypothesis to be subsequently
> tested in controlled studies. (p. 20)

Alongside this more explicitly evaluative research firmly located within a positivistic
tradition, other studies, whilst equally concerned with developing and improving
practice, have focused less on outcome and more on developing an understanding of the processes involved. As was indicated earlier, our study of an evolving

community-based mental health service was seen as making a contribution to a wider understanding of the changing nature of professional practice in the context of contemporary legislation. Other studies (see Fisher *et al.*, 1984; Howe, 1986), which have also sought to explore different patterns of service delivery and to link these with the wider organizational context of practice, offer a rich source of data for understanding more about the nature of social work and social care practices.

Working within a broadly conceived interpretative framework, such understandings can generate new ways of conceptualizing practice, thereby contributing to the development of 'practice theories'. As Curnock and Hardiker (1979) state:

> We hope our work has helped us to understand in some small ways the complex filtering processes in which social workers are engaged as they work with clients. Traditionally this has been referred to as 'practice wisdom', but we think that it can make claim to a higher theoretical status than this. This is why we have been moving towards an understanding of 'practice theories' too. (p. 172)

This reconceptualizing of theory and practice is further explored by Usher and Bryant (1989). Using the exploratory metaphor of the 'captive triangle', where theory and research are conventionally represented as the foundation or base which is then applied to practice at the apex, they argue the need to re-think this conventional representation and to 'open up' this triangle to allow a new way of thinking about these three elements without privileging any one at the expense of the other. They argue for the greater awareness on the part of practitioners to convert their practice into praxis:

> — a form of practice which is both reflective and reflexive. The essence of being reflexive is that theory and practice are dialectically interrelated. Implicit theory is brought to consciousness and continually open to change in the light of practice, which itself changes as informal theory is modified. This process, therefore, clearly utilizes the hermeneutic circle of mutually-interactive backward and forward movement between understanding and action. (p. 92)

They then go on to elaborate the nature of the relationship between formal theory and informal theory using the notion of 'review'. 'This involves accepting that the purpose of formal theory is representation and explanation, and that of informal theory is judgment, interpretation, and understanding' (p. 93).

What is important here is that both formal and informal theory are acknowledged as different and equally valid ways of knowing about the social world. This raises an issue of central concern in the development of social work theory, namely the way in which power operates through ways of knowing. It is also an area where feminist researchers have made a growing contribution. As Worrall (1990), in her study of female offenders, points out:

> The relationship between knowledge and power is crucial to any attempt to theorize women's experiences. The desire to know is a desire for power but knowledge of itself does not give power. On the contrary, it is those who have power who are authorized 'to know' and whose 'knowledge' is afforded privilege. (p. 7)

Henkel (1995) discusses similar issues around different conceptions of knowledge in the context of social work education, and identifies the need for 'critical reflection and openness to uncertainty' (p. 68) in the pursuit of reflective practice. She argues the relevance of both pragmatism and hermeneutics which, although derived from the different traditions of North America and continental Europe, have much in common.

> Both challenge the Cartesian paradigm, at the centre of which are dualistic forms of thought (mind and body; subject and object; theory and practice; knowledge and action) and the ideal of the individual knowing subject contemplating an external object. Instead they assert the active and collective nature of knowledge acquisition and development, together with the role of language and disciplinary tradition in shaping knowledge and confounding the clear cut division between subject and object. At the same time, they facilitate a review of the relationship between conceptions of knowledge as understanding and dialogue. (p. 68)

Critical Theory in particular, with its emphasis on 'dialogic communication', offers a conceptual framework for social work (and social work research) practice (Blaug, 1995). However, particular attention to either Critical Theor(ies) or feminist perspectives, both with emancipatory aims, have remained outside the scope of this paper. The main puprose of this paper has been to provide an account, to tell a story, about the development of an approach to researching social work and social care practices; an approach located within an interpretive framework and seen as one attempt at encouraging closer links between research, theory and social work practice. It has been written at a particular time and for a specific purpose. It has used autobiographical detail as a means of emphasizing the importance of self-awareness in making choices between an array of divergent approaches to social research.

In his tracing of the promise of biography, Rees (1991) confirms:

> . . . the value of developing questions over time, as part of a disciplined approach to personal and professional development. A student can be encouraged to develop questions about the present, not merely to solve an immediate problem but as a means of developing a philosophy for practice, and skills in so doing. (p. 12)

In this context, I am the student, and the process of developing a philosophy for research practice continues. Reflecting upon this account, key questions about the nature of theory, and social work theory in particular, remain unresolved. The development of feminist theory and its contribution to the formulation of feminist social work (Dominelli and McLeod, 1989) provides alternative ways of 'knowing' about the social world. Feminist approaches to research, only touched upon here, need closer consideration in the development of research practice relevant to social work and social care. However, in my view, this takes me beyond an interpretive framework (and therefore the scope of this paper) and into areas which identify the limitations of this tradition. It also begins the telling of another story, currently in the making.

References

BLAUG, R. (1995) 'Distortion of the Face to Face: Communicative Reason and Social Work Practice', *British Journal of Social Work*, **25**, 4, pp. 423–39.

BRANNEN, J. (Ed.) (1992) *Mixing Methods: qualitative and quantitative research*, Avebury, Aldershot.

BRYMAN, A. (1989) *Research Methods and Organisational Studies*, Unwin Hyman, London.

BUIST, M. (1988) 'Illuminative Evaluation', in LISHMAN, J. (Ed.), *Evaluation. Research Highlights in Social Work 8*, 2nd edn, Jessica Kingsley Publishers, London, pp. 72–81.

BULMER, M. (1982) *The Use of Social Research: Social Investigation in Public Policy-making*, George Allen and Unwin, London.

CURNOCK, K. and HARDIKER, P. (1979) *Towards Practice Theory: Skills and methods in Social Assessments*, Routledge and Kegan Paul, London.

DENZIN, N.K. (1970) *The Research Act in Sociology*, Aldine, Chicago.

DOMINELLI, L. (1991) ' "What's in a name?" A comment on "Puritans and paradigms" ', *Social Work and Social Sciences Review*, 2, pp. 231–35.

DOMINELLI, L. and McLEOD, E. (1989) *Feminist Social Work*, Macmillan, London.

EVERITT, A., HARDIKER, P., LITTLEWOOD, J. and MULLENDER, A. (1992) *Applied Research for Better Practice*, Macmillan, London.

FINCH, J. (1986) *Research and Policy: the uses of qualitative methods in social and educational research*, Falmer, Lewes.

FISHER, M., NEWTON, C. and SAINSBURY, E. (1984) *Mental Health Social Work Observed*, George Allen and Unwin, London.

GIBBONS, J.S., BOW, I., BUTLER, J. and POWELL, J. (1979) 'Clients' reactions to task-centred casework', *British Journal of Social Work*, **9**, 2, pp. 203–15.

GUBA, E.G. and LINCOLN, Y. (1981) *Effective Evaluation: Improving the Usefulness of Evaluation Results Through Responsive and Naturalistic Approaches*, Jossey Bass, San Fransisco.

GUBA, E.G. and LINCOLN, Y. (1989) *Fourth Generation Evaluation*, Sage, Newbury Park, California.

HAMMERSLEY, M. and ATKINSON, P. (1983) *Ethnography: Principles in Practice*, Tavistock Publications, London.

HENKEL, M. (1995) 'Professional Competence and Higher Education', in YELLOLY, M. and HENKEL, M. (Eds), *Learning and Teaching in Social Work: towards reflective practice*, Jessica Kingsley Publications Ltd., London.

HOLMAN, B. (1987) 'Research From the Underside', *British Journal of Social Work*, **17**, 6, pp. 669–83.

HOWE, D. (1986) *Social Workers and their Practice in Welfare Bureaucracies*, Gower, Aldershot.

HOWE, D. (1990) 'The Client's View in Context', in CARTER, P., JEFFS, T. and SMITH, M. (Eds), *Social Work and Social Welfare Yearbook 2*, Open University Press, Milton Keynes.

HUGMAN, R. (1988) 'Ethnography and social care', *Social Services Research*, **17**, 6, pp. 669–83.

HUGMAN, R. (1991) *Power in the Caring Professions*, Macmillan, London.

JORDAN, B. (1978) 'A comment on "Theory and practice in social work" ', *British Journal of Social Work*, 8, pp. 23–5.

JORDAN, B. (1990) *Social Work in an Unjust Society*, Harvester Wheatsheaf, Hemel Hempstead.

McKeganey, N.P. and Bloor, M.J. (1981) 'On the retrieval of sociological descriptions: respondent validation and the critical case of ethnomethodology', *International Journal of Sociology and Social Policy*, **1**, 3, pp. 58–69.

Mies, M. (1983) 'Towards a Methodology for Feminist Research', in Bowles, G. and Klein, R. (Eds), *Theories of Women's Studies*, Routledge and Kegan Paul, London.

Munn-Giddings, C. (1993) ' "A Different Way of Knowing": social care values, practitioner research and action research', *Educational Action Research*, **1**, 2, pp. 275–85.

Oliver, M. (1990) *The Politics of Disablement*, Macmillan, London.

Oliver, M. (1992) 'Changing the Social Relations of Research Production', *Disability, Handicap and Society*, **7**, 2, pp. 101–15.

Paley, J. (1987) 'Social Work and the Sociology of Knowledge', *British Journal of Social Work*, **17**, 2, pp. 169–86.

Parlett, M. and Hamilton, D. (1977) *Introduction to Illuminative Evaluation*, Pacific Soundings, Cardiff-by-the-Sea, California.

Powell, J. and Goddard, A. (1996) 'Cost and Stakeholder Views: a combined approach to evaluating services', *British Journal of Social Work*, **26**, 1 (forthcoming).

Powell, J. and Lovelock, R. (1989) 'The development of community based adult mental health services — a research contribution', *Bulletin of the Royal College of Psychiatrists*, **13**, 12, pp. 662–6.

Powell, J. and Lovelock, R. (1992) *Changing Patterns of Mental Health Care: A case study in the development of local services*, Avebury, Aldershot.

Ravn, I. (1991) 'What should guide reality construction?', in Steier, F. (Ed.), *Research and Reflexivity*, Sage, London.

Raynor, P. (1984) 'Evaluation with one eye closed: the empiricist agenda in social work', *British Journal of Social Work*, **14**, pp. 1–10.

Reason, P. (Ed.) (1988) *Human Inquiry in Action: developments in new paradigm research*, Sage, London.

Rees, S. (1991) *Achieving Power: practice and policy in social welfare*, Allen and Unwin, London.

Sainsbury, E. (1985) 'The contribution of client studies to social work practice', *Social Work — Research into Practice, Proceedings of the First Annual JCC/BASW Conference*, September 1985, London.

Sainsbury, E. (1987) 'Client Studies: their contribution and limitations in influencing social work practice', *British Journal of Social Work*, **17**, 6, pp. 635–44.

Schon, D.A. (1983) *The Reflective Practitioner: how professionals think in action*, Temple Smith, London.

Schon, D.A. (1987) *Educating the Reflective Practitioner*, Jossey-Bass, San Francisco.

Sheldon, B. (1978) 'Theory and practice in social work: a re-examination of a tenuous relationship', *British Journal of Social Work*, 8, pp. 1–22.

Sheldon, B. (1984) 'Evaluation with one eye closed: the empiricist agenda in social work — a reply to Peter Raynor', *British Journal of Social Work*, 14, pp. 635–7.

Sheldon, B. (1986) 'Social work effectiveness experiments: review and implications', *British Journal of Social Work*, 16, pp. 223–42.

Smith, D. (1987) 'The limits of positivism in social work research', *British Journal of Social Work*, 17, pp. 573–86.

Smith, D. (1992) 'Puritans and paradigms: a comment', *Social Work and Social Sciences Review*, 3, pp. 99–103.

Smith, G. and Cantley, C. (1985) *Assessing Health Care: a study in organizational evaluation*, Open University Press, Milton Keynes.

SMITH, G. and CANTLEY, C. (1988) 'Pluralistic Evaluation', in LISHMAN, J. (Ed.), *Evaluation. Research Highlights in Social Work 8*, 2nd edn, Jessica Kingsley Publishers, London, pp. 118–36.

STEIER, F. (Ed.) (1991) *Research and Reflexivity*, Sage, London.

THYER, B. (1993) 'Social Work Theory and Practice Research: the approach of logical positivism', *Social Work and Social Sciences Review*, **4**, 1, pp. 5–26.

USHER, R. and BRYANT, I. (1989) *Adult Education as Theory, Practice and Research: the captive triangle*, Routledge, London.

WALLACE, A. and REES, S. (1988) 'The Priority of Client Evaluations' , in LISHMAN, J. (Ed.), *Evaluation. Research Highlights in Social Work 8*, 2nd edn, Jessica Kingsley Publishers, London, pp. 58–71.

WEBB, D. (1991a) 'Puritans and paradigms: a speculation on the form of new moralities in social work', *Social Work and Social Sciences Review*, 2, pp. 146–59.

WEBB, D. (1991b) 'A stranger in the academy: a reply to Lena Dominelli', *Social Work and Social Science Review*, 2, pp. 223–41.

WORRALL, A. (1990) *Offending Women: Female Lawbreakers and the Criminal Justice System*, Routledge, London.

12 Qualitative Approaches to Data Collection and Analysis: Examinations and Schools

David Scott

With regard to the study of education, it is possible to identify four research paradigms: positivism, post-positivism, post-modernism and post structuralism (Denzin and Lincoln, 1994). The first of these, positivism, for so long the dominant influence, can be characterized in the following way: values can be separated from facts, with the researcher's task designated as uncovering and reporting those facts. They are not considered to be a part of the research and their presence is not expected to affect the quality or type of data that are gathered. Positivists further argue that there are no meaningful differences between natural and social science methodologies. Bhaskar (1989) develops this argument, though his solution is radically different from other social theorists in the research tradition under discussion. He suggests that both social scientific and scientific methodologies should be understood as one: 'both the dominant naturalist tradition, positivism, and its anti-naturalist hermeneutical foil rest on an ontology rendered obsolete by these developments (new collateral theories of philosophy and ideology). The time is therefore overdue for a "sublation" of their historic confrontation' (p. ix). Without a solution of this sort, social scientists who introduce reflexive and interpretative elements into their methodologies are deemed to have acted unscientifically and therefore without objectivity. The textual account that eventually emerges is therefore objective, separate from the value positions of the researcher and representative of an intransitive reality. Researchers working within this tradition would thus seek to privilege their accounts by ignoring the problem of reflexivity, by denying that these accounts are essentially constructed, and by minimizing through the use of certain textual and methodological devices the place of the researcher in that construction.

However, seeking to decontaminate the research experience by separating the researcher from the object of their study, involves the adoption of a particular value position, principally that data which are collected in this way effectively and adequately represent reality. Furthermore, it is difficult to imagine that those decontaminating devices do in fact separate off the researcher from what is being researched. All types of research involve selective and thus value-laden interventions of different types during their conduct. It is in this sense that the data are value-impregnated. The researcher, tacitly or overtly, has already mapped the area that they are studying, based on experience and knowledge. But within this, there is a place for change, realignment and modification. The researcher finds out things during the course of the research which they did not know. Reflexive practices are therefore considered essential elements within post-positivist, post-modernist and post-structuralist research traditions, and they relate to examination of both the researcher's own conceptual and affective maps, the way those maps mediate and structure reality for the researcher, and what is being researched. Researchers who would place themselves broadly within these traditions would accept the value-laden implications of their position, but seek to understand and conceptualize it by adopting reflexive stances. This chapter will focus on two aspects: data-collection and their analysis.

The Research Project

The empirical study which is discussed in this chapter is an investigation of GCSE coursework processes. The General Certificate of Secondary Education replaced O-level and CSE as the principal means of examination for 16 year olds in 1988 and has undergone substantial revision since (chiefly in the reduction of the coursework component). Although it is a recent innovation, it has a long developmental history. The Examination Boards as early as 1972 had explored the notion of a common examination at 16+ and feasibility studies were started the following year. Their success led to the setting up of the Waddell Committee which recommended a single system of examination (DES, 1978). In the Spring of 1979, a Conservative Government was elected. The new Secretary of State for Education, Mark Carlisle, announced soon after that the idea of a common replacement for O-level and CSE would be further explored, and would incorporate three new elements: subject criteria, differentiated examinations and a measure of teacher-assessed work. One of his successors, Sir Keith Joseph, took the process one stage further when he revealed in a speech to the Northern Education Association in January 1984 that working parties would be set up to develop subject-grade criteria, that candidates would be awarded grades in terms of positive achievement and that the examination would be criterion-referenced (Joseph, 1984). The final versions of the National and Subject criteria were published in March 1985, and the first cohort of students sat the examination in June 1988.

The project team decided to adopt the condensed fieldwork methods of multi-site case study (Walker, 1974), located within the ethnographic research tradition (Hammersley and Atkinson, 1983; Burgess, 1984; Woods, 1986). Case studies of the effects of coursework were made in six schools, across three different counties and two metropolitan districts in the United Kingdom. They were of an independently controlled mixed day/boarding school, an independently controlled single-sex (female) day school, a single-sex (female) urban comprehensive school, a mixed urban comprehensive school, a mixed rural comprehensive school and a mixed rural secondary modern school. They were chosen to represent a range of organizational and socio-economic contexts.

In each of these schools, as the sole researcher I used a variety of data-collection methods, principally interviews, observations and document analysis.

This allowed me to reconstruct events through the eyes of key participants. Interviews were conducted with senior members of staff in each school and with heads of department in all the major subject areas. Informal contact was maintained with other members of staff, and with large numbers of pupils both in class and outside. In addition, I interviewed six pupils in each school. They were chosen to give a gender balance, where this was appropriate; and to allow a variety of responses from different ability levels within each school. In four out of the six schools one of these pupils was observed throughout their timetable during a full day. Other relevant lessons (assessed practicals in the sciences, oral work in English) were also observed where I felt that this would contribute to further understanding of coursework processes. Interviews were conducted with the parents of the sample of pupils, so that the key issue of parental contributions to coursework assignments could be investigated. Each of these thirty-six pupils kept a diary over five weeks to record the extent of the work they were doing in all their subjects outside the classroom. Within each school a number of pupils were identified as failing to complete coursework requirements in some or all of their subjects and subsequently interviewed. Finally, all year 10 pupils in each setting completed a short questionnaire, which asked them to list their homework (including coursework completed at home) during one full week in the summer term of the second year of the project.

Choosing Cases

Data collection methods were not predetermined. Research processes were guided strategically by the developing theory. This is at the heart of what Glaser and Strauss (1967) call 'grounded theorizing'. A dialectical relationship exists between theory building and data collection. As fieldwork proceeds, the researcher's initial hunches, hypotheses and conjectures are gradually refined and reformulated, and this acts progressively to focus analysis and reorganize data collection methods.

Prior to this, there is what Malinowski (1922) calls the 'foreshadowed problem'. This involves clarifying and developing research ideas before fieldwork begins. Glaser and Strauss (1967) in opposition to this approach, argue that the researcher should avoid presuppositions, hypotheses and previous research studies, though they have recently modified this position. Bulmer (1979) has criticized this *tabula rasa* approach because it is difficult to achieve and it ignores the way researchers conceptualize research problems. Furthermore, all data and data collection methods include theoretical assumptions, the adoption of which occurs prior to fieldwork (Harris, 1979).

These initial hypotheses and suppositions that informed the initial stages of my research were influential in guiding the selection of cases. They were:

a)   Children in rural schools may have problems with completing history and geography coursework projects because they may have limited access to primary sources of information.

b)   Parental interventions in coursework processes would be differentially distributed and were likely to be of greater intensity in middle-class localities.

c) The amount of work students actually do may have gender implications. Coursework processes which are assessed over the two years of the course may favour the more persistent and hardworking pupils. Girls are therefore likely to benefit.

d) Coursework processes are of benefit to the taught curriculum, but reduce examination reliability and comparability. (Fieldnotes, 6.6.1988)

Though some of these themes declined in importance as fieldwork progressed, initially they were influential in research design, and extra- and intra-sampling judgments. Six case-studies of school processes were eventually made. Choosing appropriate cases though, can never be an exact operation, since practical constraints limit researchers' freedom of action (cf. Shipman, 1981; Burgess, 1983). Even if pre-sampling is undertaken, there are no guarantees that these sampling judgments accurately reflect the research design. If such guarantees were able to be made, there would be no point in completing the fieldwork, since there would be nothing new to discover. Furthermore, since the research focus is in a state of constant flux, it is difficult to prespecify appropriate cases.

In order to develop formal theory, the research programme can be used to build theory (Glaser and Strauss, 1967), or test theory (Hammersley, 1985; Hammersley and Scarth, 1986; Hammersley, Scarth and Webb, 1985), or provide detailed ethnographic description which uses theoretical elements (Burgess, 1983, 1984). Depending on purpose, different sampling judgments will be made. Cases are chosen either for typicality or for explanatory power. They are either representative of a wider whole or they illuminate theories which concern that wider setting. Hammersley (1985) describes three styles of case study research. The first style is where the researcher wants to study typical cases, which represent a larger whole or aggregate. Honigmann (1973), for instance, argues that ethnographers must identify their selection criteria to enable the reader to determine the relationship between the sample and its intended population. In a similar way, Woods (1987) cites the need to make 'the case' as representative as possible to improve external validity. The second style of case-study research cited by Hammersley (1985) is where the researcher wants to use cases to test theories. They study more and more cases until they are satisfied that the theory holds. The third style is where the researcher is not concerned with notions of representativeness, as they acknowledge the uniqueness of each case, but they are interested in how the workings of particular processes are illuminated by single cases.

This study of GCSE coursework broadly adopted this last approach. Though I formulated a series of tentative hypotheses (see above), these were used to guide the selection of cases. These cases were not representative of all schools in the country, though they did include schools which could be distinguished from each other by sets of identifiable characteristics — single sex/mixed, independent/state, urban/rural, selective/comprehensive, day/boarding, high/low socio-economic status of parents, and compacted/extended catchment areas. The theory that I subsequently generated is not generalizable to every other case, because my six schools were not chosen for typicality. They were chosen because their distinguishing features allowed specific investigation of those aspects of the research problem (understanding coursework processes) that pre-fieldwork hypothesizing had suggested would be important. Mitchell (1983) refers to this as theoretical sampling. The intention therefore, was to develop theories which illuminate processes in that wider universe. Formal theory emerges which has explanatory power but it is based on the uniqueness of each case. Furthermore, it quickly became apparent that the case as an holistic entity could not be a school because coursework processes were subject bound. Thus a progressive refocusing of 'the case' took place as fieldwork proceeded and as it became clear that departmental processes were of greater significance than school processes.

Negotiating Access

Gaining access to research settings involves far more than simply being granted permission to begin research. It is a continuous series of negotiations and re-negotiations, with different personnel at different levels within the organization. Indeed, though access may be granted by the principal gatekeeper, this may not reflect the interests and wishes of all members of that organization. Having been granted permission to conduct research at Lampton Independent School by the headteacher, I was enjoined to:

> Go where you want; go into any classroom. We are a completely open school. We have nothing to hide. Interview who you want. We will find the time for you.

Though I subsequently encountered little opposition, it was clear from one tentative enquiry that I would not be welcome in her classroom. Having successfully negotiated access with other members of staff, I chose not to pursue the matter. Gaining initial access therefore is only the beginning of a process (Woods, 1986) which stretches throughout the fieldwork and has consequences for both the research methods employed and the subsequent account that the researcher eventually submits. They therefore, cannot assume a neutral value-free position, but are fundamentally a part of the written account that is finally completed.

The initial means of gaining access to the six case-study schools was by letter. Due to lack of time this was changed to telephoning and three schools were approached only by this method. There was no correlation between method and success rate. Two schools that I telephoned, without sending an initial letter, subsequently granted access. Another did not reply, so I telephoned to ask for an interview with the headteacher, which was granted. Access was subsequently refused. Once an interview had been arranged, and it was not necessarily with the headteacher, it was usual for permission to be granted at that interview. Clearly the decision had been made in those cases before the interview took place, using the information available in the initial letter. In other cases headteachers initiated consultation procedures with their staffs. This resulted in successful access in some cases, but failure in others.

The reasons given for my failure to gain access (in four schools) provide insights into the social organization and operational state of particular settings. The headteacher of one of the schools refused entry because of pressure from the unions. This was a single-sex girls' school in an urban area of high unemployment and extensive social deprivation. It had just gone through a period of sporadic union action, and was threatened with closure due to falling numbers. My presence as a researcher would have increased the pressure on participants.

Undergrove School, on the other hand, suffered from none of these disadvantages, except that teacher unions were taking industrial action in all schools at this time. I received a prompt letter explaining that: 'It would take me several hours to explain to you in detail the reasons, but if I say to you time and other commitments of colleagues, I am sure you will understand.'. The Headteacher of Grove Priory failed to reply to my letter. The school secretary of Abbotsbury telephoned to say that it was 'inconvenient and unnecessary'. Teachers may fear outsiders, because they could expose shortcomings in their professional practice. As Woods (1986) puts it: 'Teachers may fear disturbance of their own delicately balanced survival equilibrium. Outsiders can only be perceived as a threat to this' (p. 28). The extent of this threat is determined by the perception of the headteacher in each of the schools. However, as Wolcott (1973) acknowledges, a school study can not be completed openly without seeking permission from the headteacher. But this has repercussions, since the level at which the researcher enters will influence the conduct of the fieldwork and the type of data that is gathered. Though Simons (1987) advocates a democratization of research methods where research programmes are constructed to meet the needs of all the participants in what are inevitably stratified situations, in the initial stages of gaining access democratic goals cannot be met.

As a researcher, I used a number of familiarity devices to facilitate access. What I said, what I looked like, how I behaved — the ephemera of role — were all designed to establish trust and thus ease the process of entry (cf. Hammersley, 1979; Delamont, 1984). I deliberately used my extensive experience as a teacher as a device to reassure. I claimed privileged knowledge of the research setting because I had taught in comprehensive schools for thirteen years. There are, though, dangers of over-familiarity. My fieldnotes record such an incident:

> I notice two girls sitting outside the headteacher's study, reading books. At my last school pupils sent out of classrooms for misbehaviour were sometimes picked up by the head and made to work for the rest of the day outside his study. I assume these two girls have fallen foul of some teacher. (Lorton School for Girls)

Later I am disabused of such a notion:

> The Deputy Head tells me that they try to welcome visitors by always having two girls on duty outside the head's study, whose task it is to welcome visitors and ask them politely who they would like to see.

Burgess (1984) argues that the degree of familiarity or strangeness found in research settings has been polarized in some of the literature. He suggests that in his
research he found within the same social setting a series of situations which were
both familiar and strange. Whatever the degree of real familiarity with the six case-
study schools where I did my research, I assumed a persona that was familiar with
the mores and codes of school life. Since gatekeepers operate with expectations
about the researcher's identity and intentions (Hammersley and Atkinson, 1983),
role-playing that assumes empathetic understanding of a school's culture is more
likely to persuade gatekeepers to grant access. In the case of Austell School,
an independent boys' school, I deliberately mentioned the fact that I had been
educated in a fee-paying boarding school. The headteacher asked me about its
headteacher whom he knew. Knowledge of particular settings has to be carefully
and sensitively 'reached'; gaining access therefore requires the adoption of strategies which are able to penetrate the protective skin which surrounds them.

One device I used to gain entry was the submission of a research brief to the
gatekeeper or gatekeepers. Commentators (cf. Burgess, 1984) have argued against
this approach for a number of reasons. Since it is usual to have only a limited
understanding of the complete research programme at the beginning of the research
and since methodology and data-collection operate in a dialectical fashion, the researcher is rarely in a position to provide a full account of their purposes to the
relevant gatekeeper. Furthermore, as Hammersley and Atkinson (1983) suggest, it
may not be prudent to give a full picture because 'unless one can build up a trusting
relationship with them relatively rapidly, they may refuse access in a way that they
would not do later in the fieldwork' (p. 71). On the other hand, providing minimal
information about the research design simply puts in writing what is said anyway
at initial access meetings. The site brief that I used included a clear specification
of the ethical safeguards I was prepared to build into the investigation. In all but
one of the cases they were accepted without argument. In my fieldnotes after my
initial interview with the headteacher of St Thomas' School for Girls, I wrote: 'she
seemed to trust that I wouldn't be insensitive to confidences, that I would build in
a system of anonymity to the reporting'. The degree of frankness, even indiscretion,
was high. The headteacher of Lorton School described her deputy as someone who
should have retired years ago. The Headteacher of Carseley High School described
his staff as willing, hard-working, but essentially apolitical; but he did say that
there were one or two members of staff who were very outspoken, and gave an
indication of who they were.

In one school, the issue of confidentiality and anonymity assumed a position
of central importance in my initial discussions. Austell is an independent boys'
school, and the headteacher's fear was that unsubstantiated comparisons would
be made between state and independent schools. In order to gain access, I had to
negotiate further ethical safeguards, ones which I did not initially want to make.
This involved agreeing to

> submit to you (the headteacher of the school concerned) before publication of any
> article or paper that I write, so that you may check for inaccuracies or bias; and

so that we can, if it proves to be necessary, reach a compromise about what should go in the article. The article will of course not mention your school by name, nor any of the teachers in it by name; but the above stipulation will apply to any part of that article which concerns itself with your school.

In order to maintain momentum, I was prepared to relax the principle articulated in the site brief of the researcher owning the data. In the end, for reasons not connected with the negotiated process of gaining access, I decided that the school would not be an appropriate place in which to work. Thus intra- and extra- sampling judgments reflect both the original research design and the contingencies of agreeing access.

Ethical Concerns

Having successfully negotiated initial access to each of the six case study schools and having done so with the aid of a site brief which contained certain ethical safeguards, it was important to put these into effect during the fieldwork. In my fieldnotes, I listed those areas of the project which involved me in ethical undertakings:

1 Since I am dealing with children as well as adults, I need to set up mechanisms which allow teachers and students to say what they feel.
2 It is important that I do not misrepresent individual contributions in my final account of coursework processes.
3 I have a responsibility to protect particular individuals because insensitive handling of their data may harm them. This goes further than simply agreeing to negotiate the release of data, because such negotiations are always going to take place on an unequal basis.
4 I have an obligation to the public: to place in the public domain information I have gathered about coursework processes.
5 I have an obligation to the school to protect its interests. Anonymity can partly fulfil this responsibility.
6 I have been commissioned by an external sponsor. They have certain expectations.
7 Finally I have a responsibility to certain ethical principles of conduct; that I should tell the truth for instance. (Fieldnotes, 5.5.1988)

This list was not able to serve as a working model for a number of reasons. Some of these obligations are in conflict with each other. Telling lies may be necessary to maintain confidentiality. In granting anonymity to schools and research participants, I was involved in a number of small deceptions and evasions. When asked, for instance, by the headteacher at Lampton about the identity of a particular teacher whose practice he disapproved of, I declined to answer. Moral obligations are always conditional; that is they have consequences outside of themselves which cannot be subsumed absolutely under the aegis of any moral prescription. Given the fluid nature of the principles that researchers can use to guide them in their endeavours, as a general rule therefore, ownership of the data resides with the researcher. This can be contrasted with more democratic approaches to data ownership in which research participants retain rights of veto over publication, and the narrative that is eventually produced is in effect a negotiated account between researcher and participants.

There are a number of problems with this. First, because the needs of different participants may not be known at the beginning of the research process, there are bound to be initial decisions made about methodology which will structure the type of data that is collected. Second, there is a temptation on the part of the researcher to present their negotiated account as a neat and coherent view of reality because they are operating in the public domain. Third, negotiating with participants (especially with children) can never be negotiating between equals. The researcher understands the consequences of release and publication better than the participant. Finally, the manner of negotiation may be determined by the implicit structures of the institution. Burgess (1984) reminds us that 'people respond to the structured situations in which they are located'. Negotiation of the release of data in non-democratic research situations therefore serves to generate more data, whereas for democratic researchers it serves to construct the reality of the situation.

From the outset, I was determined that my research should be as open as possible. There was never any intention on my part to engage in secret or covert research, where participants are unaware their behaviour is the subject of scrutiny (Homan, 1980). Even when researchers feel it is necessary to adopt covert stances, they may still express reservations (Bulmer, 1979). The British Sociological Association in 1992 clarified their position on covert research:

> As far as possible sociological research should be based on freely given informed consent of those studied. This implies a responsibility on the sociologist to explain as fully as possible, and in terms meaningful to participants, what the research is about, who is undertaking and financing it, why it is being undertaken and how it is to be disseminated. (p. 2)

However it has to be acknowledged that all research necessarily entails a hidden element (Roth, 1962). Since researchers are unlikely to have a clear idea of what exactly they want to research at the beginning of the investigation, they can only provide participants with a limited account of their purposes. The giving of consent by participants is always subject to the power/knowledge differential that exists between participant and researcher. As the British Sociological Association (1992) acknowledges:

> Wherever possible they (researchers) should attempt to anticipate, and to guard against, consequences for research participants which can be predicted to be harmful. Members are not absolved from this responsibility by the consent given by research participants. (p. 2)

Protecting the interests of participants in research projects though, is difficult. Individuals and locations cannot be disguised completely, though it is easier to deceive outsiders than insiders. Anonymizing individual responses enabled me to protect participants from external scrutiny, and in a project such as this, this was important. For instance Sarah, a fifth year pupil at Tidehill, would not have wanted her remarks about her well-developed work avoidance techniques to be heard by her teachers:

> You can get away with not doing homework. I have got away with not doing a load of homework for certain subjects. They have a look at my homework diary and they see that I am getting work. Usually the teachers give you work and I write it in my book, and then in my homework diary I would add another extra amount; so they were thinking I was getting enough. So after that if I didn't have any, I would put in something that I had been doing in lessons.

There are always tensions between confidentiality and portrayal. Burgess (1984) writes: 'it is evident that whatever precautions are taken to protect those involved in a field study, nothing is foolproof' (p. 206).

Fieldwork Relations

Though I used a site brief which was read by the key gatekeepers in each school, this did not prevent a temporary breakdown in relations half way through the initial fieldwork period in one of them. This hiatus served to underline the need to nego-tiate and re-negotiate access at every level of the organization. Indeed, access may need to be negotiated with representatives from staff bodies, who may not even play a significant part in the research project.

Having initially been granted access by the headteacher, to whom I had outlined a programme of action, I was passed across to the deputy head (Curriculum) who proceeded to organize a schedule of interviews with key personnel in the school. These were timetabled during free lessons and were located in the library. They included both staff and pupil interviews. Having assumed that the site brief would at this stage have been read, I accepted this pattern of working, and decided that I would use these interviews both as data-collection sessions and as opportunities to negotiate further access to classrooms and laboratories. I also, as I had done with the other schools, asked pupils to keep a diary of activities that related to coursework processes. Allport (1942) has categorized the use of diaries in three ways; as int-imate journals, as memoirs and as logs. Though these three uses are not mutually exclusive, I was interested in their capacity to document accounts of processes which I could not observe. Coursework completion involves extra- as well as intra-classroom and school processes. I was not able to be present at completion pro-cesses which occurred outside the school. I was therefore only able to gain access to them by dint of retrospective interviews and personal diaries.

Having completed a week of interviews which included gaining permission to visit a number of classes and the promise by my cohort of pupils to keep a diary over a six week period, I was then taken aback at the beginning of the next week to be told that I could not continue with my fieldwork, because 'the unions are hopping mad and I can't afford to upset them' (Deputy Head [Curriculum]). He went on to argue that in my initial planning interview with him I had not told him I wanted to visit classrooms, and I had not told him that I wanted 'to snoop behind teachers' backs by getting pupils to spy on teachers'. Considerably shaken by these events, I was on my way out of the school when I was stopped by a teacher whom I had already interviewed who told me, 'This has been brewing for months. He is using you to get the unions on his side. He's under a lot of pressure at the moment'. Lack of time meant that I was not able to pursue the micropolitical implications of this, but it does point to the potentiality of research projects to be hijacked for overt political purposes. There is within any research project a momentum for exploitation of the researcher by teachers within the school. Indeed in many cases the researcher is quite happy to accept a degree of exploitation. In this case it threatened to prevent further fieldwork in the school. I was only able to resume data collection by going back to the headteacher and re-opening access procedures. In the end I was able to complete my fieldwork, when the headteacher was persuaded to transfer gatekeeping duties from the original deputy to another.

Interviews

The primary data collection method that I used during fieldwork was interviewing. Burgess (1983) offers three reasons for concentrating upon interviewing at the expense of making further observations. Interviews can allow the researcher access to past events. They can allow access to situations at which the researcher is not able to be present (see above). Thirdly, they can allow access to situations where the teacher refuses permission for the researcher to be present. In a project which sought information about fieldwork trips, parental contributions to coursework projects, pupil experiences over a two year period, it was never going to be possible to be present at more than a limited number of these important events. Interviewing and diary keeping were therefore used as substitutes to direct observations.

I did not use schedules during the interviews, but relied on the ebb and flow of conversation with the occasional use of pointers to focus the interview. This technique more closely corresponds to Stenhouse's (1982) notion of a conversation rather than interrogative questioning. My interviews though, were not unstructured. My specific time-bound concerns and perceptions of coursework served to structure the interviews and impose an agenda on them. The way I was perceived by interviewees, the role they perceived me as playing, acted to give shape to their answers. Finally, data collection methods operate in a dialectical fashion with data analysis, and are therefore constantly changing. Different themes and different areas of interest were pinpointed at different phases of the fieldwork.

Furthermore, interviewer and interviewee do not operate on a level plane. Despite arguments that the gap between adult and child can be bridged if the researcher adopts particular roles, it is doubtful whether the differences in age, size and status can be successfully overridden. It would be false to assert that the interviews

I conducted with pupils were entirely open. Though some of the pupils took me into their confidence and told me things they would not have told their teachers (see above), in the main they were only too well aware of the proper relations they should maintain with guests to the school. Even with teachers, 'the asymmetrical relationship between interviewer and interviewee', identified by Ball (1983), acts to structure the type of data that emerges. This is an inevitable consequence of the outsider seeking to discover meanings and understandings shared by practitioners within particular institutions.

Observations

I attended a variety of lessons which were relevant to coursework processes, and this served to supplement data gathered from the interviews. My role in these lessons could usefully be described as 'participant-as-observer' (Gold, 1958). Gold identifies four types of observer field roles. The 'complete participant' conducts covert observations of participants and settings. The 'participant-as-observer' accepts the inevitable contamination of natural settings as a result of their presence; but develops relationships with informants and makes no attempt to conceal their purposes. Researchers, conducting classroom ethnographies anyway, are unable to conceal their role, and thus cannot make 'complete participant' observations. A third type, identified by Gold, is 'observer-as-participant'. Here the researcher formalizes their role and sets limits to the amount and type of contact they have with participants. In classroom situations, the researcher makes little effort to interact with pupils and teachers, though they may use interview techniques to gather data about the processes they have just observed. Finally, there is the 'complete observer' role, in which interaction between researcher and researched is limited to gaining and sustaining access. In some classroom situations it is difficult for the researcher to maintain an 'observer-as-participant' role, because teachers and pupils naturally and without being asked invade the researcher's 'space'.

My preferred style corresponded more closely to the 'participant-as-observer' role, as I listened, watched and took notes. I also at appropriate moments walked round the class and talked to pupils about their work. Though formal and systematic observation category systems have been developed (Flanders, 1970; Delamont, 1984) and used (Galton, Simon and Croll, 1980), commentators (Woods, 1986; Burgess, 1984) have suggested that pre-defining category instruments limit the data that can be collected, pre-specify the types of meanings that can be developed, and may easily misrepresent the complex social setting that is being explored. For these reasons, ethnographers (Fuller, 1984; Woods, 1986) either use such instruments in limited ways or abandon them altogether. I did not employ formal and explicit category systems, but simply took detailed notes of observations. This does not mean that my observations were unstructured. As theory was developed during the fieldwork, I focused on different aspects of classroom activities. My time- and space- bound presence influenced intra-sampling judgements, which acted to structure observational data. At Tidehill for instance, some parts of the geography coursework programme preceded my period of fieldwork. Finally my direct inter-ventions in lessons (talking to pupils when they were engaged in writing up course-work projects) served to change the 'natural' setting, and acted as a means of organizing the experiences that I was seeking to understand.

Theory Development

I have already suggested that data are value-impregnated, and therefore, as Harris (1979) argues, are never free of the concerns, interests and conceptual frameworks of the researcher. If this is so, then reflexive processes are essential and would involve examination of both the research processes by which data were collected (see above), and as importantly, the epistemological status of those data. It is with the latter that we are now concerned.

What follows is a description of theory-development in the project. Examina-tion syllabuses can be read to support the following agenda: examinations with coursework elements are fair and equitable, not arbitrary, guarantee some measure of predictive validity, enable reasonable comparisons to be made between students by positing similar assessment environments, and allow improvements in curric-ulum strategies which maximize learning opportunities. Teachers in the case study schools conformed to this agenda in full, or rejected parts of it. Table 12.1 contrasts belief or non-belief in this agenda with teachers' attitudes towards examination rule-following. Six situational stances were formulated, and each is briefly described below. This use of typologies is common in qualitative research (Woods, 1986).

Table 12.1: Typology of attitudes about examinations amongst teachers teaching GCSE coursework

Belief	Type of Rule-following	Situational Stance
Belief in agenda	Rigid observance	Conformist
Belief in agenda	Elastic observance	Adaptive
Belief in agenda	Non-observance	Oppositional
Non-belief in agenda	Rigid observance	Ritualistic
Non-belief in agenda	Elastic observance	Transformative
Non-belief in agenda	Non-observance	Non-conformist

Conformist teachers believe that public examinations with coursework ele-ments are useful and meaningful devices. Conformists attach great importance to observing rules and procedures, and are likely to treat texts in 'readerly' ways (Barthes, 1975). They will accept meaning frames as given and will not seek to discover alternative interpretations. They are likely to want to adjust their practice in line with such textual readings. Adaptive stances are similar in that the teacher has confidence in formal examination systems, even if they do include coursework elements. They are different because such teachers are prepared to reinterpret examination rules so that they conform to their notion of good practice. They are likely to treat texts in 'writerly' ways (Barthes, 1975), and to protect pedagogical strategies if they feel they may conflict with examination rules. Oppositional stances combine belief in an examination agenda which implies that certain rules have to be followed with an apparent disregard for those rules in practice. The stance therefore can be said to be oppositional because it counter-positions belief and rule following. Examinations, including those with a coursework element, can provide fair, accurate and predictively valid accounts of pupil aptitudes, but if through non-observance of those rules other ends may be achieved, an oppositional stance is sustained.

Those teachers adopting ritualistic forms of behaviour attach more importance to observing rules and procedures than in achieving the purposes for which those rules exist. This has been referred to as a form of goal displacement (Merton, 1957). Juxtaposing non-belief with rule following may create tensions at the level of practice and disregard for those rules. But the textual reading is still 'writerly' (Barthes, 1975), even if the practitioner is not prepared to translate such a stance into elastic rule-following or disregard for those rules. Those teachers who do not accept that examinations can be fair and equitable, and who furthermore believe that they may damage the curriculum, may reinterpret but not reject the rules that underpin that agenda. This transformative stance combines a sceptical attitude towards formal examinations with an elastic approach to rule-following. Finally, there are non-conformist practitioners who are prepared to ignore examination rules. Since they do not believe in the examination agenda, they do not see the need to follow its rules anyway.

Contextualising these Accounts

It is important to place in context these different readings. Phenomenological analysis gives priority to people's accounts of intentionality and subjective meanings. This is the phenomenological researcher's first and only point of reference. Those who dispute the adequacy of this seek to go beyond subjective meanings and argue that there is an important difference between 'things seeming to be the case to the actor and things being the case' (Sharp and Green, 1975, p. 21). In other words, phenomenological researchers fail to come to terms with the social structures that underpin and position actors' intentional behaviours. Society, as far as Bhaskar (1989) is concerned, 'is the ensemble of positioned practices and networked inter-relationships which individuals never create but in their practical activity always presuppose, and in so doing everywhere reproduce or transform' (p. 4). Bhaskar argues that social behaviour or activity may depend on or involve four conditions which are outside the consciousness of the individual actor. They are: unacknowledged conditions, unintended consequences, the exercise of tacit skills, and unconscious motivation. Social practices therefore are never reducible to the content of human consciousness, but must always incorporate a material dimension.

The gap between actors' perceptions of processes and what actually occurred is further complicated by two important features: the time dimension of such accounts; and the place, role and temporal insertion of the researcher in that process. Table 12.2 describes the chronological sequence of events that concerns us here.

Table 12.2: *Chronological sequencing in the implementation and research process*

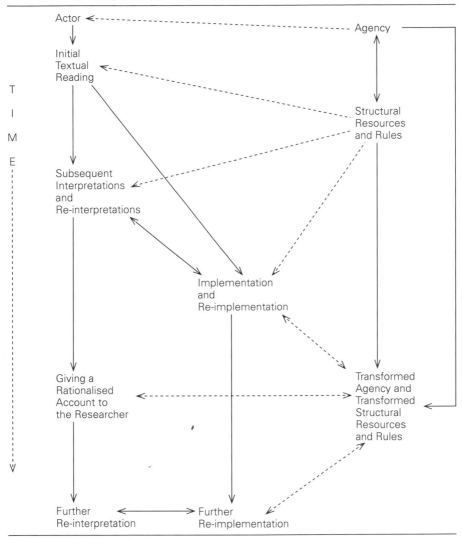

The teacher's initial textual readings or their initial confrontation with the ideas implicit in the new text draws upon both those internalized rules which actors reproduce in their day-to-day working lives and those structural resources which position actors within set frameworks. Those elements of structure that are relevant to the matter in hand condition but do not determine actors' responses (Archer, 1982). Initial textual readings give way to subsequent interpretations and reinterpretations of coursework processes, and all the various readings are implicated in the implementation and reimplementation of coursework strategies. The dialectical interplay between structure and agency is transformed into new forms of structure and agency, and produces, in Archer's word, 'elaboration' — that is, both elaborated structure and transformed agency. This cycle of activity at different moments and in different guises influences actual implementation of processes.

The researcher comes to the process after it has happened, though re-interpretation and re-implementation of processes is on-going and may happen after the rationalized account has been given to the researcher, and indeed may be influenced by that rationalization. What the researcher is doing therefore, is retrospective analysis. Those teacher perspectives which concern us here are not descriptions or formulations of intentions. They are actors giving accounts of how they feel they should have behaved, as well as how they feel they did behave. They are therefore likely to be normative. It is not possible to argue that teacher stances on examinations caused those actors to act in the way they did, because first, the chronological sequence of events makes this impossible, and second, since they are likely to be post-hoc rationalizations, they do not coexist in a simple naming relationship with the events they seek to describe.

They are also subject to the mediating effects of the research process. The researcher offers a time and place specific perspective on that slice of reality which concerns them. Their positioned account implies a gap between those sets of rationalized perspectives and the researcher's narrative report, in the same way as we have argued here that there is necessarily a gap between agents' accounts of processes and what actually happened.

Conclusion

The central focus of this chapter has been to document how qualitative research methods may be used to examine school practices. By focusing on the processes of data collection (foreshadowing the research problem, constructing a research plan, gaining access to fieldwork sites, negotiating access within those sites, choosing which data collection methods to adopt, sampling within each case, adopting ethical and thus by implication epistemological frameworks, adapting the design to fit the burgeoning theory and analyzing the data), and on epistemological questions concerning those data, it is possible to show that these practices are essentially social and rooted in relationships between researcher and researched. This is in contrast to those working within research traditions which argue that data can be theory-free and independent of the values of the researcher. Qualitative research practitioners on the other hand, would argue that the adoption of such a stance involves a profound misunderstanding of the real relationship between data, methods and theory.

References

ALLPORT, G.W. (1942) *The Use of Personal Documents in Psychological Sciences*, Bulletin No. 49, New York: Social Science Research Council.

ARCHER, M.S. (1982) 'Morphogenesis versus Structuration', *British Journal of Sociology*, **33**, 4, pp. 455–83.

BALL, S. (1983) 'Case study research in education: some notes and problems', in HAMMERSLEY M. (ed), *The Ethnography of Schooling*, Driffield: Nafferton.

BARTHES, R. (1975) *S/Z*, London, Jonathan Cape.

BHASKAR, R. (1989) *Reclaiming Reality*, London, Verso.

BRITISH SOCIOLOGICAL ASSOCIATION (1992) *Statement of Ethical Principles and their application to Sociological Practice*, London, British Sociological Association.

BULMER, M. (1979) 'Concepts in the analysis of qualitative data', *Sociological Review*, **27**, 4, pp. 651–77.

BURGESS, R.G. (1983) *Experiencing Comprehensive Education: A Study of Bishop McGregor School*, London, Methuen.

BURGESS, R.G. (1984) *In the Field: An Introduction to Field Research*, London, Allen and Unwin.

DELAMONT, S. (1984) 'The old girl network: Reflections on the fieldwork at St Luke's', in BURGESS R.G. (ed) (1984), *The Research Process in Educational Settings: Ten Case Studies*, Lewes, Falmer Press.

DENZIN, N. and LINCOLN, Y. (1994) (eds.) *Handbook of Qualitative Research*, London, Sage.

DEPARTMENT OF EDUCATION AND SCIENCE (1978) *Part 1 School Examinations: Report of the Steering Committee established to consider proposals for replacing the GCE 'O' level and CSE examinations by a common system of examining (Waddell Report)*, London, HMSO.

FLANDERS, N.A. (1970) *Analyzing Teaching Behaviour*, New York, Addison-Wesley.

FULLER, M. (1984) 'Dimensions of gender in a school: reinventing the wheel', in BURGESS R.G. (ed), *The Research Process in Educational Settings: Ten Case Studies*, Lewes, Falmer Press.

GALTON, M., SIMON, B. and CROLL, P. (1980) *Inside the Primary School Classroom*, London, Routledge and Kegan Paul.

GLASER, B.G. and STRAUSS, A.L. (1967) *The Discovery of Grounded Theory: Strategies for Qualitative Research*, Chicago, Aldine.

GOLD, R. (1958) 'Roles in sociological field observation', *Social Forces*, **36**, 3, pp. 217–23.

HAMMERSLEY, M. (1979) 'Data Collection in ethnographic research', block 4, part 3 of course DE304', *Research Methods in Education and the Social Sciences*, Milton Keynes, Open University Press.

HAMMERSLEY, M. (1985) 'From Ethnography to Theory: A programme and paradigm for case study research in the Sociology of Education', *Sociology*, **19**, 2, pp. 187–211.

HAMMERSLEY, M. and ATKINSON, P. (1983), *Ethnography: Principles in Practice*, London, Tavistock.

HAMMERSLEY, M., SCARTH, J. and WEBB, S. (1985) 'Developing and testing theory: the case of research on examinations and pupil learning', in BURGESS R.G. (ed), *Issues in Educational Research*, London, Falmer Press.

HAMMERSLEY, M. and SCARTH, J. (1986) *The Impact of Examinations on Secondary School Teaching*, School of Education, Open University.

HARRIS, K. (1979) *Education and Knowledge*, London, Routledge and Kegan Paul.

HOMAN, R. (1980) 'The Ethics of Covert Methods', *British Journal of Sociology*, **31**, 1, pp. 46–59.

HONIGMANN, J.J. (1973) 'Sampling in ethnographic fieldwork', in BURGESS R.G. (ed), *Field Research: A Sourcebook and Field Manual*, London, Allen and Unwin.

JOSEPH, K. (1984) Speech to the North of England Conference, Sheffield, January, quoted in Secondary Examinations Council (1985), *Report of Draft Grade Criteria Working Party: English*, London, SEC.

MALINOWSKI, B. (1922) *Argonauts of the Western Pacific*, London, Routledge and Kegan Paul.

MERTON, R.K. (1957) *Social Theory and Social Structure*, Chicago, Free Press.

MITCHELL, J.C. (1983) 'Case and Situation Analysis', *The Sociological Review*, 1, pp. 187–211.

ROTH, J.A. (1962) 'Comments on "Secret observation"', *Social Problems*, **9**, 3, pp. 283–84.

SHARP, R. and GREEN, A. (1975) *Education and Social Control*, London, Routledge and Kegan Paul.

SHIPMAN, M. (1981) *The Limitations of Social Research*, London, Longman.

SIMONS, H. (1987) *Getting to know schools in a democracy: the politics and process of evaluation*, Lewes, Falmer Press.

STENHOUSE, L. (1982) 'The conduct, analysis and reporting of case study in educational research and evaluation', in MCCORMICK R. (ed), *Calling Education to Account*, London, Heinemann.

WALKER, R. (1974) 'The conduct of educational case studies', in DOCKWELL B. and HAMILTON D. (Eds), *Rethinking Educational Research*, London, Hodder and Stoughton.

WOLCOTT, H. (1973) *The Man in the Principal's Office: An Ethnography*, New York, Holt, Rinehart and Winston.

WOODS, P. (1986) *Inside Schools: Ethnography in Educational Research*, London, Routledge and Kegan Paul.

WOODS, P. (1987) 'Ethnography at the crossroads: A reply to Hammersley', *British Educational Research Journal*, **13**, 3.

13　Grounded Theory — Its Basis, Rationale and Procedures

Dean Bartlett and Sheila Payne

Introduction

Grounded theory is most commonly thought of as a method of qualitative data analysis and is therefore distinguished from more traditional quantitative methods which, as Berg (1989) points out, are often given more respect due probably to the exalted view of science held by the educated public and its tendency to regard science as related to numbers and implying precision. Qualitative researchers often appear, therefore, to be suffering from an inferiority complex as they feel it necessary to defend their enterprise, often by attacking the perceived alternative of quantitative research, referring, for example to Kaplan's famous statement 'if you can measure it, that ain't it!' (cited in Berg, 1989; p. 2).

However, grounded theory is much more than simply a method of data analysis and legitimizing its use by reference solely to the quality/quantity debate does scant justice to the approach which actually adopts a far more sophisticated and persuasive rationale. In order to fully understand the rationale behind the grounded theory approach and the power it confers we must examine more closely the theoretical basis of research in the social sciences.

The Theoretical Basis of Research

Psychology and other social sciences have conventionally adopted the scientific meta-theory of empiricism and have therefore relied almost exclusively on the hypothetico-deductive logic of statistical inference which may be graphically represented as in Figure 13.1, below.

Starting from a body of theory, research hypotheses are formulated by a process of deductive inference and are then operationalized in an experimental design where the appropriate dependent and independent variables are measured and controlled for in a particular representative sample of the target population.

This formulation of the research process leads to a natural emphasis on the accurate measurement and recording of valid and reliable empirical data, while the task of the researcher is crystallized in the host of methodological problems such an endeavour engenders. As Agar (1986) points out, the questions which

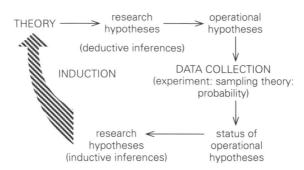

Figure 13.1: The Research Process Under the Hypothetico-Deductive Paradigm

need to be addressed in formulating a research problem are the product of the researchers' 'received view' of science: 'What is the hypothesis?' 'How do you measure that?' 'How large is your sample?' 'Did you pre-test the instrument?'. According to Levy (1981), psychologists have become preoccupied with methodological subtleties to the neglect of more substantive issues concerning the meaning of what researchers do:

> The organism we study is a complex system. It is capable of presenting us with many faces' postures, strategies, rule systems or whatever, depending upon what we do with it.
>
> . . . measurement is not another methodological problem: it is a matter of substance — of the meaningfulness of the assignment of numbers and of their selected properties to behaviour — and that requires some theorizing about behaviour and not reference to some handbook of methodology. (p. 269)

Similarly in 1953, C. Wright Mills criticized the 'abstracted empiricism' of quantitative research for being atheoretical (cited in Silverman, 1993) and the critique of positivism has continued since this time, becoming ever more impassioned.

Denzin (1989) lists five characteristics of the positivistic paradigm which, he claims, 'divorce the researcher from the world under study' (p. 23) and which assume: (1) that 'objective reality' can be captured, (2) that the observer can be separated from what is observed, (3) that observations and generalizations are free from situational and temporal constraints, (4) that causality is linear and (5) that inquiry is value-free. Because of concerns about the applicability of these positivistic assumptions to human mental and social life, and as a result of the loss of meaning in an effort to maintain scientific rigour, there has, in recent decades been a shift by many psychologists and other social scientists towards an alternative qualitative and interpretive school of thought.

Silverman (1993) contrasts two schools of thought which he labels positivism and interpretive social science respectively, the former utilizing concepts of social structure, facts and quantitative hypothesis-testing while the latter is concerned with social construction, meanings and qualitative hypothesis-generation. However, other authors reject the supposed distinction between qualitative and quantitative approaches (e.g. Dabbs, 1982; Bryman, 1988). In any case, the reactionary nature of the debate does not, in and of itself, provide a convincing argument for the value of qualitative methods such as grounded theory because, as Silverman goes on to note, 'it became increasingly clear that "positivists" were made of straw since very few researchers could be found who equated the social and natural worlds or believed that research was properly theory-free' (p. 21). Similar criticisms were made by Levy (1981) who, in his presidential address to the British Psychological Society, said that:

> . . . we have a simplified view of science, perhaps due — for understandable socio-historical reasons — to our anxious desire to receive the accolade of being 'scientific'. Perhaps the amount of scientific progress in psychology is inversely proportional to the time we spend arguing about it. I believe that science is much more a process of social exchange than many of us are prepared to admit. We shun the thought that scientific knowledge may be ideologically flavoured, yet ideologies as an aspect of the structure of personal and social knowledge, are properly part of psychology's interests. We prematurely separate data and theory, sometimes calling data 'fact', when both data and theory are obviously intertwined in the processing of experience and ideas. We employ barely defensible notions of objectivity and subjectivity. We speak of 'validating' rather than 'discovering the meaning of'. And we are tempted to speak of such things as objectivity, truth, proof and methodology where I believe we mean to refer to the more human and social qualities of communicability, generalizability, plausibility and interpretability. (p. 269)

Despite the criticisms of philosophical naivety which have been levelled against psychologists and other social scientists it is still possible to distinguish between traditional, positivistic, quantitatively oriented research and research which adopts an alternative paradigm. Thus there has developed a 'paradigm dialog' (Guba, 1990) in the social sciences between traditional positivism, on the one hand, and a host of qualitative and interpretive alternatives that have emerged to challenge it, on the other. As Phillips (1987) writes, 'at the meta-level, expressions such as "crisis in the social sciences", "uneasy social science", "paradigm clash", "hotbeds of pluralistic activity", "garrulous and vacuous contributions" — and worse — are common, and indicate that important issues are being hotly debated' (pp. vii–viii).

Alternative paradigms are often referred to broadly as qualitative methods, naturalistic approaches or any other of several ill-defined collective terms, however, despite the gamut of 'alternatives' which exist, they do share some common features, as noted by Marshall and Rossman (1989), for example. They characterized qualitative research as involving immersion in the everyday life of the chosen setting for the study, valuing participants' perspectives on their worlds and seeking to discover those perspectives, viewing inquiry as an interactive process between the researcher and the participant, being primarily descriptive and relying on people's words as the primary data. While Marshall and Rossman's characterization of alternative paradigms gives a useful indication of the nature of qualitative research, it does little to illuminate the underlying philosophical issues which lie at the heart of the different approaches to social research. These issues revolve around two, or possibly three, sets of questions: ontological, epistemological and, according to Guba (1990), methodological. That is, the researcher needs to know what is knowable, the nature and status of knowledge claims and how to discover them. In order to highlight the different positions held on each of these issues by researchers in each of the paradigms and also to avoid the criticism of philosophical naivety, let us examine briefly recent developments in the philosophy of science.

Positivism adopts a realist ontology, that is it assumes that there exists a reality driven by immutable natural laws, and the object of science is to discover those laws and thereby describe the true nature of reality by the process of empirical experimentalism. This method grapples with the complexity of the natural world by controlling for confounding variables and it is committed to an objective epistemology; if there is one true world 'out there', then it is possible to know about it (discover the truth) by eliminating subjective experimenter bias.

This represents the scientific world view commonly held by many psychologists but, as Phillips (1987) has noted, stemming from the work of Popper, Kuhn, Lakatos and others, a new understanding of the logic of science has been forged in recent decades. Popper showed that, because empirical support for theoretical propositions relied upon statistical sampling and inductivist principles, the logic of experimentation must rest on falsificationism, rather than verificationism. The classic example is that of the white swan. As it is never possible for someone to observe all swans, they must select a sample of swans. If all the swans in this sample are white, it does not necessarily follow that all swans are white; this particular observation has not verified the proposition that all swans are white, it has merely not refuted or falsified it. Later Hanson (cited in Phillips, 1987) demonstrated the theory-laden nature of observation claiming that the background knowledge held by an investigator strongly influences what is observed. Thus positivism was shown to be fallible in that the accumulation of evidence permits a host of alternative theories to coexist, but does not compellingly disqualify any.

A further development in the philosophy of science stemmed from the growing respect for the historiocity of science in the work of Kuhn (1962) for example. Kuhn's central thesis was that the key concepts of a science and the methodological rules to be followed are dependent upon the particular paradigm within which a scientist works and therefore when a paradigm shift occurs, the old concepts and rules are no longer valid. Thus, within any particular science, the knowledge accrued within any particular paradigm at any given time can not really represent absolute knowledge or 'truth', as it is necessarily relative and changes when another paradigm shift occurs. While Kuhn's work has been criticized, largely because of his postulate concerning the incommensurability of different paradigms, it certainly highlighted the important dynamic quality of ongoing scientific programmes and this theme was taken up by Lakatos who acknowledged the dynamic nature of science and proposed that it is guided by a 'positive heuristic' under which it is improved as it increases its scope to account for new facts.

Thus it can be seen, from our brief excursion into the philosophy of science, that the psychologist's belief in a positivistic ontology and epistemology as the basis of scientific research is indeed naive as we are now in a post-positivistic era. Post-positivism maintains that scientists employ exactly the same type of fallible reasoning as other types of intellectual endeavours, adopting a justificationist epistemology and seeking justified belief in knowledge claims (Phillips, 1990). Thus claims of knowledge are accepted because they are soundly based, either by the experience of observation (empiricism) or by appeal to reason (rationalism). To argue that qualitative research is better than quantitative research simply on the grounds that quantitative research is positivistic and therefore inappropriate for social science is naive and ill-founded. It may well be that the types of quantitative research in which psychologists and other social scientists currently engage in under the banner of science are inappropriate for the study of human social and mental life, however such a position must surely be justified on the basis of a refutation of the methods of science due to their incompatibility with the nature of the object of study.

If one examines the historical development of science beginning with the increased interest in classical thought of the Renaissance, one can see that science was never developed as a method of investigating such things as human thought processes. Prior to the Greek philosophers, people generally believed that things were explainable in terms of a supernatural influence. Aristotle challenged this idea and proposed that every event had a given cause (or rather causes, for he proposed that any object or event has four causes: the material cause which is what it is made up of, the efficient cause which is the force or agent which moves the object or causes events to happen, the formal cause which is the pattern or form of the object and final cause which is its end or purpose). During the Renaissance some philosophers rejected final causes for explaining natural phenomena as they involved the ascription of intention or purpose to objects. Similarly, formal causes were rejected as they merely provided different ways of classifying or describing objects or events rather than explaining them. This reformulation enabled the very rapid accumulation of knowledge and advancement of the natural sciences. Thus the purpose of science as developed from the period of the Renaissance was to explain natural (i.e. physical) phenomena, but this is rather different from explaining people, where formal and final causes are extremely important. For example, if final causes are excluded then one is forced to understand agency merely in terms of goal-directedness according the satisfaction of motivational drives, rather than as human engagement in purposeful activity, and we are left with a 'hopelessly reductive human science, in which goals such as survival and reproduction are the ultimate explanatory factors, and issues of significance are ignored altogether' (Benner and Wrubel, 1989; p. 32). The problem remains, however, that exactly what constitutes these 'issues of significance' is, as yet, unknown as psychologists have failed to come up with an adequate account of what it is to be a conscious human being. The nearest they have come to such an account may be something like the socio-cognitive account of mental functioning (e.g. Fiske and Taylor, 1984) which is really considered to be something akin to a paradigmatic approach rather than an account of the nature of human beings. In any case, this account is far from universally held by even a majority of psychologists who cling to the reductionism of the natural sciences which, in conjunction with Lockian notions of the person as a passive receptor of information from the environment, and Cartesian dualism, has resulted in theories of mechanistic human mental functioning, even to the extent that, in the most extreme form of cognitivism, the mind is viewed as analogous to a computer.

The socio-cognitive model of human functioning draws on theory and data from the fields of both cognitive and social psychology and assimilates the two areas into a new, hybridized whole. The paradigm relies on no single theoretical framework, but socio-cognitive research shares a set of assumptions about the nature of human beings as social thinkers, naive scientists and cognitive misers. Social cognition is mentalistic and process-oriented, focusing on elements such as attribution, attention, inference, memory and schemata and, from its origins in both phenomenology and experimental cognitive psychology, is able to relate the private and subjective life-world of the individual to the general cognitive processes common to all people.

Given such an account of human functioning and the aims of science to search for justified belief in knowledge claims, the hypothetico-deductive method of empirical experimentalism, while useful as part of the 'tool-kit' of the social scientist, does not provide the sole solution to method in the social sciences. In the words of Lincoln and Guba (1985), its neglect of the subjective life-world of individuals 'has produced research with human respondents that ignores their humanness, a fact that has not only ethical but also validity implications' (p. 27).

Grounded theory adds to the tool kit of the social scientist by allowing the investigator to enter the life-world of participants' own understandings while maintaining the search for justified belief central to a scientific enterprise. In the words of Corbin and Strauss (1990),

> grounded theorists share a conviction with many other qualitative researchers that the usual canons of 'good science' should be retained, but require redefinition in order to fit the realities of qualitative research and the complexities of social phenomena . . . significance, theory-observation compatibility, generalizability, consistency, reproducibility, precision and verification. (p. 4)

In contradistinction to the emphasis on verification of the hypothetico-deductive system of logic, grounded theory utilizes induction directly in an attempt to build theory from observation. In this sense, it is not incompatible with the deductive theory-testing of the hypothetico-deductive system as depicted in Figure 13.1, but it is truly driven by observation of the phenomenon under study and turns the chain of logic on its head with inductivism taking the primary role and deductive inferences following on from this. In the preface to their seminal work *The Discovery of Grounded Theory*, Glaser and Strauss (1967) explained how grounded theory was complementary to the theory testing prevalent in most social science research and aimed towards the generation of theory:

> Attempts to close the gap between theory and research have concentrated principally on the improvement of methods for testing theory . . . Our book is directed

toward improving social scientists' capacities for generating theory . . . What is required, we believe, is a different perspective on the canons derived from vigorous quantitative verification on such issues as sampling, coding, reliability, validity . . . conceptual formulation, construction of hypotheses and presentation of evidence. We need to develop canons more suited to the discovery of theory. These guides, along with associated rules of procedure, can help release energies for theorizing that are now frozen by the undue emphasis on verification . . . Although our emphasis is on generating theory rather than verifying it, we take special pains not to divorce these two activities, both necessary to the scientific enterprise. (p. vii)

Having thus examined how grounded theory fits in with the theoretical underpinnings of social science research, we are now able to appreciate the usefulness of such an approach in the post-positivistic scientific endeavour of the search for justified belief in knowledge claims. We now turn to examine the emergence of grounded theory, not only as a method of data analysis, but as a method of investigation from the inception of a research project through decisions about sampling and data collection to analysis and finally the presentation of results. In order to achieve this, we firstly take a brief look at the historical development of grounded theory and then examine in more detail some of the procedures it adopts.

The Discovery and Development of Grounded Theory

Grounded theory was first presented to the research community in Glaser and Strauss's 1967 book which described how theory could be constructed from data by the development of *in vivo* categories and their properties using the method of constant comparison (see below). Glaser and Strauss also described the process of theoretical sampling and how one moves from substantive grounded theory, relating to the particular context under study, to formal grounded theory which is more general in its scope. Finally, they discussed how insight on the part of the analyst aids theory construction.

Glaser and Strauss aimed to legitimize and encourage the generation of theory, set out the general method of comparative analysis which they advocated and finally, to stimulate others to publish their own methods for generating theory (Glaser and Strauss, 1967). Interestingly, in a later article written with Juliet Corbin, with whom he has published much subsequent work, Strauss claims rather different aims of the book, namely that it aimed to offer a rationale for theory that was grounded, suggest the logic and specific procedures for generating grounded theories and to legitimate qualitative research in general (Strauss and Corbin, 1994). In fact, since the publication of their seminal work in 1967, when they collaborated on research in the School of Nursing at the University of California into American health institutions and related topics such as dying, there has been something of a split between the two researchers. Stern (1994) reports that even back in the 1960s and 70s, students of Glaser and Strauss 'knew the two had quite different *modus operandi*, but Glaser only found out when Strauss and Corbin's *Basics of Qualitative Research* came out in 1990, whereupon Glaser wrote his second solo book on grounded theory' (p. 212), however, the title of a recent (1991) article by Glaser, *In Honor of Anselm Strauss: Collaboration*, would suggest that the two were not quite as inimical as Stern implies.

In any case, following the publication of *Discovery*, Glaser (1978) produced a volume entitled *Advances in the Methodology of Grounded Theory: Theoretical Sensitivity* to give it its full name, or just *Theoretical Sensitivity* for short. This volume went beyond the scope of *Discovery* by developing ideas concerning the social psychology and creativeness of the analyst which merely surfaced in the final chapter of their original work. Theoretical sensitivity is a quality of the analyst which allows him or her to think analytically and transcend the data to produce theoretically dense grounded theories and will be explained more fully in the following section. In this volume, Glaser also explains the nature and process of memoing, theoretical coding, sampling and sorting and the write-up and generation of formal grounded theory.

Nearly a decade after Glaser's solo volume, Strauss (1987) published a solo volume of his own entitled *Qualitative Analysis for Social Scientists* which discussed in detail the basic analytic procedures of grounded theory. In the preface to this book Strauss wrote of Barney Glaser that he 'teaches and uses [grounded theory] in research essentially as I do. There are some differences in his specific teaching tactics and perhaps in his actual carrying out of research, but the differences are minor' (p. xiv).

Since this time, Strauss and Corbin have collaborated on several publications about grounded theory (e.g. Strauss and Corbin, 1994; Strauss and Corbin 1990; Corbin and Strauss, 1990) which document the development of the grounded theory approach, outline its theoretical basis and assumptions and provide clear guidelines on how to actually perform and evaluate grounded theory research. In the preface to their book on the subject, Strauss and Corbin (1990) write that:

> This is the fourth in a series of books on grounded theory [referring to Glaser and Strauss (1967), Glaser (1978) and Strauss (1987) as the other three] . . . If you read and study each of these books, which we strongly advocate, you will find that some of their terminology and specific recommended procedures are not always identical . . . Basically, however, all of the books express an identical stance towards qualitative analysis and suggest the same basic procedures. (p. 8)

It wasn't until the publication of Glaser's second solo book in 1992 that the differences between the two researchers referred to by Stern (1994) became glaringly obvious, with Glaser suggesting that the Glaserian and Straussian methods should be distinguished and even given different names. While these differences are significant, it is still possible to refer to a corpus of information which one may label 'grounded theory' and which is set out in the following section.

As Turner (1981) noted, the initial formulation of grounded theory by Glaser and Strauss met with only limited interest, while it took a further two decades before those doing qualitative research showed much appreciation for the explicit and systematic conceptualization of grounded theory. Notwithstanding the differences in opinion about grounded theory between the original authors, along with an increase in popularity comes the diffusion of a method and, as highlighted by Strauss and Corbin (1994), the diffusion of grounded theory methodology 'seems recently to be increasing exponentially in numbers of studies, types of phenomena studied, geographical spread and disciplines (education, psychology, nursing and sociology, for example)' (p. 277). Strauss and Corbin go on to note the risks attending such diffusion such as the tendency to label a study as adopting grounded theory merely because it has become fashionable to do so. This leads to a bastardization of the original method which compromises its integrity and therefore potentially weakens it, as evidenced by the title of Stern's (1994) recent article, 'Eroding Grounded Theory'. Stern claims that one reason for the erosion of grounded theory stems from what she calls the 'menace of minus mentoring', that is the learning of grounded theory from a book or book chapter rather than the face to face training seminars advocated by Glaser (1978). Thus she ironically concludes her article about grounded theory with the injunction 'Get thee to a mentor'.

Strauss and Corbin (1994) also go on to highlight a second problem of the rapid diffusion of grounded theory which derives from its piecemeal adoption and which means that it may be used inappropriately when other methods may serve the purpose better. Indeed the piecemeal adoption of different methods is rife in qualitative research as pointed out by Morse (e.g. 1994) who refers to the practice of 'muddling methods' and Baker *et al.* (1992) who suggested that 'method slurring' often occurs between grounded theory and phenomenology.

A further problem associated with the widespread diffusion of grounded theory stems from the way it was initially presented in *Discovery* and relates to its inductive nature. According to Glaser and Strauss's original formulation, the investigator can go out into the field without having reviewed the existing literature. This is a corollary of the inductive nature of grounded theory and the desire not to 'contaminate one's effort to generate concepts from the data with preconceived concepts that may not really fit . . . The danger is to force the data in the wrong direction if one is too imbued with concepts from the literature' (Glaser, 1978; p. 31). This is a very attractive proposition for the novice researcher or post-graduate student as it legitimizes doing the fun bit of research (going out into the field) without having to first do the boring bit (sitting in the library), however, Glaser goes on to note that 'when reading for his research, the analyst should read for ideas . . . [which] . . . of course, make one theoretically sensitive, and . . . make the analyst sensitive to what he may discover in his data' (p. 32). There is indeed some controversy over when is the correct time to review the literature. However, in the current authors' opinion it is necessary to perform a literature review of previously published material in the area; if this were not performed, how would the researcher know that his or her project had not already been undertaken? The skill of the grounded theorist lies in reading around the project in order to become theoretically sensitive, while at the same time phenomenologically 'bracketing' specific theoretical knowledge while actually performing the analysis. The necessity to perform at least some degree of literature review before collecting data is supported by the comments of Strauss and Corbin (1994) who write:

> because of the partly rhetorical purpose of that book (Glaser and Strauss, 1967) and the authors' emphasis on the need for grounded theories, Glaser and Strauss overplayed the inductive aspects. Correspondingly, they greatly underplayed . . . the unquestionable fact (and advantage) that trained researchers are theoretically sensitized . . . Many people still get their conceptions of grounded theory from the original book, and have missed the later more realistic and balanced modifications of that book's purposeful rhetoric. (p. 277)

Thus, since its original formulation in 1967, grounded theory has evolved and matured with each successive generation of researchers and there are those who work more or less closely to its original canons as expounded by Glaser and Strauss. The original grounded theory derives its theoretical underpinnings from Pragmatism and Symbolic Interactionism (Corbin and Strauss, 1990), although others have labelled it as an interpretive method which has phenomenology as its philosophical basis (e.g. Stern, 1994). While it is true that grounded theory and phenomenology do share several features in common such as exploiting the rich, thick description of human experience and seeking understanding of a problem through the participants' own words and frames of reference, as Baker *et al.* (1992) point out, the two approaches 'are based on different intellectual assumptions and, flowing from these, have clear differences in purpose and methodological prescriptions' (p. 1355). The legitimacy of adopting only parts of the grounded theory method, or any other method for that matter, must ultimately rest upon the justifications put forward by individual researchers, however perhaps there are a core of procedures and stages of analysis which define grounded theory as implied by Glaser (1978) who wrote, in reference to the production of theoretical memos, that 'if the analyst skips this stage by going directly from coding to sorting or to writing — he is not doing grounded theory' (p. 83). For this reason the current authors reserve the term 'grounded theory' for those analyses which closely resemble the original definition of the method in that they include all of the stages advocated by both Glaser and Strauss with only minor modifications, while analyses which include only some of the stages are labelled 'grounded analyses'. Alternatively, Strauss and Corbin (1994) consider that the definitive features of the grounded theory method consist of the grounding of theory upon data through the process of 'data-theory interplay', the making of constant comparisons, the asking of theoretically oriented questions, theoretical coding and the development of theory, however they go on to comment that:

> no inventor has permanent possession of the invention — certainly not even of its name — and furthermore we would not wish to do so. No doubt we will always prefer the later versions of grounded theory that are closest to or elaborate our own, but a child once launched is very much subject to a combination of its origins and the evolving contingencies of life. Can it be otherwise with a methodology? (p. 283)

Having given a brief outline of the history of grounded theory and discussed some of the issues its subsequent evolution has raised, we go on, in the next section, to examine the procedural details of how to do grounded theory by describing and explaining a number of processes through which a grounded theory study progresses. However, before this can be done, a word of warning is in order. As we have seen, different authors have used various interpretations of grounded theory in different ways, even to the extent that there is disagreement between the original authors, and it must be noted, therefore, that the following guidelines represent the current authors' interpretation of the grounded theory method, based primarily on reading the work of each of its two inventors, Barney Glaser and Anselm Strauss.

The Procedures of Grounded Theory

The procedures used in grounded theory may be succinctly summarized in the form of a table such as that which may be seen in Table 13.1. While the table implies a series of stages, it is not our intention to imply that these stages are discrete, or

Table 13.1:   The Processes of A Grounded Theory Study

Process	Activity	Comments
1	Collect Data	Any source of textual data may be used but semi-structured interviews or observations are the most common.
2	Transcribe Data	It is necessary to produce full transcriptions of the data in order to analyze it.
3	Develop Categories	Categories are developed from the data by open coding of the transcripts.
4	Saturate Categories	Further examples are gathered as one proceeds through the transcripts until no new examples of a particular category emerge.
5	Abstract Definitions	Once the categories have been saturated, formal definitions in terms of the properties and dimensions of each category may be generated.
6	Theoretical Sampling	From the categories which have emerged from the first sample of data, choose theoretically relevant samples to help test and develop categories further.
7	Axial Coding — The development and testing of relationships between categories	Using the method of axial coding, possible relationships between categories are noted, hypothesized and actually tested against data which is being obtained in ongoing theoretical sampling.
8	Theoretical Integration	A core category is identified and related to all the other subsidiary categories by means of the coding paradigm, and links with existing theory are established and developed.
9	Grounding the theory	The emergent theory is grounded by returning to the data and validating it against actual segments of text.
10	Filling in gaps	Finally, any missing detail is filled in by the further collection of relevant data.

that they follow each other in a strict linear sequence. As noted by Glaser (1978) 'as one moves forward, one constantly goes back to previous steps' (p. 16) and similarly, Strauss (1987) writes that 'the essential procedures for discovering, verifying, and formulating a grounded theory ... are in operation all through the research project and ... go on in close relationship to each other, in quick sequence and often simultaneously' (p. 23). Obviously some stages must logically precede others, for example one cannot develop any categories unless one has gathered some data, however, the table below represents merely a heuristic device which may be used to describe the family of inter-related procedures used to generate grounded theory and, while we may talk of stages, progression and previous and subsequent procedures, the dynamic and iterative nature of grounded theory is hereby noted. Having made our apologies, we now go on to discuss the first stage of any grounded theory, that of data collection.

Stage 1. Data Collection

As previously mentioned, grounded theory derives its theoretical basis from symbolic interactionism. Symbolic interactionists suggest that individuals order and make sense of their world according to shared meanings which they develop through a process of social interaction and which are conveyed by the reflexive use of symbols. Thus, according to Morse (1992), grounded theory 'provides a means for eliciting these meanings and for describing the psychological and social processes that have been developed to assist people make sense of their world' (p. 257). Grounded theory is therefore able to exploit the richness and thick description of human experience through the participants' own words and frames of reference and, for this reason, the primary source of data in a grounded theory is the semi-structured interview, although the actual method of analysis can be used to analyze any form of textual data, such as observations, newspaper reports or diary entries. Thus with respect to both the source of data and how to actually go about gathering it, grounded theory offers little advice, other than to suggest one refers to the ethnographic interview and fieldwork literature in order to follow the usual procedures to avoid biasing responses and to assure credibility (Corbin and Strauss, 1990).

Stage 2. Transcription of Data

It is very important to produce full transcriptions of your data in the initial stages of data collection, however, once analysis has begun on the first few interviews, the researcher already has the beginnings of an emerging theory. Just as theoretical sampling (see Stage 6 below) guides what kind of data you sample, so your emerging theory may guide exactly what data should be transcribed. Strauss and Corbin (1990) advise that one should be selective and transcribe only as much as is necessary, however this merely reformulates the question of how much to transcribe. There is no point in transcribing reams of data which is irrelevant, but until enough data has been collected to allow the theory to emerge, one must transcribe everything as, until one has an idea of the story which the data tells, one does not have the criteria necessary for selectivity. Finally, Strauss and Corbin advise that if this is your first grounded study, or you are still quite inexperienced, then it is wiser to transcribe all the data. Ultimately, however, the decision rests with the individual researcher who is under an obligation to justify why some bits of data were not transcribed.

We will just mention briefly the format in which the data is transcribed, which involves using only the left hand side of the page. This leaves the right hand side of the page free to write your codes on. Also, it is useful to number the lines of text for future reference and using double spacing makes the process of reading and coding the transcripts easier. Finally, because the process of coding involves taking chunks of text and sorting them according to the categories which are developed, it is necessary either to have several photocopies of each transcript which are cut up into segments of text at various stages or to use a computer which is able to search and gather chunks of text for you and then print them out. The current authors' preferred aid to analysis consists of a qualitative analysis computer software package called 'The Ethnograph' (Seidel *et al.*, 1988). This package allows one to produce as many soft or hard copies of the data as necessary and greatly speeds up the mechanics of analysis, however packages such as these cannot do anything that could not be done with several copies of your data, a pair of scissors and gallons of glue; they do not 'do' the analysis for you, they merely make the mechanics of analysis easier and quicker, thereby freeing up your intellectual capacities to concentrate on the actual analysis itself.

Stage 3. The Development of Categories

The development of categories lies at the heart of the grounded theory method and begins as soon as the first interview has been recorded and transcribed. Thus data collection and analysis go on simultaneously in grounded theory, with the analysis producing the emergent theory which in turn guides data collection. Categories are developed using the method known as open coding which consists of reading through the transcripts line by line and breaking down the data into discrete parts known as chunks or segments. A segment may consist of an idea, an event, a name or something that represents a particular phenomenon, but it generally consists of a concept. Thus open coding involves reading through the data and conceptualizing it into meaningful units of analysis. As for what constitutes a 'meaningful unit of analysis', this depends on the research questions you are asking. In open coding it is important to analyze the data minutely and the current authors therefore generally take the *smallest* meaningful unit of analysis, by which we mean a chunk of text which stands on its own and which is meaningful and therefore interpretable in isolation from its context. An initial reading through of a transcript may generate literally hundreds of such chunks, segments, or concepts.

The next stage of open coding consists of categorizing the concepts which means gathering similar concepts, i.e. concepts which relate to the same phenomenon, together and labelling this group of concepts. The conceptual categories are at a higher level of abstraction than the individual concepts, or exemplars, of a category. A quick note about terminology here: the terms 'concept' and 'category' are often used interchangeably by grounded theorists as a category is merely the collection of specific ways in which a concept has appeared in the data.

Coding is an art and is very difficult to learn how to do properly, however as Strauss (1987) points out, 'the excellence of the research rests in large part on the excellence of the coding' (p. 27). In open coding it is important to think analytically, that is one must not merely describe the data or paraphrase it, but one must 'see with analytic depth what is there' (Strauss and Corbin, 1990; p. 76) and in order to do this, one needs theoretical sensitivity. Theoretical sensitivity opens up our thinking about the phenomenon we are studying and is a characteristic of the researcher which consists of having insight into the data and the capacity to understand and see what is actually there in the data. It enables us to shake loose the blinkers which we habitually wear and which are composed of assumptions, experience and immersion in the technical literature.

Paradoxically, our personal and professional experience, as well as a knowledge of the technical literature, can provide the source of theoretical sensitivity in that they make us aware of the sort of assumptions which we may hold. We must step back from and question those assumptions, bracketing them in order to maintain an attitude of scepticism towards anything which is not directly suggested by the data themselves. It therefore allows us to formulate theory which is faithful to the reality of the phenomenon under study. Strauss and Corbin (1990) offer a number of techniques for stimulating and enhancing theoretical sensitivity which aim to steer your thinking out of the confines of both the technical literature and personal experience, avoid standard ways of thinking about phenomena, stimulate the inductive process, focus on the data and not take it for granted, prevent rushing past 'diamonds in the rough' when examining data, and discover properties and dimensions in the data. These techniques consist of asking a series of fundamental questions of the data such as who does it relate to, who is it about, who else is involved, what is it about, what is going on, how and why is it occurring, when does it occur, who controls it . . . and a whole series of questions about the particular phenomenon of the form who?, when?, where?, what?, why?, how? and how much? Questions such as these are asked of the word, phrase or sentence and it can be an eye-opening and fascinating experience asking these questions, formulating tentative answers to them and checking out these provisional answers by referring back to the data.

A second technique for enhancing theoretical sensitivity consists of the making of comparisons. As has been mentioned, grounded theory is often called the constant comparative method because one is constantly making comparisons between a particular concept and other concepts and categories, looking for similarities and differences. This assists the researcher to guard against bias and produce valid and reliable analyses because as each category is being developed, it is constantly being verified and refined or else rejected according to whether or not it is present in the data, how pervasive it is and what different forms it may take. Thus, as Glaser (1978) points out, categories must *earn* their way into the theory by systematic generation from the data. Similarly, by asking questions of the data and coming up with provisional answers, we are going beyond the data to produce provisional hypotheses which must then be verified by returning to the data. Thus our tentative answers are only ever provisional and must be checked out and either rejected or confirmed by the data, or else revised to fit the reality of the situation under study.

As well as comparing concrete segments of data with other segments of data, the researcher must also think abstractly about it and make comparisons against hypothetical categories and concepts. For example, using the 'flip-flop' technique, one compares a concept which has emerged from the data with its hypothetical opposite along any particularly salient dimension. It will be useful here to consider an example piece of text to see how it is coded. The following piece of text was taken from a study by one of the current authors (DTB) about minor forms of stress:

I: Right and how do you react when this sort of thing happens?

S: Um, well, basically if I get annoyed I feel like I could tell them to put it right and, um, if somebody else is not doing their job and they should be doing their job and sorting it out, for instance we just got to Waterloo station on our way here today and when you get there, there's no information you can find which is relatively simple and so I just said to somebody else, I said the way they run this station, you know, sort it out its just ridiculous.

Now, looking at this piece of data, we can see that the participant mentions some-one doing their job, so we might suggest the category 'meeting responsibilities'. Now, by examining the data closely and thinking about the data analytically using the questioning and comparison techniques that have been discussed, one is able to pick out the properties or attributes of the category and its dimensions. By thinking about this example and looking at other examples in the same category, we may notice that it appears to have the attribute of frequency, that is how often are responsibilities met which may appear to vary along the dimension always-never. Another property of meeting responsibilities may be extent — that is — to what extent are responsibilities met, and this may vary along the dimension 'not at all' to 'exceedingly well'. This process is known as dimensionalizing the data and is used to help define the categories in Stage 5 of the analysis where the provisional properties and dimensions are either confirmed or disconfirmed by their presence or absence in actual data.

Now, in the 'flip-flop' technique of making comparisons, we compare an incident with a hypothetical extreme along a salient dimension, so for example in thinking about how the fact that the station administrators at Waterloo were not meeting their responsibilities we can see that this made the participant angry and made him want to complain. Now, if we compare this to a hypothetical case where the responsibility of providing clear and easy to understand information was at the other end of the dimension of the property 'extent' and was performed exceedingly well by, for example, an efficient, user-friendly interactive computer terminal, how would this make the participant feel? Would he still feel annoyed? What is it about whether or not an individual meets his or her responsibilities that causes annoyance? Is it a matter of principle, that the participant feels a moral code is being violated? Or does it only annoy him when it affects him or his plans directly? I recall that I have another category called 'planning', so how does this category relate to the plans the participant has made in catching the train? How would meeting responsibilities exceedingly well in this case affect him? Would he still want to complain? Would he congratulate the station staff? What motivates him to complain? . . . We can see that by making this sort of comparison, we have managed to think deeply and analytically about the data, discovered some of its salient properties and dimensions, uncovered possible relationships between other categories and generated further questions which need verification. Open coding, in which the data is analyzed minutely, enables us to create conceptually dense theories, while the techniques described to enhance theoretical sensitivity aid the generation of theoretically dense explanations because they open up our creative thinking abilities, giving us new avenues to explore and therefore new insight into the data.

The types of comparisons which are made may be far-out or close-in so that, for example, in comparing one category with another, we may compare catching a train with catching a bus. This is a close-in comparison because each activity has much in common and shares many of the conceptual properties, however, we could also compare catching a train with swimming at the local swimming pool. This is a far-out comparison because it seems far removed from the phenomenon under study. Upon initial consideration the making of such comparisons may appear to be quite ridiculous and a waste of time, but if we think about the sort of issues and questions such a comparison raises we can see that it is actually a useful technique to encourage analytic thought, an integral part of theoretical sensitivity. For example, swimming at the local pool is a leisure activity, but catching a train is not. Or is it? It can be; what does this depend on? We often feel relaxed while swimming at the local pool, but not when catching a train. Why is this? When we catch a train we are bound by the timetable but this is not so when we are swimming; is this anything to do with it? We have control over when we start or stop swimming, but not over when the train runs; is this relevant? There exists a literature about control and its relation to stress. Does it have anything to say about this particular incident? Have any of the concepts it refers to already emerged from the data? This may be interesting to look at during later stages of analysis, but for now, I will bracket my knowledge about control theory and concentrate on what my data says. You can see that the use of such comparisons really stimulates the train of thought and allows us to go beyond an individual segment of data and think creatively, whilst always making sure that we return to our data in order to ground our emerging theory in it.

The techniques described enable the researcher to think analytically rather than descriptively about the data and help to make the analysis theoretically and conceptually dense by helping to generate provisional categories and their dimensions and think about generative questions and the inter-relationships between categories. One can see that open coding is time-consuming but is also fascinating, triggering off creative, stimulating, exciting and complex trains of thought. By scrutinizing the document very closely, line by line or even word by word, and producing concepts which seem to fit the data, but which are only, as yet, provisional the analyst quickly produces enormous numbers of questions and amounts of information relating to the data and in order to help us keep track of our thoughts and the progression of the analysis, we need to use the adjunctive procedures of memos and diagrams. Memos are simply notes to ourselves and may be code notes, theoretical notes or operational notes. In open coding we use only code notes which are memos about concepts and categories and their properties and dimensions. They consist of a dated memo with a heading to indicate what type of memo it is and to what concepts and categories it pertains. They can contain short quotes or phrases in the form of segments of text but are conceptual in nature in that they are not about specific people or incidents, but about abstractions of incidents, events or happenings to which particular concrete examples pertain. This is a result of the nature of grounded theory which may be represented by the 'concept-indicator model' (Strauss, 1987). This model may be seen in Figure 13.2, below and represents the way in which conceptual coding is guided by a set of empirical indicators.

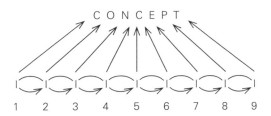

Figure 13.2:   The Concept-Indicator Model (Strauss, 1987)

The model shows how events or happenings observed in the data serve as empirical indicators of a concept which the analyst derives from them, initially only provisionally, but later with more certainty. The indicators are compared to each other and from these comparisons, those that share similarities are taken to be indicators of an emergent abstract concept or category, the nature of which is indicated by the nature of those features which the indicators have in common. The indicators are then compared directly to the category along with additional indicators which occur in the data and the category is thereby refined as further properties of it are generated and the code becomes verified and saturated (see Stage 4). Thus a further question to ask which increases theoretical sensitivity when doing open coding is 'what category does this incident indicate?' (Glaser, 1978).

Code notes refer, then, to the abstract category, but may contain examples of empirical indicators. They may also include lists of and questions about the attributes and dimensions of a particular category and its possible relationship to other categories. Operational memos on the other hand are simply reminders about things you have to do, such as look up a particular reference, make a list of codes, sort and order previous memos or consider a particular sample to interview next, for example. Theoretical memos and diagrams are discussed more fully below under Stage 7 of the analysis. Having gone through the basic procedures associated with open coding we now turn to look at the next stage of analysis, that of the saturation of categories.

Stage 4. Saturate Categories

Open coding is the predominant type of coding in the initial stages of data collection and analysis, but may come to a temporary stop when the categories have been saturated. Glaser and Strauss (1967) and Strauss (1987) called this 'theoretical saturation' and describe it as the point at which additional analysis no longer contributes to discovering anything new about the data and thus it is not really a discrete stage of the research or something which you actually do; it just happens that at some time in the analysis you are not learning anything new about a category. At this point, new instances of the category are not coded since this 'only adds bulk to the coded data and nothing to the theory' (Glaser and Strauss, 1967; p. 111) and 'the researcher feels confident that he or she is fully aware of what is meant when any new phenomena encountered are classified into the category in question' (Turner, 1981; p. 236). Glaser and Strauss (1967), in their original formulation, also used the term 'theoretical saturation' as a threshold criterion which determined how many groups should be sampled for each theoretical point, stopping theoretical sampling when data from the different groups did not lead to any development of a particular category. Saturation will occur at different times for different categories and is ultimately a decision for the individual researcher. Once a category is saturated, the researcher may progress on to the next stage of the research.

Stage 5. Abstract Definitions

This stage of research involves formulating an abstract definition of each of the categories in terms of their properties, dimensions and subcategories. By this stage, the researcher will have saturated the categories and constant comparisons will have generated an accumulated knowledge about each of the categories in the form of a number of code notes relating to them and their properties and dimensions. At this point the researcher must formulate an explicit abstract definition of each category by integrating those properties in terms of the qualities which are being implicitly recognized each time a new incident of the category is recognized. The process of defining categories is exacting and demanding but, as pointed out by Turner (1981), often develops a deeper and more precise understanding of the nature of the phenomenon being studied and may cause the researcher to decide that theoretical saturation has not been reached and further open coding or theoretical sampling is therefore required.

Stage 6. Theoretical Sampling

Theoretical sampling refers to the process of deciding on analytic grounds what data to collect next and where to collect it by sampling particular groups of people according to their significance to the development and testing of the emergent theory. Theoretical sampling is perhaps the least discrete of all stages in the grounded theory research process as it occurs right from when the first open coding is complete up until the final stages of filling in the gaps. It refers to the types of questions which are asked of participants, and the types of participants who are asked, and particular questions or samples of people are chosen because of their proven theoretical relevance in terms of their repeated presence or absence which has been noted in the process of constant comparison. They are also chosen to permit comparison between more or less similar groups which not only determines the generalizability of the emerging theory, but also increases theoretical and conceptual density by maximizing the possibility of discovering new relevant categories and also of finding differences at the dimensional level between properties of a particular category. Sampling may cease only when one has achieved full theoretical saturation not only of each of the categories, but of the theory as a whole and this occurs in the final stage of filling in the gaps.

Stage 7. Axial Coding

Axial coding refers to the process of making connections between categories by use of a 'coding paradigm'. The coding paradigm is a heuristic device used to generate questions and provisional answers and hypotheses about the relationships between categories and may be represented graphically as in Figure 13.3, below.

Causal Conditions — > Phenomenon — >
Context — > Intervening Conditions — >
Action/Interactional Strategies — >
Consequences.

Figure 13.3:   The Coding Paradigm (Strauss and Corbin, 1990)

The diagram shows a set of possible relationships that may exist between categories or between categories and their subcategories. The paradigm is therefore also used in Stage 5 of the grounded theory process, abstracting definitions. It consists of a model of the conditions, interactions and consequences surrounding the particular phenomenon under study and has several components. Causal conditions refer to the events or incidents that lead to the occurrence or development of a phenomenon, while the context represents both the specific properties of the phenomenon and the specific conditions under which the sequences of action and interaction it stimulates take place. Intervening conditions refer to the broad and general conditions which influence the sequences of action and interaction. Action and interaction refer to the ways in which an individual or group of individuals respond to the phenomenon in terms of the purposeful, goal-oriented strategies they adopt to manage or deal with the phenomenon. Finally, the consequences refer to the outcome of the occurrence of the phenomenon and the action and interactional strategies that were adopted to deal with it.

Categories are related to each other and to their subcategories by means of the same techniques that were discussed under Stage 3, the development of categories, namely the making of constant comparisons and asking of questions. The questions that are asked derive from the coding paradigm and relate to the potential relationships which it depicts, thus to return to the example above, we may ask is the category of meeting responsibilities related to the category of planning, and, if so, how? In this case, the phenomenon is planning and the collection of information may be an action/interaction strategy in the context of others having control over the availability of that information. Others meeting their responsibilities constitutes an intervening condition which leads to the consequence of the experience of stress when you try to obtain the information. We then return to our data to see if these hypothesized relationships are borne out by evidence in the form of incidents and events that support our hypotheses. In cases where the hypothesized relationships are not supported we ask why not and consider additional factors, such as extra intervening conditions which may explain the anomaly. In this way we gain depth of understanding and our emerging theory gains variation and density.

The paradigm is also used to link categories at the dimensional level by examining the relationships that exist between the various categories at different dimensional locations, thus we may examine how the occurrence and experience of stress varies according to the nature and degree of planning and the extent to which others meet their responsibilities to the individual actors or group of actors. This allows us to make further connections between various categories at the dimensional level and increase theoretical density and sophistication by elaborating upon the processes that occur.

These ideas are recorded in the form of theoretical memos, some of which may have already been accumulated during the process of open coding when certain questions or possible relationships began to emerge. Theoretical notes suggest relationships and verify them with pieces of evidence consisting of actual segments of text from the data. These memos link categories to other categories and their subcategories, explore and describe the nature of these relationships and the conditions under which they hold and pull other theoretical notes together as the emerging theory takes form. Some of the ideas that we come up with are better represented graphically in the form of either flow charts or conditional matrices and these products of analysis constitute one of the major ways in which the results of a grounded theory study are communicated (see Miles and Huberman (1984; 1994) for more details on how to present data graphically).

You will note that in axial coding, as indeed in open coding, one is constantly moving between inductive and deductive logic, using concrete examples or empirical indicators from the data to suggest possible categories and their relationships and then verifying these against other data. Thus to label grounded theory a wholly inductive method is slightly misleading as it does make use of deductive logic, however, it is inductive at the level of analysis depicted in Figure 13.1.

As axial coding progresses the researcher moves towards greater and greater theoretical density and theoretical integration until, at some point, it is time to progress onto the stage where one actively attempts to integrate the emerged theory.

Stage 8. Theoretical Integration

Theoretical integration is the actual formulation of a grounded theory in its entirety. It involves identifying the story line of your research, that is identifying the central phenomenon of interest and relating it to all of the categories that you have identified and validating those relationships. At this stage you will have identified and defined the categories and noted the most important ones which are significant to your storyline. Theoretical integration is achieved by the process of selective coding. This involves firstly selecting a core category, that is the one category which identifies what your research is about. This is achieved by asking questions such as: what are you studying and what are your findings, and a useful technique is to produce a short (few lines) general descriptive overview of the research which is then compared to a list of the important categories that have emerged and the one which is abstract enough to encapsulate your story line is chosen as the core category. Only one core category must be chosen, which is related to all the other subsidiary categories that have emerged. This is achieved by use of the coding paradigm shown in Figure 13.3.

The categories are arranged and rearranged in terms of the paradigm until they seem to fit the storyline. The ordering of the categories is dependent upon the logic of the story line and the patterns and relationships that emerged during axial coding. One then begins to selectively code by hypothesizing relationships between the core category and all the other categories according to the coding paradigm and then validating these relationships by going back to the data. Thus, selective coding uses exactly the same techniques as axial coding, but relates all the categories to the core category and the categories are then related not only at the conceptual level, but also at the property and dimensional levels as discussed in the previous section.

Stage 9. Grounding the Theory

The theory is then grounded by applying it as a whole to the data. This is achieved by laying it out in the form of theoretically sorted memos and integrative diagrams and then validating it against the data by individually validating all the statements which support the individual relationships in the theory and by testing the theory through looking at individual cases in their entirety. If one comes across cases which do not fit the theory, one asks why and looks for additional intervening conditions which may explain the variance, or else adjusts the theory to accommodate such cases. It is unlikely that the researcher will achieve a perfect fit with every individual case and thus the aim is to produce the best fit for the highest number of cases; if the analysis has been done well, there should be a good fit to most cases.

Stage 10. Filling in the Gaps

Once the theory has been integrated and grounded, thereby satisfying the researcher that the theoretical framework holds up to scrutiny, the analyst is able to go back to the categories and fill in any missing detail. This involves identifying those aspects of the theory for which not much data exists and going back into the field to collect this data and analyze it in the usual way in order to give the final theory conceptual density and specificity. Once this stage of analysis has been complete, the researcher may finally write up the study (see Meloy (1994) for advice on this).

Conclusion

In conclusion, we have seen that grounded theory provides a powerful and robust method for constructing theory. In contrast with assumptions to the contrary based on a naive conception of science, it is consistent with the search for justified belief in knowledge claims and constitutes not only good, but valuable science. It enables researchers to generate theory which is true to the data and, because of its emphasis on inductive logic, closes the theory-data gap. Finally, we should like to give two warnings to the potential grounded theorist. Firstly, grounded theory is incredibly time-consuming and secondly it is incredibly complex. Those of you who are not daunted by hard work will have no fear of taking up the grounded theory method; those of you who are should avoid it at all costs. In relation to its complexity, we may take comfort in the words of its originators, Glaser and Strauss:

> Not everyone can be equally skilled at discovering theory, but neither do they need to be a genius to generate useful theory.

References

AGAR, M. (1986) *Speaking of Ethnography*, London, Sage.

BAKER, C.B., WUEST, J. and STERN, P.N. (1992) 'Method Slurring: The Grounded Theory/ Phenomenology Example', *Journal of Advanced Nursing*, **17**, pp. 1355–1360.

BENNER, P. and WRUBEL, J. (1989) *The Primacy of Caring: Stress and Coping in Health and Illness*, NY, Addison-Wesley.

BERG, B.L. (1989) *Qualitative Research Methods For Tthe Social Sciences*, London, Allyn and Bacon.

BRYMAN, A. (1988) *Quantity and Quality in Social Research*, London, Unwin Hyman.

CORBIN, J. and STRAUSS, A. (1990) 'Grounded Theory Research: Procedures, Canons and Evaluative Criteria', *Qualitative Sociology*, **13**, 1, pp. 3–21.

DABBS, J.M. (1982) 'Making Things Visible', in VAN MAANEN, J. (Ed) *Varieties of Qualitative Research*, California, Sage.

DENZIN, N.K. (1989) *Interpretive Interactionism*, Volume 16, Applied Social Research Methods Series, London, Sage.

FISKE, S.T. and TAYLOR, S.E. (1984) *Social Cognition*, NY, Random House.

GLASER, B.G. (1978) *Advances in the Methodology of Grounded Theory: Theoretical Sensitivity*. California, Sociology Press.

GLASER, B.G. (1991) 'In Honor of Anselm Strauss: Collaboration', in MAINES, D.R. (Ed), *Social Organization and Social Process: Essays in Honor of Anselm Strauss*, New York, Aldine de Gruyter.

GLASER, B.G. (1992) *Basics of Grounded Theory Analysis*, California, Sociology Press.

GLASER, B.G. and STRAUSS, A.L. (1967) *The Discovery of Grounded Theory: Strategies for Qualitative Research*, London, Weidenfield and Nicolson.

GUBA, E.G. (1990) *The Paradigm Dialog*, London, Sage.

KUHN, T.S. (1962) *The Structure of Scientific Revolutions*, Chicago, Chicago University Press.

LEVY, P. (1981) 'On the relation between method and substance in psychology', *Bulletin of The British Psychological Society*, **34**, pp. 265–70.

LINCOLN, Y.S. and GUBA, E.G. (1985) *Naturalistic Inquiry*, London, Sage.

MARSHALL, C. and ROSSMAN, G.B. (1989) *Designing Qualitative Research*, London, Sage.

MELOY, J.M. (1994) *Writing the Qualitative Dissertation: Understanding by Doing*, Hove, Lawrence Erlbaum.

MILES, M.B. and HUBERMAN, A.M. (1984) *Qualitative Data Analysis: A Sourcebook of New Methods*, Beverly Hills, CA, Sage.

MILES, M.B. and HUBERMAN, A.M. (1994) *Qualitative Data Analysis: An Expanded Sourcebook*, (2nd edition), London, Sage.

MORSE, J.M. (1992) *Qualitative Health Research*, London, Sage.

MORSE, J.M. (Ed). (1994) *Critical Issues in Qualitative Research Methods*, London, Sage.

PHILLIPS, D.C. (1987) *Philosophy, Science and Social Inquiry: Contemporary Methodological Controversies in Social Science and Related Fields of Research*, Oxford, Pergamon Press.

PHILLIPS, D.C. (1990) 'Postpositivistic Science', in GUBA, E.G. *The Paradigm Dialog*, London, Sage.

SEIDEL, J.V., KJOLSETH, R. and SEYMOUR, E. (1988) *The Ethnograph*, California, Qualis Research Associates.

SILVERMAN, D. (1993) *Interpreting Qualitative Data: Methods for Analyzing Talk, Text and Interaction*, London, Sage.

STERN, P.N. (1994) 'Eroding Grounded Theory', in MORSE, J.M. (Ed), *Critical Issues in Qualitative Research Methods*, London, Sage.

STRAUSS, A. (1987) *Qualitative Analysis for Social Scientists*, Cambridge, Cambridge University Press.

STRAUSS, A. and CORBIN, J. (1990) *Basics of Qualitative Research: Grounded Theory Procedures and Techniques*, London, Sage.

STRAUSS, A. and CORBIN, J. (1994) 'Grounded Theory Methodology: An Overview', in DENZIN, N.K. and LINCOLN, Y.S. *Handbook of Qualitative Research*, London, Sage.

TURNER, B.A. (1981) Some Practical Aspects of Qualitative Data Analysis: One Way of Organising the Cognitive Processes Associated With the Generation of Grounded Theory, *Quality and Quantity*, **15**, pp. 225–47.

14 Action Research in Information Systems

David E. Avison

Introduction

Chapter 7 outlines many research methods appropriate to information systems: conceptual study, mathematical modelling, laboratory experiment, field experiment, surveys, case studies, phenomenological research/hermeneutics, ethnography, grounded theory, longitudinal study and action research. Other chapters have looked at some of these in more detail, for example, grounded research is discussed in Chapter 13 and participant observation in Chapter 15.

Traditionally, information systems research has been based on laboratory-based experimentation or field surveys, with much emphasis on statistical analysis. However, there are only a limited number of factors that can be studied under laboratory conditions and such an approach does not simulate the 'real-world' environment which is the domain of information systems. Further, it is difficult, if not impossible, to allocate meaningful values on 'people factors', the domain of information systems and any of the social sciences. The numbers that are produced from such statistical analysis might seem accurate, however, and have credence that they do not deserve. Such research work might lead to publications, but is unlikely to make a real contribution.

In this chapter we look at a research approach which I have found particularly useful in information systems because I am interested in problems in their organizational context. However, as Trist and Murray (1990) show, it is well suited to research in the social sciences generally, including inter-disciplinary work. This paper describes action research and then shows how action research was used in my own research in the description of Multiview, a framework for developing information systems, and then a particular action research project as part of this research. Potential advantages and disadvantages of action research are discussed and some issues related to action research for debate are introduced.

What is Action Research?

In action research, described in Checkland (1981), researchers test and refine principles, tools, techniques and methodologies to address real-world problems. It is characteristic of action research that the practitioners as well as the researchers participate in the analysis, design and implementation processes and contribute as much as the researchers in any decision-making. Thus there is a synergy between the researchers and practitioners, the researchers building up theories and modifying them on the basis of practical experience and the practitioners using and modifying research ideas for solving real-world problems.

Action research is often confused with case study research, but, as Benbasat *et al.* (1987) have shown, whereas case study research examines phenomena in its natural setting with the researcher an independent outsider, in action research the researcher might be a participant in the implementation of a system and simultaneously evaluate a particular approach. In action research, the researcher ought to be 'useful' as well as an observer. The justification for action research is based on the acceptance of the subjective processes and the possibility that knowledge is socially constructed.

The history of the development of action research has been traced by Warmington (1980), who attributes the first explicit use of the method as that applied to social problems by the social psychologist Kurt Lewin in the 1940s (Lewin, 1946). He used action research in a number of projects, for example, relating to the promotion of less-desirable cuts of meat in wartime. It was used by Collier (1945) in the area of race relations. In Warmington's account, the implicit use of the method by researchers such as F.W. Taylor and Elton Mayo in solving practical organizational problems predates Lewin's work.

Other versions of the method were used in the 1960s at the Tavistock Institute in developing a socio-technical view, and that at Lancaster in soft systems and these have been particularly influential in information systems.

Hult and Lennung (1980) argue that:

> Action research simultaneously assists in practical problem-solving and expands scientific knowledge, as well as enhances the competencies of the respective actors, being performed collaboratively in an immediate situation, using data feedback in a cyclical process aiming at an increased understanding of a given social situation, primarily applicable for the understanding of change processes in social systems and undertaken within a mutually acceptable ethical framework.

Action research therefore attempts to link theory and practice, thinking and doing, achieving both practical and research objectives. Gaining this knowledge is seen as an active process, so that beliefs may be redefined in light of the outcomes. A representation of reality is not so much desired, but rather is a means for dealing with reality. Action research is a pragmatic approach which desires to 'come to terms' with the world. This emphasis on the pragmatic is further reflected by Susman (1983), who states that action research builds on a learning cycle. His learning cycle is diagnosis, action planning, action taking, evaluation and the specification of learning. The people involved in action research, be they called researchers, actors, participants or subjects, begin in a real situation and return to it at the end of the learning cycle.

This type of learning represents the enhanced understanding of a complex problem. Information about a particular situation and a particular environment have

David E. Avison

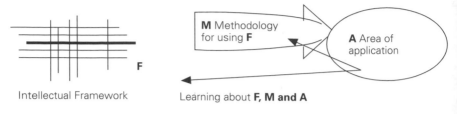

Intellectual Framework   Learning about **F, M and A**

Figure 14.1:   Organized use of rational thought (source: Checkland, 1985)

been obtained, which gives a contingent value to the truth learned. The researcher expects, however, to generate knowledge which will further enhance the development of models and theories. The aim is the understanding of the complex human process rather than a universal prescriptive truth.

The mutually accepted ethical framework mentioned in the quote from Hult and Lennung (1980) may cause some concerns. If the goals of the researcher and client differ drastically, there is tension. As Willcocks and Mason (1987) show, coercive situations are not uncommon in information systems work. Where these tensions do occur, some method for satisfying each of their goals needs to be found (Warmington, 1980; Jackson, 1987).

Finally, in the process of learning, an explicit clear conceptual framework which is acceptable to the researcher and the organizational actors in the action research study must exist. This is needed so that the explicit lessons will emerge from the research cycle.

In comparing action research to other research methods, three important distinctions can be brought out:

1   The researcher is actively involved, with expected benefit for both researcher and organization.
2   Knowledge obtained can be immediately applied. There is not the sense of the detached observer, but that of an active participant wishing to utilise any lessons learned based on an explicit clear conceptual framework.
3   The research is a cyclical process linking theory and practice.

The above discussion can be seen within Checkland's intellectual context: the 'organized use of rational thought' (Checkland, 1985). This context is based on a simple model of a cycle of continuous inquiry where theory interacts with practice.

Depicted in Figure 14.1 is the use of a theory: an intellectual framework of linked ideas (**F**), through a methodology or an intervention process (**M**), to an application area (**A**). In going through a cycle, learning can be generated about **F**, **M** and **A**.

The implications can also be seen in comparison to the other methods and the comparison of two extremes, laboratory experiments (positivist science) to action research, is shown in Figure 14.2.

Points of Comparison	Positivist/Scientific	Action Research
Value position	Methods are value neutral	Methods develop social systems and release human potential
Time perspective	Observation of the present	Observation of the present plus interpretation of the present from knowledge of the past, conceptualization of more desirable features
Relationship with units	Detached spectator, client system members are objects of study	Client system members are self-reflective subjects with whom to collaborate
Treatment of units studied	Cases are of interest only as representative of populations	Cases can be sufficient sources of knowledge
Language for describing units	Denotative, observational	Connotative, metaphorical
Basis for assuming existence of units	Exist independently of human beings	Human artefacts for human purposes
Epistemological aims	Prediction of events from propositions arranged hierarchically	Development of guides for taking actions that produce desired outcomes
Strategy for growth of knowledge	Induction and deduction	Conjecturing, creating settings for learning and modelling behaviour
Criteria for confirmation	Logical consistency, prediction and control	Evaluating whether actions produce intended consequences
Basis for generalization	Broad, universal and free from control	Narrow, situational and bound by context

Figure 14.2: A comparison of positivist science and action research (source: Susman and Evered, 1978)

Action Research in Information Systems development

I illustrate action research through research concerned with the development of information systems undertaken by the author with others. The whole research cycle is illustrated in Figure 14.3. There has been a proliferation of information systems development methodologies (1) over some years and this has led to practitioners, researchers and teachers being confused about which methodology is 'best'. This is the 'area of concern' that I investigated. A significant part of the work has therefore been comparing and classifying information systems development methodologies (2). This is published in, for example, Avison and Fitzgerald (1985 and 1995), Avison, Fitzgerald and Wood-Harper (1988) and Avison *et al.* (1992).

However, our research suggests that it is unreasonable to rely on one approach. Each of the themes has strengths and weaknesses and our practical work suggests that tools and techniques appropriate for one set of circumstances may not be appropriate for others. The appropriate methodology will depend on the problem context (3), that is, the organization itself and the users and analysts who are developing information systems. It is not feasible for analysts to know a number of methodologies sufficiently well enough to choose one for each particular problem

David E. Avison

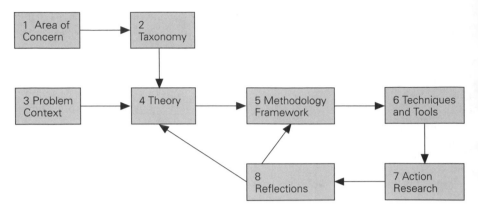

Figure 14.3:   Learning cycle of action research (adapted from Avison and Wood-Harper, 1991)

situation. On the other hand, it is also unreasonable for analysts and users to choose teachniques and tools without any methodology framework to guide their choice. There are too many possible alternatives and too many decision points. A compromise is to use an approach where the choice of techniques and tools can be made within a loose methodology or framework (4). At least, that is one of the theoretical bases of Multiview.

As a result of this research, the methodology framework known as Multiview (5) was refined and defined. This is partly a synthesis of many of the themes discovered in the research, and includes techniques and tools (6) and their later modification. Multiview is described in Avison and Wood-Harper (1990 and 1991) An important aspect of this research has been to use Multiview in a number of problem situations (7) in different types of organisation. Six such projects are described in Avison and Wood-Harper (1990). The next stage is evaluation. There were a number of lessons learned from the experience of using Multiview in various problem situations and these have led to modifying the Multiview framework. The conclusions about the methodology framework, its use in various problem situations and of action research in information systems, is carried out in the last formal stage (8) (see also Schön, 1983) but there is feedback to stages 3, 4 and 5, so that the whole process is cyclical in nature. This feedback process of theory, action, reflection, modification of theory and further action is described in Avison (1990).

An Action Research Project

Having looked at a cycle of research which is centred on the action research approach, I will look at an example of the approach used in a problem situation. This is discussed in much more detail in Avison and Catchpole (1988) and is one of the six cases discussed in Avison and Wood-Harper (1990).

The project was carried with the Darlington Health Authority and concerns information systems provision in the community care sector. It involved the analysis, design and prototyping of an information system which fulfils some of the local needs of fourteen nursing and para-medical professions working in the community in a district health authority, whilst satisfying the statutory requirements of the UK National Health Service (NHS) Körner steering group for those professions. The work leading to the implementation of a prototype computer information system was achieved through the participation of those professionals who would eventually use the system. This prototype system covers the chiropody and school nursing staff groups. The case study illustrates the contingency aspect of Multiview, that is, the choice of tools and techniques within the framework and the adaptation of the structure of the framework itself to suit the needs of a particular problem situation.

The health care activity of the community health services creates tens of thousands of health care interactions annually. These relate to a whole range of activities, from the domiciliary midwifery service to the domiciliary care of a terminally ill elderly patient. The previous system in the health authority had involved several discrete manual record systems. There was little comprehensively organized information available and it was difficult to evaluate how effective the services were. The need for the systematic collection, collation and analysis of information would be a valuable information base for planning and organizing health care activities, providing feedback to the professionals working in the area and fulfil the statistical requirements of the central government in order to control the National Health Service (the Körner requirements). Data relating to the total community care services could provide valuable epidemiological and demographic information.

In current discrete information systems which have operated for many years, data has been collected on forms relating to the provision of services in the community. Individual practitioners submit data on their activities to managers, usually on a monthly basis. A characteristic of this data is that it is of high volume, which means that it is very difficult if not impossible to process manually into meaningful information. Data collection is often duplicated by different staff groups. Returns made by staff are frequently stored away for many years without use being made of them. The recording of this data is often carried out merely to fulfil statutory requirements or for no good reason at all.

An increasing emphasis is being placed on caring for clients in the community situation and the potential of community information systems is large. At this particular health authority the number of beds in the district general hospital is 750. One community service, school nursing, has 20,000 registered clients. This data could provide valuable epidemiological and demographic information. The opportunity is presently being lost.

Our remit was to analyze, design and implement a prototype of an appropriate information system for the community health services of the health district, whilst fulfilling the related statutory requirements of the NHS Körner steering group.

The purposes of this particular action research project were many. From the researchers' point of view, it was a further opportunity to test the Multiview approach to information systems development in 'action' so that problems with using the approach could be looked at and, perhaps, refined Multiview could bed so that it would be more suitable for other applications in this area. The differences in the description of the approach found, for example, in Wood-Harper, Antill and Avison (1985) and in Avison and Wood-Harper (1990) stem from the tuning processes that came from using the approach in action research projects such as this. From the users' point of view, the purpose was to develop a prototype information system for community health workers in a local area health authority. From senior management's point of view, it was to fulfil the requirements of government to provide statistics related to community health.

One of the principles embodied in the Multiview approach is that stakeholders in any information system ought to have control over their work environment. This is at odds with more conventional approaches to information systems development which tend to preclude real participation (as against 'lip-service participation') of the stakeholders, the methodology being a straight-jacket preventing them from contributing effectively. User groups, for example, participated at all stages in the development of the information system (not only in the design of the human-computer interface, which is now the limit of even the more enlightened conventional approaches). Another requirement of the researchers was to enable prototyping in a natural environment (Avison and Wilson, 1991). This facilitates the demonstration of aspects of a potential information system to be made without any irreversible work being done to the operational system.

The first phase of Multiview is an analysis of human activity systems. Our familiarization process had two strands. We carried out a survey of computer applications for the community aspects of the NHS and also talked to the professionals working in community health for the health authority and went on visits with them to clients. It was obvious from our survey that there was no existing information system that could be used 'off the peg', we would have to develop our own.

The Multiview framework used to develop the system lends itself to participation of user groups and at all stages of the development of the information system, not only the design of the human-computer interface. A second and related requirement was to enable prototyping. This facilitates the demonstration of aspects of a potential system to be made without any irreversible work being done on the real system. There are a number of application generators and fourth generation languages which facilitate prototyping. A quick delivery of a skeletal working system can be made which will test out design principles of a system with users, who can then be involved participatively in the construction of the system. A prototype can be used as a tangible starting point for discussions. It may be possible to use the prototype as a basis for the operational system, it 'becomes' the operational system after many iterations when users regard it as being satisfactory. A final requirement of the methodology was to enable the setting-up of the database in such a way that it could be useful to the various professional groups and managers at the health authority and fulfil the Körner requirements. As authors of Multiview, we claimed that it would support these requirements. The claim needed to be tested.

Two staff groups, chosen at a meeting by the representatives of all community care groups, carried out the initial pilot studies. One nursing group (school nurses who carry out 'group session' type activities) and one para-medical group (chiropodists as they carry out 'face-to-face contact' type activities) were particularly suitable as they tested different parts of the system. The way the system was developed led to modifications of the Multiview framework. This is almost inevitable if the researchers are using action research methods: the practitioners have as much influence on decision-making as the researchers and therefore are likely to change the researchers' theories.

We were fortunate to receive the full co-operation from user groups. These included management grades, such as the director of nursing services for the community, the six assistant directors of nursing services, the senior clinical medical officers, and district heads and non-management grades such as health visitors, school nurses, community midwives, district nurses and dietitians. These formed design groups meeting regularly to decide on overall strategy as well as detailed designs.

Users were also happy to try new tools and techniques such as portable hand-held data recorders as an alternative to the redesigned forms. The portable data recorders, no bigger than hand calculators, enable direct data entry into the computer system. This experiment was not imposed on staff — we as *facilitators* made the staff groups aware of the various ways of collecting data and the staff groups chose to try these and the redesigned forms in our prototypes.

The applications were produced with reports and screens providing information about the community care service. The prototype was evaluated from the point of view of effectiveness, that is how the system met objectives and goals, and efficiency, that is some measure of the 'mechanical' aspects of the system such as the accuracy, timeliness, and speed of access to information. We also wished to review the training and design process, essentially reviewing the participative and prototyping approach to information systems development, and opinions were solicited about the system from the senior managers, user groups, individual users and clients. The methods used for this purpose included questionnaires, individual interviews and group discussions. This feedback included comments on the methods used to develop the application, the training and education aspects, as well as the information system itself.

The results are discussed in detail in Avison and Catchpole (1988). Comments such as: '. . . as it is the community health professionals who have to use the system, we are in the best place to help design it; we know what information is important and relevant for recording'; 'It is good to be involved with developing new system'; 'I feel I have been able to make a valid input in the designing of a systems which meets our needs'; and 'I have been made aware of the difficulties in the systems design process' were positive. These comments are not surprising, it is their system, not that of the technologists alone. They considered the alternatives, contributed to the design and implemented it with the help of the researchers, who were seen by them partly as facilitators. However, the usefulness of this type of response is open to debate. There are parallels with the meaningless questions asked of athletes after winning a race or of a parent following the death of a son in a car crash: 'What does it feel like?' (Silverman, 1990).

It may be helpful to show the types of lessons and conclusions that have been drawn from the action research that led to the definition and tuning of the Multiview information system development framework. These are explored further in Avison (1990) and Avison and Wood-Harper (1990 and 1991).

- *Lesson 1 — A methodology takes time to define and test*: The initial formulation of the Multiview framework, which is described in Wood-Harper, Avison and Antill (1985), took some years to develop through practice and field work. The description in that text is developed further in the 1991 text and is being further tuned through action research projects undertaken since that time.
- *Lesson 2 — The traditional model is inappropriate*: As evidenced by our field work, information systems development does not, in practice, exhibit the step-by-step, top-down nature of the traditional 'waterfall' model, sometimes referred to as the systems development life cycle. None of the action research cases have exactly followed the Multiview approach espoused in either text. Further, in the real-world cases undertaken, some phases of the approach were omitted and others were carried out in a different sequence from that expected.
- *Lesson 3 — The political dimension is important*: The manipulation of power, that is, the political dimension, is important in real-world situations. This transcends the rationale of any methodology. Most of the case studies show decisions being made which were influenced by considerations beyond those that are implied by the Multiview framework.
- *Lesson 4 — Responsible participation is contingent*: A high level of responsible participation, *where appropriate*, is a positive ingredient of successful information systems development. In other case studies, some potential users were apprehensive about the proposed information system and did not cooperate fully.
- *Lesson 5 — the methodology is interpreted by users/analysts*: The users/ analysts affect the perception of the situation and they interpret the methodology. This effect is highlighted in professional analysts and users, where cultures, education, background, and so on, will greatly effect the interpretation of the methodology itself and the way it is used.

Conclusions that might be drawn from the above lessons might include:

- *Conclusion 1 — The Multiview methodology is in a continuing state of development*: Information Systems is a comparatively new discipline, the diversity of approaches is caused to some extent by the background and cultures of their authors and none is all-inclusive. The methodologies address a moving target in that the technology, along with tools and techniques supporting it, develop relentlessly. We therefore regard Multiview as defined as part of a process of improving information systems practice. Multiview is an *exploration* in the development of information systems rather than a methodology, because the latter term implies a formal, fixed and inflexible approach.

- *Conclusion 2 — Defining an information system is contingent*: Defining an information system is contingent on the methodology, the situation and the information systems development team. In some of the case studies not all of the stages of Multiview were used because of the situation (in one case there was no computer system developed). In any situation where an information system might be appropriate, there are factors such as culture, language and education which have to be taken into consideration. Sometimes the political and social climate is such that participation is difficult to achieve. In other situations particular tools and techniques are not appropriate to the problem situation. The use of an information system methodology in practice is a hermeneutic process in which the situation is 'read' by the problem solvers (Argyris, Putman and Smith, 1986).

The above lessons and conclusions are not of the type that might be drawn from more conventional research. They may seem disappointing to readers expecting some exact correlation between variables or some other definite conclusion. But I would claim that this research has made a valuable contribution to information systems research and practice.

Advantages and Problems of Action Research in Information Systems

Action research allows the researcher great potential to utilize the ideas of users and change concepts and methods as the work develops. Researchers and subjects co-operate in solving a real-life problem. It is particularly useful that action research allows work to take place in its natural setting and it gives the researcher an insight into real-life practical areas. Feedback from the practical application of techniques can be used to refine and improve those techniques and their description. Although the results of action research are of a qualitative nature, they do offer a degree of external validity because the theory developed can be interpreted and refined by others in other real-world situations.

Action research has proved helpful to the development of Multiview. The weaknesses in the descriptions of some of the techniques were revealed when using them in one action research project described in Avison and Wood-Harper (1990). The practicality of using techniques and tools contingent on a particular problem situation as suggested by Multiview, can only be revealed by its use in different situations. Major omissions in the exposition of Multiview were revealed in a number of projects. Some assumptions in Multiview, such as the users' enthusiasm for participation and the low relative importance of the technical dimension have also been questioned through this experience. The part played by researchers as active players in the problem situation (not merely 'impartial' observers), along with users and analysts, has meant that both researchers and practitioners have together influenced the practice (by implementing change in the problem situation) and the theory (by changing the Multiview approach).

However, there are disadvantages of action research. The lack of impartiality of the researcher has led to its rejection by a number of researchers and academic departments. The lack of scientific discipline in such research makes it difficult for the work to be assessed for the award of research degrees and for publication in academic journals. A particular difficulty that researchers have is persuading research funding bodies that this type of research is as valid and as useful as conventional methods of scientific research. Further, although the researcher's intent is to conduct research while effecting change, the approach is sometimes branded with the description 'consultancy' and not research. The open-endedness of such research and the consequent flexibility necessary in writing a research proposal also provide additional difficulties. Further, a major consequence of the choice of the action research method is that the research is context-bound as opposed to context-free. It is difficult to determine the cause of a particular effect, which could be due to environment (including its subjects), researcher, or methodology. This has been made explicit in some research, but it can mean that action research produces narrow learning in its context because each situation is unique and cannot be repeated. This is a major criticism of action research — it does not produce generalizable learning 'naturally'.

However, there are attempts to reconcile the narrow learning that can come from action research with the need for generalizable research (Warmington, 1980). The findings from the Multiview research (discussed in this chapter) has resulted in other researchers and practitioners applying the Multiview theory in other problem situations, and by taking into consideration the learning that emerges in the complex process of developing an information system, generalizing these findings.

Issues

In this chapter, I have provided an overview of action research, describing the action research cycle in the context of my own research in information systems, then looking at a particular action research project before considering some of the advantages and disadvantages of the approach. Readers are warned that it has necessarily been simplistic: there are many forms of action research (Elden and Chisholm, 1993), although there is a broadly-shared definition of the approach. In this final section, I wish to raise some issues which might be used to start a debate about action research. I will restrict my list to just a few issues, though there are many. My list is not only limited but opinionated, so I trust other issues will be raised and counter-views will be forthcoming! Questions are asked which may also be used to start the debate.

1 *Is there any alternative?* There are a number of research methods appropriate to information systems. The traditional, empirical research more suited to the natural sciences, is not so consistently appropriate to the social sciences. I believe that the less conventional action research approach proved to be appropriate for research in information systems development and the definition of Multiview. In particular, it proved appropriate to understanding information systems in organizations and assessing their impact on people and organizations. However, I leave it to the reader to decide or, preferably, debate with others whether other methods could have been equal to the task. Case study research (Yin, 1994) is possibly the most plausible alternative, and, along with the survey approach, a particularly well-used research method in information systems.

2 *Research or Consultancy?* In my view, many people who say they are doing action research are failing to adhere to its tenets. Typically, the 'researcher' carries out a consultancy project at an organization and writes it up afterwards as a paper. The term action research is used because the 'researcher' is involved in the process with practitioners (and wants the work to be academically respectable), but the term is not justified. First, the practice is not developed from thinking into the development of a theory and is not used to test and modify this theory. There is, in short, 'action' but no 'research'. Multiview was developed from ideas and, although a novel development, is steeped in the literature (see Figure 14.3). Second, the basis of the work is not compatible with action research. The 'researcher' is working for and paid by the organization in order to do a job. The employer expects the work to be done as he or she wishes. In the Health Authority project discussed above, the managers and other staff were aware that we were researchers wishing to test and modify our theories, this has to be established at the beginning. However, through working with us, practitioners could achieve some improvement of their work situation. You may debate whether being paid for the work is incompatible with the ideals of research.

3 *Differing world views*: It is very difficult, if not impossible, to work in situations in which researchers and practitioners have radically opposing views about the project. If, for example, the managers wish to develop a computer information system to 'dehumanize' the workplace or to 'downsize', I would find it difficult to participate. In the Health Authority project discussed above, the managers and other staff agreed with the researchers that an emphasis would be placed on providing information to and for the community care workers (though it was also providing data for government). This stance may by regarded as naive, indeed impossible to sustain absolutely, for it is unlikely that all ethical views will match neatly. Situations will often be pluralist, and sometimes coercive (where one group dominates another), and it is often difficult to establish common ground on objectives to be sought. However, in such situations, particularly coercive ones, I am not sure how action research can proceed.

David E. Avison

Acknowledgments

Multiview was designed with Trevor Wood-Harper and the case study developed with Paul Catchpole.

References

ARGYRIS, C., PUTMAN, C.R. and SMITH, D. (1986) *Action Science*, Jossey-Bass, San Francisco.

AVISON, D.E. (1990) *A Contingency Framework for Information Systems Development*, PhD thesis, Aston University.

AVISON, D.E. and CATCHPOLE, C.P. (1988) 'Information Systems for the Community Health Services', *Medical Informatics*, **13**, 2.

AVISON, D.E. and FITZGERALD, G. (1995) '*Information Systems Development: Methodologies, Techniques and Tools*', 2nd edition, McGraw-Hill, Maidenhead.

AVISON, D.E. and FITZGERALD, G. (1985) 'Information Systems development: Current Themes and Future Directions', *Information and Software technology*, **30**, 8.

AVISON, D.E., FITZGERALD, G. and WOOD-HARPER, A.T. (1988) 'Information Systems Development: A Tool-kit is not enough', *Computer Journal*, **31**, 4.

AVISON, D.E., SHAH, H.U., POWELL, R.S. and UPPALL, P.S. (1992) 'Applying Methodologies for Information Systems Development', *Journal of Information Technology*, **7**, 2.

AVISON, D.E. and WILSON, D. (1991) 'Controls for Effective Prototyping', *Journal of Management Systems*, SA-58.

AVISON, D.E. and WOOD-HARPER, A.T. (1990) *Multiview: An Exploration in Information Systems Development*, McGraw-Hill, Maidenhead.

AVISON, D.E. and WOOD-HARPER, A.T. (1991) 'Information Systems Development Research: An Exploration of Ideas in Practice', *Computer Journal*, **34**, 2.

BENBASAT, I., GOLDSTEIN, D. and MEAD, M. (1987) 'The Case Research Strategy in Studies of Information Systems', *MIS Quarterly*, February, 1987.

BURRELL, G. and MORGAN, G. (1979) *Sociological Paradigms and Organisational Analysis*, Heinemann, Oxford.

CHECKLAND, P.B. (1981) *Systems Thinking, Systems Practice*, Wiley, Chichester.

CHECKLAND, P.B. (1985) *Systems Theory and Information Systems*, in: BEMELMANS, T.M.A. (Ed.) (1984) *Beyond Productivity: Information Systems Development for Organizational Effectiveness*, North Holland, Amsterdam.

COLLIER, J. (1945) 'United States Indian Administration as a laboratory of ethnic relations', *Social Research*, 12.

ELDEN, M. and CHISHOLM, R.F. (1993) 'Emerging varieties of action research: introduction to the special issue', *Human Relations*, **46**, 2.

HULT, M. and LENNUNG, S. (1980) 'Towards a Definition of Action Research: A Note and a Bibliography', *Journal of Management Studies*, **17**, 2.

JACKSON, M.C. (1987) 'New Directions in Management Science', in JACKSON, M.C. and KEYS, P. (Eds) *New directions in management science*, Gower, London.

LEWIN, K. (1946) 'Action research and minority problems', *Journal of Social Issues*, **2**, 4.

SCHÖN, D.A. (1983) *The Reflective Practitioner: How Professionals Think in Action*, Basic Books, New York.

SILVERMAN, D. (1990) 'Six Rules of Qualitative Research: A Post-Romantic Argument', *Symbolic Interaction*, **12**, 2.

Susman, G. (1983) 'Action Research; A Sociotechnical Systems Perspective', in Morgan, G. (Ed.), *Beyond Method: Strategies for Social Research*, Sage, Beverley Hills.

Susman, G. and Evered, R.D. (1978) 'An assessment of the scientific merits of action research', *Administrative Science Quarterly*, 23, December.

Trist, E. and Murray, H. (Eds) (1990) *The Social Emergence of Social Science: A Tavistock Anthology*, University of Pennsylvania Press, Philadelphia.

Warmington, A. (1980) 'Action research: Its methods and its implications', *Journal of Applied Systems Analysis*, 7.

Willcocks, L. and Mason, D. (1987) *Computerising Work*, Paradigm, London.

Wood-Harper, A.T., Antill, L. and Avison, D.E. (1985) *Information Systems Definition: the Multiview Approach*, Blackwell Scientific Publications, Oxford.

Yin, R.K. (1994) *Case Study Research: Design and Methods*, 2nd edition, Sage, Thousand Oaks, California.

15 Issues in Participant Observation — A Study of the Practice of Information Systems Development

Joe Nandhakumar

Introduction

In recent years, there has been increasing recognition of the importance of social and organizational aspects of information systems. This has provided new insights into the application of information systems in organizations, and has led to a growing interest in interpretive approaches to information systems research. The interpretive approaches are based on rather different assumptions about the nature of the world and the way we can know it than traditional positivist research. A number of authors such as Boland, 1985; Zuboff, 1988; Boland and Day, 1989; Orlikowski, 1992; 1993; Jones and Nandhakumar, 1993; Walsham, 1993; Jones, 1994; DeSanctis and Poole, 1994, have adopted interpretive epistemology to seek to throw some light on the complex process of IS development practice.

Several different methods of data collection are considered as being suitable for use in interpretive information systems research. Interviews are perhaps the most widely used method. Observation may also be carried out directly with the observer being either a passive or active member of the research setting. Active involvement in which the observer does not seek to influence the situation more than would be expected from other participants is described as *Participant Observation* (Taylor and Bogdan, 1985; Atkinson and Hammersley, 1994). It may be distinguished from Action Research (Reason, 1994) in which the researcher seeks deliberately to intervene in the situation, often by employing specific techniques, in order to achieve a particular outcome.

Rather than attempting to review the suitability of each of these methods, in this chapter, I seek to identify a range of epistemological, methodological and practical issues raised by the application of participant observation in interpretive research, since it appears to be used relatively rarely in information systems research. In order to illustrate this, I shall first describe my experience in conducting a participant observation study of the Executive Information Systems (EIS) development process in a large manufacturing company (LMC — a pseudonym).

A Participant Observation Study of EIS development

This study involved me working full-time for a six month period as a salaried member of the EIS development 'team' based in the headquarters of LMC Europe.

At the time of the research, this team consisted of the leader William, a former analyst from the Systems (Computing) Division, three other Systems analysts (Mark, Luke and David), and a trainee (Phil). Because one of the members had recently moved to another area of the company as part of LMC's staff rotation policy, the team was temporarily short-staffed. A replacement was not expected for five months and this made it easier for me to persuade the team manager that I could help them out in clearing the backlog of development work as well as providing an outsider view of their activities. In addition, as I had previously been employed as a member of the EIS team for a short period and had considerable software development experience the manager knew that I would quickly be able to make an effective contribution.

During initial discussions with LMC about research access, concern was expressed about confidentiality as an article, written by a former consultant to LMC, had recently appeared in a business magazine describing problems with one of the projects in which the EIS manager had been involved. It was therefore necessary to explain the nature of the participant observation study being proposed to remove these fears. It was also agreed that the EIS manager would be able to see and approve the case description produced from the research and that no attempt would be made to talk to executives directly.

The LMC EIS was based on company-standard personal computers (PCs) which provided a touch-screen, colour, graphical user interface through which executive reports could be accessed and a mainframe-computer based systems which managed the cataloguing and distribution of the reports to the PCs. New reports were regularly added to the EIS by team members, based on data provided by different divisions of the company. The development of a new report was referred to as a 'project'. In addition, the EIS team was responsible for maintenance and support activities, such as fixing hardware and software-related problems, software upgrades, documentation, and security.

During the research period I was fully involved in the EIS team's activities, being given charge of development and maintenance of a number of EIS projects. I was also given the same facilities as the other team members, including access to all documents and support staff involved in data provision, technical support and systems security. However, I was allowed to spend a few days a month to write up the research and meet with my academic supervisor to discuss progress.

During the study at LMC Europe I maintained a daily log to record activities of EIS team members, events, meetings, discussions, and other observations. An extract of the log is given below.

> Luke was again prevented from making progress with upgrading any EIS PCs and spent most of the day again on reading general magazines and talking with Steve (*another analyst in the Systems Division*). This was noted by William who had a lengthy discussion with him about the situation. . . . . . .

> Mark spent most of the day assessing the performance of the new logon procedure and then carried out extensive checks to ensure that the EIS was running correctly. He found by chance that there were errors in the Daily Production Report and

corrected this. He also dealt with a technical problem with one of the EIS PCs in accessing the external news services which he found to have been caused by a loose cable. . . . .

Phil continued writing the program for Personnel-EIS project while David was on leave. . . . . .

Joe had to revise the Product Development-EIS prototype again as the data providers wanted to test the system before a presentation to their managers. As a result Joe could not carry out any further work on the Inventory-EIS prototype as planned, and it was evident that it would not be ready that week. Joe then spent time on catching up with office work, sorting out his PC, and learning to use the new graphical capabilities of the upgraded software. . . . .

The team members also debated who should carry out the upgrading of the executive PCs in one of the overseas branches, which was situated in a holiday resort.

At the start of the research period I attempted to record activities every hour. This was found to be impractical because of the volume of data to be recorded and the time available, so I resorted to writing up the log at the end of each day. Occasionally discussions were specifically arranged to enable me to obtain other participants' accounts of their actions. Data were also sought from other key players such as support staff. Data on the historical context were also gathered from the staff at LMC and from company documents.

The study resulted in hundreds of pages of log containing a large amount of data which was then written up in the form of a case study soon after the field study was completed. This described the development process in the order that events happened, and recorded many aspects of the real-life context. The case study was sent to William for comments. Although analysis and interpretation of the data presented in the case was made during the period of participant observation the final comprehensive analysis happened after the field study was completed.

Discussion

The above briefly outlines how I applied participant observation to study the EIS development at LMC. A number of issues may be identified from the use of participant observation in this study. This section therefore seeks to examine a range of epistemological, methodological and practical issues raised by the application of participant observation in interpretive research.

Epistemological and Methodological Issues

In the introduction to this chapter, I stated that interpretive approaches are based on rather different assumptions about the nature of the world and the criteria for constructing and evaluating knowledge about it than traditional positivist approaches. Interpretive research assumes that 'reality' is ultimately a human construction and therefore subjective (e.g. see Chua, 1986; Orlikowski and Baroudi, 1991; Easterby-Smith *et al.*, 1991). For example, organizational structures and hierarchical levels as typically represented in an organizational chart, are seen as existing through human action rather than being external and objective. They can therefore be understood only through interpreting the meanings that individuals reveal through their inter-actions. The interpretive researcher therefore attempts to understand the phenomena of interest through accessing the meaning that participants assign to them. Under-standing social phenomena is therefore concerned with studying them from the perspective of the human actors involved in a particular social context. This implies that the researcher first needs to have access to the actors themselves. Even if re-searchers are able to gain direct access to the actors, however, their ability to obtain an understanding of actors' interpretations may be limited in a number of ways.

First, the researcher cannot assume that he or she understands the actors description of their behaviour and interpretations in a particular social setting. For cxample, many terms used by actors in a particular setting may appear identical to those used in everyday life, but may have different meanings in that setting (Taylor and Bogdan, 1985). Relying on actors' verbal descriptions alone can there-fore lead to misinterpretation of what is said. Similarly, social rules and norms identical to those in other settings, may have different meanings in a particular setting.

Second, actors may provide a distorted account of their behaviour because their ideas as to what ought to happen in the situation may differ from what actually goes on (Taylor and Bogdan, 1985). This is not to say that there is a true view of what should happen in a situation or of what actually happens, but that actors may interpret their own behaviour in terms of dominant perceptions (Becker and Geer, 1957).

Third, actors may seek to deliberately mislead the researcher or may not talk to them about certain issues and activities because they may feel that discussing these might be impolite or too sensitive (Van Maanen, 1979).

Finally, actors may be unable to give an account of their actions because they form part of social routines of which they are only tacitly aware. Giddens (1984) distinguishes between practical and discursive knowledge and argues that actors know more than they can say.

Access to actors' interpretations
Through participation in the EIS team's activities I was able to overcome, at least to some extent, the above barriers to understanding. Thus the meanings of particu-lar terms and activities in the LMC context could be learned from daily observation of the behaviour of the team members. For example, the term 'travelling-man' was used by team members to describe the new divisional vice president who took over responsibility for the EIS. This was explained as meaning that he was rarely in his office and was therefore thought unlikely to make as much use of the EIS as his predecessor. As a result, team members became concerned about a possible loss of

senior executive support for the EIS and several meetings were held to discuss how they should respond to this development.

The term 'closed-door-meetings' was also used in conversations to describe urgent meetings in LMC, but this also had a wider meaning in that you should 'keep your distance' from the manager because something was wrong, such as someone was being made redundant or adverse data on departmental performance was being published. The actual door slamming was used by managers to convey this message to their staff. When activities were delayed such as a demonstration of a new EIS project which was repeatedly cancelled because managers were engaged in 'closed-door-meetings', its meaning was understood and accepted by team members. By observing these rituals over time an understanding of their meanings and their effects on the development process could be developed.

Through participating in the activities I was able to appreciate for myself the subjective experience of work such as motivation and time pressure in EIS development and to understand the ways that team members responded to them. For example, when restrictions were imposed on the LMC employees' overseas travel in response to the outbreak of the Gulf War, this contributed to a loss of motivation among the team members. They therefore fulfilled only the minimum requirements and spent most of the time on reading magazines/software manuals and occasionally engaged in disputes with other team members (especially with junior members) on development standards.

By getting to know the team members personally I was also able to gain insights into the reasons why individuals interpreted situations in a particular way. For example, when William asked Mark to find out executives' needs from their secretaries he complained that they would not talk to the EIS team members and treated them like maintenance workers. Luke, however, did not share this view. This may have reflected the fact that Mark had made his way up from the shop floor while Luke was a graduate who had been recruited from Finance division.

The problem of misrepresentation and non-disclosure was reduced by participant observation in a number of ways. For example, it enabled me to check team members' statements against observed behaviour and also gave me access to internal memos, company documents and other staff, which could be compared against observation and initial interpretations. This was illustrated when the EIS team sought to spread a story that the suspension of one of the EIS by the data providers' division was to hide the adverse stock performance figures resulting from a major strike. It subsequently transpired, however, that the suspension was largely due to the inability of the EIS to support the changing needs of the data providers' division. The EIS team had seen this as bad for their image in the company and had therefore encouraged an alternative story which cast the blame for the suspension elsewhere. It was not possible, however, to sustain the deception with a team member for any length of time.

Many of the practices of the EIS team were also confidential and could not have been discovered without being involved in development work. For example, the EIS team did not talk about the systems security to anyone outside the department because tight security was essential to safeguard the confidential reports and win the support of data providers. In practice, however, security was compromised by many issues such as the inability of the software to provide the necessary password security and the reluctance of executive users to use many levels of passwords. Team members therefore covered this issue up to project an image of a secure EIS. For example, they followed an elaborate password allocation procedure to satisfy other interested parties such as data providers and users that the EIS complied with company practices. These informal practices were not concealed from me, but rather they involved me in them. By comparison they usually gave a well rehearsed version of the 'EIS story' to outside researchers.

The influence of unstated cultural norms on EIS development could also be observed through the sustained involvement offered by participant observation. For example, LMC had a strong organizational hierarchy that prohibited direct contact between EIS team members and executives. Thus when one of the EIS team members was seen in a Vice President's office, the Systems Executive demanded an explanation from the EIS area managers. This meant that team members had to guess what executives' requirements might be during the design of EIS and that it was not possible for them to question executives about the usefulness of EIS applications.

Being an observer as well as a participant, however, I was able to notice and question aspects of the social routine of which the participants were hardly aware unless interruptions occurred. For example, expectations of timing and location of many activities such as report updates and team meetings were embedded in the social context. The deeper structure of these phenomena was understood only by noticing these activities through involvement and inquiring about their origins.

Involvement of the researcher

Although the above discussion illustrates that participant observation seems to provide the kind of access to actors' interpretations implied by an interpretive research approach, this method is often seen as intervening in the research context too much and hence distorting the data. For example, my participation in the work of the EIS team clearly meant that I influenced their activities. The most tangible evidence of this was the various EIS projects in which I played a major development role. I also sought to introduce a number of new design conventions for EIS projects. Although not all of these were accepted, some helped to influence other team members' practice.

While team members fairly rapidly accepted me as an ordinary colleague, and did not treat me differently because of my status as a researcher, my presence may still have affected their interpretations more than normal. My questions about team conventions and practices may have encouraged members to pay particular attention to these. My occasional absences to write up the research may also have served to remind them of my dual status.

My perceptions of the development process were inevitably influenced by my prior beliefs, values and interests and by my personal involvement in the activities under investigation. By maintaining contact with my academic supervisor throughout the study, and by seeking to continuously develop my theoretical approach it was hoped to promote a reflective attitude towards my own interpretations.

It could be argued that since the interpretive approach assumes that the researcher cannot stand outside the research context, and that detailed knowledge of this context is necessary (see e.g. Walsham, 1993), close engagement of the researcher in the research site is seen as desirable. Sensitivity towards the ways in which this may affect the social phenomena being studied is therefore necessary. A reflective attitude concerning the extent to which the researcher's interpretations are shaped by their own preconceptions is also appropriate.

Further, since the researcher has his or her own interpretations, their influence on the research context is also not seen as neutral. The interpretive approach therefore views the process of research as value laden.

Time and context

The interpretive approach believes that interpretations are time and context dependent and these may shift as meanings are formed, transferred and used (Orlikowski and Baroudi, 1991). In order to understand how interpretations may change over time, the researcher therefore needs to be exposed to the situation for an extended period rather than obtaining occasional snapshots of the process. This implies a longitudinal study. The context dependence of the phenomena also requires that the researcher gains a thorough knowledge of the social setting to appreciate its influence (Geertz, 1973).

At LMC, through participating in the developers' activities in the company setting over a period of time I was able to get insights on how processes were changing and also how they were sustained. For example, the way in which design standards used for EIS interfaces and working practices were enforced could be observed as well as the way in which they evolved. The six month research period also allowed the complete development process for an EIS project to be studied from the initial concept through to its implementation as a working component of the EIS. As the timing of work on this project changed frequently in response to other events and pressures on team members' time, continuous participation was necessary to be able to observe the whole process. While some potentially significant activities may occur too infrequently to be observed in a period of six months, others may be happening every second. A decision had therefore to be made about the level of detail in which to record and interpret the development process. For example, micro-ethnographic techniques such as Discourse Analysis (Stubbs, 1983) could be applied to investigate the second to second process. However, these techniques may be too detailed to be feasible for a longitudinal study of the processes over the course of a whole information systems development project. Our experience with participant observation demonstrated the complexity of dealing with a large amount of data even from our level of detail. Further, such techniques make it even more difficult to address the broader historical and social context, which we found to be an important element in understanding information systems in organizations.

Generalizability and validity

Because interpretations are time and context dependent, generalizability cannot be extended reliably from a sample to the population. The ideas and theories generated in one setting can therefore provide only a basis for understanding similar phenomena in other settings rather than enabling the prediction of behaviour in other contexts. As interpretations are seen as changing over time, replicating interpretive research on different occasions will also not yield the same results. The validity of interpretive research therefore depends on gaining sufficient access to the knowledge and meanings of actors to enable a plausible representation of their interpretations to be generated.

Practical and Ethical Issues

Having considered some of the epistemological and methodological issues raised by the use of participation observation in our study, I will now focus on some of the practical and ethical issues.

Gaining access to an organization

Gaining access to an organization of interest was difficult because many practitioner managers were unaware of the nature of academic research. Some believed that organizational research would always involve questionnaire surveys or interviews, and were suspicious about the reasons for a researcher getting involved in organizational life. Others feared that researchers' involvement and subsequent publications might bring bad publicity to their organization. At LMC, it was therefore necessary to explain the nature of the participant observation study being proposed, to alleviate these fears. It was also agreed that the EIS manager would be able to see and approve the case description produced from the research.

Coping with the dual role

The data collection and interpretation may require the researcher to retain a commitment to being a researcher while being an employee in the company. I had to clarify my role in the company in advance because over-commitment in work might have restricted my ability to collect data. I kept close contact with the academic base and research supervisor throughout the field work period and also took time off to write up data. My previous experience in the systems development enabled me to fit comfortably in the employment role.

Dealing with constraints for data collection and presentation

Data collection was affected by the inevitable selection process during the study. For example, at LMC the way data were gathered was affected by practical constraints such as not being able to be in two places at the same time to observe some activities, especially when the activities were carried out in a foreign branch. Because I could not record much during office hours, the way data were recorded was affected by memory limitations to recall events at the end of the day. I therefore had to use many mechanisms to get around these practical constraints. For example, in order to overcome the practical limitations of only being able to observe activities in which I was involved, I initiated conversations with other team members, often during lunch hours or evenings, about their activities. During formal team meetings the team members also provided a brief description of their activities and problems. The team members' 'daily task list', a list (informally and openly) maintained to record outstanding tasks and their execution, was another source of data. In order to recall events I also maintained a diary to jot down key events and activities when I paused between tasks, and in conversations, I tried to remember a few key words, such as 'boring design', 'crowded screen' and 'difficult environment', to recall the discussion later.

There were also ethical dilemmas such as writing about colleagues' activities and confidentiality agreements which limited which items could be recorded explicitly. Any ambiguity on the company's requirements about the confidentiality was clarified before starting the field work. This enabled me to work around this constraint from the beginning to convey the level of details I intended.

Other selection processes also shaped the presentation of the data. For example, the transcription of the log into the main case study and subsequently into a published version involved considerable selection. In this process some issues were expanded while others were filtered out. The way these data were interpreted was also influenced by our prior assumptions, beliefs, values and interests. The whole process was further influenced by our personal involvement in the project. The effect of this process is illustrated below.

> *Log entry*:
> Luke was again prevented from making progress with upgrading any EIS PCs and spent most of the day again on reading general magazines and talking with Steve (*another analyst in the Systems Division*). This was noted by William who had a lengthy discussion with him about the situation. . . . . . .

> *Case Study entry*:
> . . . Although many EIS PCs had been upgraded with the new software during that period, Luke's progress in this was constantly affected. Because of the company convention that development staff should not work on an executive's PC while they were in their office, Luke had to wait until one of the executives was away to upgrade the software on his PC. He therefore spent his time on other activities and was fulfilling only the minimum requirements.

> *Case entry for publication*:
> . . . Because of the hierarchical norms Luke had to wait until one of the executives was away to upgrade software. This was noted by William who had a lengthy discussion with him about the situation.

> *Interpretation*: (discussion on management control and team members' autonomy).
> . . . however, tighter control on team members' activities did not appear to improve productivity. For example, the company rules on access to executives seriously affected Luke's ability to complete his work and reduced his motivation as William noted . . .

Funding for the study

Another issue of concern was funding for the participant observation. Observation in organizations may be expensive. Participation in the activity of the organization being studied, however, may provide some compensation to the organization for their (researchers) participation and also, as in my case, help to fund the study itself.

Conclusions

As discussed in the introduction, the primary aim of this chapter was to explore issues raised by the application of participant observation in interpretive information systems research. The evidence presented also indicates the value of participant observation in providing the kind of data implied by interpretive research approach. In particular, it provides direct access to actors' interpretations and allows in-depth exposure to the research context over time. The under-utilization of participant observation in information systems research may therefore be seen as a deficiency of the current information systems literature. This chapter, however, does not promote participant observation as a panacea. Participant observation provides a particularly clear challenge to many traditional criteria of research design and places significant demands on researchers in terms of both collecting and reporting their findings. This chapter also illustrates that participant observation has a number of practical difficulties that seem likely to deter its widespread adoption.

Acknowledgments

I should like to thank Matthew Jones, Cambridge University, for his valuable contribution towards the development of this chapter.

References

ATKINSON, P. and HAMMERSLEY, M. (1994) 'Ethnography and Participant Observation', in DENZIN N.K. and LINCOLN Y.S. (Eds) *Handbook of Qualitative Research*, Sage, London, pp. 248–61.

BECKER, H.S. and GEER, B. (1957) 'Participant Observation and Interviewing: A Comparison', *Human Organization*, **16**, 3, pp. 28–32.

BOLAND, R.J. (1985) 'Phenomenology: a preferred approach to research on information systems', in MUMFORD, E.; HIRSCHHEIM, R.; FITZGERALD, G. and WOOD-HARPER, A.T. (Eds) *Research Methods in Information Systems*, North Holland, Amsterdam, pp. 193–201.

BOLAND, R.J. and DAY, W.F. (1989) 'The Experience of System Design: A Hermeneutic of Organizational Action', *Scandinavian Journal of Management*, **5**, 2, pp. 87–104.

CHUA, W.F. (1986) 'Radical Developments in Accounting Thought', *The Accounting Review*, **61**, 4, pp. 601–32.

DESANCTIS, G. and POOLE, M.S. (1994) 'Capturing Complexity in Advanced Technology Use: Adaptive Structuration Theory', *Organization Science*, **5**, 2, pp. 121–47.

EASTERBY-SMITH, M., THORPE, R. and LOWE, A. (1991) *'Management Research: An Introduction'*, Sage: London.

GEERTZ, C. (1973) *The Interpretation of Culture*, Basic Books, New York.

GIDDENS, A. (1984) *'The Constitution of Society'*, Polity Press, Cambridge.

GILL, J. and JOHNSON, P. (1991) *'Research Methods for Managers'*, Paul Chapman, London.

JONES, M.R. and NANDHAKUMAR, J. (1993) 'Structured development? A structurational analysis of the development of an Executive Information System', in AVISON, D. KENDALL, J.E. and DEGROSS, J.I. (Eds), *Human, Organizational, and Social Dimensions of Information Systems Development*, North-Holland, Amsterdam.

JONES, M.R. (1994) 'Learning the Language of the Market: Information Systems Strategy Formation in a UK District Health Authority', *Accounting, Management and Information Technologies*, **4**, 3.

ORLIKOWSKI, W.J. (1992) 'The Duality of Technology: Rethinking the Concept of Technology in Organizations', *Organization Science*, **3**, 3, pp. 299–326.

ORLIKOWSKI, W.J. (1993) 'CASE tools as organizational change: Investigating incremental and radical changes in systems development', *MIS Quarterly*, **17**, 3, pp. 309–340.

ORLIKOWSKI, W.J. and BAROUDI, J.J. (1991) 'Studying Information Technology in Organizations: Research Approaches and Assumptions', *Information Systems Research*, **2**, 1, pp. 1–28.

REASON, P. (1994) 'Three Approaches to Participative Inquiry', in DENZIN, N.K. and LINCOLN, Y.S. (Eds) *Handbook of Qualitative Research*, Sage, London, pp. 324–39.

STUBBS, M. (1983) *'Discourse Analysis: The Sociolinguistic Analysis of Natural Language'*, Blackwell, Oxford.

TAYLOR, S.J. and BOGDAN, R. (1985) *'Introduction to Qualitative Research Methods: The research for meanings'*, (2nd Edition), John Wiley, New Work.

VAN MAAANEN, J. (1979) 'The Fact of Fiction in Organizational Ethnography', *Administrative Science Quarterly*, **24**, pp. 539–50.

WALSHAM, G. (1993) *'Interpreting Information Systems in Organizations'*, John-Wiley, Chichester.

ZUBOFF, S. (1988) *'In the Age of the Smart Machine; The Future of Work and Power'*, Heinemann, Oxford.

16 Enigma Variations: Uncertainty in Social and Economic Research

George McKenzie

Introduction

One of the great works on the epistemology and methodology of social and eco-nomic research is Joseph Schumpeter's *History of Economic Analysis* (1954). Al-though the focus of his volume is the detail of the nature and structure of economic thought from Greco-Roman times until the 1950s when he died, it is much more than an encyclopedia. Schumpeter was ringing the warning bells for the increas-ingly specialized nature of social and economic research that has characterized the latter half of the twentieth century. He is keen to emphasize that research is open-ended, that it is highly subjective, that it is prone to prejudice and that it generates discourse that may take on a life independent of the social and economic problems being investigated. He warns that there is the danger that sophisticated methods can become the tools of those seeking influence rather than knowledge and understand-ing. In this chapter, I seek to use the *History of Economic Analysis* as a launching pad to discuss recent trends in social and economic research. I shall highlight some of the comments made by Schumpeter, Descartes, Weber, Marshall, Keynes and Friedman in so far as they relate to issues concerning research practice. In doing so, however, my ultimate aim is to focus upon the application of statistical methods in the social sciences. When Schumpeter died, their use was still in infancy. How-ever, many of the problems which he discussed are particularly relevant to this area of practice which has attracted widespread attention during the latter half of the twentieth century. The question that is central to what follows is: what meaning(s) can we attach to the results obtained from statistical investigations?

It is significant that Schumpeter first addresses one of the most fundamental methodological questions: what is a science? Is it possible to apply the methodo-logy of the physical sciences to the social sciences? He deals with this by defining science in such a way that it is all-encompassing:

> . . . a science is any kind of knowledge that has been the object of conscious efforts to improve it. (p. 7)

In other words, any conscious thought process designed to enhance understanding is a science. For Schumpeter, this universal theory of science was itself a social phenomenon. The methodology of social and economic research is a product of history:

> ... Whatever the field, the problems and methods that are in use at any one time embody the achievements and carry the scars of work that has been done in the past under entirely different conditions. ... Scientific analysis ... is an incessant struggle with the creations of our own and our predecessors' minds and it 'progresses', if at all, in a criss-cross fashion, not as logic, but as the impact of new ideas or observations or needs, and also as the bents and temperaments of new men, dictate. (p. 4)

For the contemporary social scientist, these thoughts will no doubt appear worrisome since they emphasize that the *objectivity* which we seek in our research is but an illusion. Not only are our investigations highly subjective but the results that we achieve may influence our environment and thence feed back onto our *subjective* interpretations of that environment.

The social scientist of today has cloaked the uncertainty of her or his research activities in the mantle of truth, rationality, certainty and objectivity in the pursuit of personal, social and career development and thus ultimately in the pursuit of power. As Schumpeter wrote in commenting upon the Battle of Methods (Methodenstreit) that took place in Germany in the late nineteenth century, schools of thought had their own sociological realities:

> Victory and conquest, defeat and loss of ground are in themselves values for such schools and part of their very existence. They will try to appropriate labels that are considered honorific — in our case, both parties laid claim to such epithets as 'empiric', 'realistic', 'modern', 'exact' — and to affix derogatory labels — 'speculative', 'futile', 'subordinate' — to the work of the enemy. (p. 815)

The previous discussion is but a caricature designed in part to inform but primarily designed to disconcert. Let us now examine more closely what we can actually expect to achieve. In so doing, I will continually place emphasis upon the pervasiveness of uncertainty in what we are investigating and hence in what we are able to achieve.

The Casino

The application of statistical method in economic and social research involves the explicit assumption that the world around us acts *as if* it were a casino. The notion of *as if* modelling plays a central role in social science research. For the moment, we shall simply concentrate upon the analogy. In a game such as roulette, we know for certain the exact, objective probabilities of the various possible outcomes from spinning the wheel. We also know the exact probability that the casino will win. Thus it is possible to calculate the expected return from any bet or any series of bets. We will not know the exact outcome, but we can calculate the average outcome and its probability. In statistical analysis, by contrast, a model is constructed which is designed to represent how a group of people will behave *on average*. The model is not exact in the sense that errors are represented in the model. These errors are assumed to be generated by a probability distribution in much the same way that the outcomes of the roulette wheel are generated by a probability distribution. For example, consider the following equation designed to represent the conjecture that the money supply, denoted Ms, influences total expenditure on goods and services, denoted Y.

$$Y = a_0 + a_1 M_s + \epsilon \qquad (1)$$

a_0 and a_1 are the parameters of the model which the statistician wishes to estimate and ϵ is the random variable designed to capture the influence of all other variables. Such errors or deviations from the model structure are usually assumed to be generated by a normal distribution such as that shown in Figure 16.1. The sources or reasons for the errors are taken to be outside the scope of the investigation. But that does not mean that they are unimportant. The flatter is the distribution, the weaker the ability of changes in the money supply to explain changes in expenditure, and conversely.

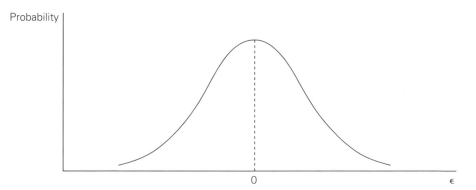

Figure 16.1: Normal Distribution

Although at first glance this procedure appears different from Descartes' method it remains in the same spirit. Instead of focusing upon a unique outcome of the investigation (i.e. perfect certainty), the emphasis shifts to the certainty in the probability of outcome. The analysis appears to become richer but it also becomes problematic. If the assumptions of the modelling procedure are valid, then it can be argued that there is a universal representation of social and economic behaviour which can be used to predict, and consequently can be used for, the purpose of formulating policy. Errors will be involved but they are assumed to be unsystematic. Any systematic errors will be recognized and corrected. Thus over time, it is claimed that the representation will be correct, on average.

Two of the most influential economists of the twentieth century, Frank Knight and John Maynard Keynes were both sceptical of this approach since they believed that the world was clouded by uncertainty. That is, they believed that it was not possible to assume that there existed a known, objective probability distribution driving the model. Consequently it would not be possible to *verify* or *falsify* conjectures. For Keynes, there existed no universal theories which could apply at all times. Rather, there existed many partial theories which might be valid at some point in time but not for all time. A theory could be used to inform and enhance understanding but it could not be used for prediction. Following the Great Depression of the 1930s, Keynes had outlined a framework which he believed would assist in enabling economic recovery. However, he did not believe that this model would be valid during periods of rapid expansion and/or inflation. In terms of equation 1, he would have argued that the parameter a_0 was very small during a depression although it might be quite large during an inflation. In addition, he would have argued that an additional variable, government expenditure, should be added to the equation, viz

$$Y = a_0 + a_1 M_s + a_2 G + \epsilon \tag{2}$$

According to his theory a_2 would be very important during times of recession and/or severe depression but relatively small during times of inflation. These views were particularly apparent following the publication in 1939 by the Dutch economist Jan Tinbergen, of an econometric model of the UK economy. Tinbergen had sought to base his investigation upon Keynes' influential *General Theory*. However, Keynes was furious. In correspondence with Roy Harrod, he wrote

> In chemistry and physics and other natural sciences the object of experiment is to fill in the actual values of the various quantities and factors appearing in an equation or a formula; and the work when done is once and for all. In economics this is not the case, and to convert a model into quantitative formula is to destroy its usefulness as an instrument of thought. Tinbergen endeavours to work out the variable quantities in a particular case, or perhaps in the average of several particular cases, and he then suggests that the quantitative formula so obtained has general validity. Yet in fact, by filling in figures, which one can be quite sure will not apply next time, so far from increasing the value of his instrument, he has destroyed it. . . . He works out a figure for it and proposes to predict by using the result, regardless of the fact that his own investigations clearly show that it is not constant, in addition to the strong *a priori* reasons for regarding it as most unlikely that it can be so.
>
> The point needs emphasizing because the art of thinking in terms of models is quite difficult — largely because it is an unaccustomed — practice. The pseudo-analogy with the physical sciences leads directly counter to the habit of mind which is most important for an economist proper to acquire.
>
> I also want to emphasize strongly the point about economics being a moral science. I mentioned before that it deals with introspection and with values. I might have added that it deals with motives, expectations, psychological uncertainties.

One has to be constantly on guard against treating the material as constant and homogeneous.

Many, indeed most, contemporary statisticians would not go as far as Keynes. However, they too are seeking to inform about the limits and potential pitfalls of quantitative modelling. For example, two prominent British econometricians, David Hendry and Grayham Mizon, follow Weber in the sense that they recognize the subjective origins of all conjectures. For example, they suggest that whim is a valid basis for conjecture. They then suggest that competing theories should be compared. This involves the construction of what is termed an encompassing model, i.e. a model that encompasses all the characteristics of the competing theories. The performance of each theory is compared against the general model. However, Hendry and Mizon emphasize that their modelling method does not yield a true model. Their interpretation is much more limited. They argue that the best that any statistical model can achieve is to capture a process generating the data. It is not necessarily to be the true process. Indeed it is highly unlikely to be the true process. All tests are conditional. Different theories can be compared but at the end of the day, the acceptance of one structure over another is conditional upon the structure of the model and the statistical assumptions.

Just as during the *Methodenstreit* of the nineteenth century social scientists were propelled into a battle for the victory of one idea over another, so today statistical method seems to invite the investigator to engage in exercises that will reveal one model to be superior to another. Within the Hendry/Mizon perspective this either/or approach is replaced by an and/both approach. It is possible that the 'best' model on the basis of their subjective criteria could include elements of all competing models. In a sense a new model is constructed. The Hendry/Mizon approach recognizes that the search for truth is not a valid objective. However, they believe that procedures designed to seek to identify order within data series is a valid objective and can inform. However, at the end of the day we must remain uncertain and sceptical about what our subjective attempts to structure the data really mean. Let us seek to develop some of the themes relating to uncertainty in social and economic research in greater detail.

States of Mind

For Keynes, the existence of uncertainty meant that decisions taken in markets could not be thought of as objective. Consequently, it was not possible to model them as if they were objective. Consider his views about the operation of financial markets:

> ... the vast majority of those who are concerned with the buying and selling of securities know almost nothing whatever about what they are doing. They do not possess even the rudiments of what is required for a valid judgment, and are the prey of hopes and fears easily aroused by transient events and as easily dispelled.

This is one of the odd characteristics of the capitalist system under which we live, which, when we are dealing with the real world, is not to be overlooked.

But there is also a further reason why it may often profit the wisest to anticipate mob psychology rather than the real trend of events, and to ape unreason proleptically . . . so long as the crowd can be relied on to act in a certain way, even if it be misguided, it will be to the advantage of the better-informed professional to act in the same way — a short period ahead. Apart, moreover, from the calculations of greater or less ignorance, most people are too timid and too greedy, too impatient and too nervous about their investments, the fluctuations in the paper value of which can so easily obliterate the results of so much honest effort, to take long views or to place even as much reliance as they reasonably might on the dubieties of the long period; the apparent certainties of the short period, however deceptive we may suspect them to be, are much more attractive.

Because of this uncertainty, emotional influences would come to dominate and these could not be modelled in any systematic fashion. His models were conditional upon a particular emotional state of mind. Thus during an economic depression, people would appear to be 'bearish', that is pessimistic and negative. Any optimism about a recovery is only temporary. Consequently, Keynes argued that direct government intervention in the form of increased spending would be needed to break the emotional negativism of a depression. On the other hand, during periods of economic expansion, people would be 'bullish', that is, euphoric. And in both states, because of uncertainty, herd behaviour would come to dominate as people sought to identify in the behaviour of others the true state of the world. Because of this uncertainty, any attempt to model behaviour over time would itself be uncertain.

The Lucas Critique

A similar conclusion can arise from another line of reasoning. In 1976 Robert Lucas argued that if a model is used to formulate policy, people will realize this and take it into account in their own behaviour.

. . . given that the structure of an econometric model consists of optimal decision rules of economic agents, and that optimal decision rules vary systematically with changes in the structure of series relevant to the decision maker, it follows that any change in policy will systematically alter the structure of econometric models.

In other words, the structure of the economy would be continually changing so as to render the use of empirical investigations virtually meaningless for policy purposes.

Superficially, it might appear as if Keynes and Lucas are saying the same thing. In point of fact, their motivations are really quite different. Keynes was arguing that in certain circumstances government had a role to play in stabilizing the economy. However, the same set of policies could not be applied universally. Different policies were relevant to different conditions. Lucas, on the other hand, is attempting to develop a neutrality theorem. This is one of a large number of neutrality theorems in economics designed to present a case that government policy will have no effect. For example, in my own area of research, the behaviour of financial markets, it is noted that financial institutions often change their behaviour so as to avoid the effects of new regulations and policies. This will usually involve the design of new financial instruments which are not covered by the regulations. As a result, the regulators are frequently in the position of having their objectives thwarted. For example, if a central bank seeks to reduce the money supply so as to reduce the rate of inflation, banks may seek to create new types of assets that are not subject to the control of the central bank. These assets cannot usually be used to carry out transactions but they can easily be sold to generate funds as and when required. Thus they are pretty close substitutes for money. As a result of this innovation, monetary policy becomes less effective. To deal with this, the central bank begins to widen its definition of 'money' to include the new financial instruments. New data series are published and used as targets for control. But this simply induces commercial banks to introduce further innovations.

Verification and Falsification

The issues that we have recognized so far are well-recognized by statisticians under the guise of *Type I* and *Type II* errors. These are explained in detail in any good introductory statistics textbook. However, they are frequently overlooked in actual research practice. Hence it is important to outline the nature of these errors. Any statistical test involves a comparison between two alternative conjectures: the theory or model is true or it is not true. The case where it is not true is referred to as the null hypothesis. If we knew the truth there would be no problem. But since we are not privileged in this way, we run the risk of committing errors. Thus there is the possibility of rejecting a model when it is true (but we do not know when this is the case) and of accepting a model when it is false (but we do not know this either). The possibilities are illustrated in Table 16.1. Note that statisticians, unlike social scientists, are careful never to use the terms *verify* or *falsify*. They use the very conditional terms *accept* and *reject*, respectively, so as to reflect the subjective nature of the investigation.

Table 16.1

	H0 True	H1 True
H0 Accepted	Correct Decision	Type II Error
H1 Accepted	Type I Error	Correct Decision

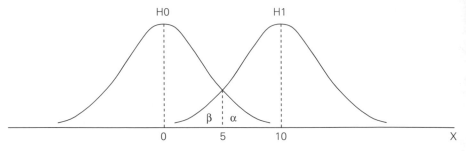

Figure 16.2:   Type I and Type II Errors

For the purposes of this paper it is important to examine the detail of the problem. Readers totally unfamiliar with statistical theory may wish to refer to a good introductory statistics textbook and skip this section for the moment. As above we consider two hypotheses, say one where the expected value of a variable, denoted x, is ten and the other where it is zero (i.e. the null hypothesis). Thus in Figure 16.2, I have drawn two identically shaped distributions, one centred on the mean of zero (H0) and the other on the mean of ten (H1). The question is: if we observed a value for x of three or of eight, how would we know from which distribution it was drawn. The answer is that we do not. Standard practice involves creating a subjective decision rule. For example let us suppose that any value of x greater than five is assumed to be drawn from H1 whereas any value less than five is drawn from H0. The probability of making the two types of errors can now be identified. The probability of making a Type I error, i.e. the probability that x is greater than 5 (thereby leading to the acceptance of H1) when H0 is actually true, is equal to the area denoted by α. Similarly, the probability of making a Type II error, i.e. the probability that x is less than 5 (thereby leading to the acceptance of H0) when H1 is actually true, is equal to the area denoted by β. We can of course increase or decrease the benchmark criterion from 5 so as to change the ratio of α to β but we have no scientific basis upon which to make this decision. The tools of hypothesis testing do not provide us with a basis for either falsification or verification.

It is here that the methodology of Karl Popper falls apart. Following Popper, many economists believe the purpose of research is to falsify. Indeed, he argued that rules should be established which only admit hypotheses than can be falsifiable (1965, p. 49). However, Popper avoided discussions of probability and statistics like the plague. As I discussed in Chapter 2, in a sense, he was applying the logic of Descartes. He was seeking certainty in falsification. However, for the social scientist, only relatively uninteresting propositions are capable of falsification. In social sciences, auxiliary hypotheses are added to the main hypothesis of interest. For example, the errors are normally distributed or the decision criterion is 5, as in the above example. Hence, any test is conditional upon these auxiliary statements as well. Since the auxiliary assumptions are frequently untested and the decision criteria are subjective, there can be no certain falsification.

Predictability

There is yet another variation on this theme. Milton Friedman (1953) has suggested that the criterion for model selection is its ability to predict and that it does not matter if its assumptions are unrealistic.

> ... the relevant question to ask about the 'assumptions' of a theory is not whether they are descriptively 'realistic', for they never are, but whether they are sufficiently good approximations for the purpose in hand. And this question can only be answered only by seeing whether the theory works, which means that it yield sufficiently accurate predictions.

So far we have acknowledged the fact that the assumptions of a model or theory *may* be unrealistic. Because of uncertainty we will never know. Friedman, however, suggests that we should persevere even if we know with certainty that the assumptions are incorrect. But this is logically unsound. If we know that the assumptions of our analysis arc false, then we cannot claim any universality for the conclusions derived through a process of deduction.

Statisticians recognize this problem under the heading *spurious correlation*. A good example of this was discussed in a famous tongue-in-cheek paper by Jerzy Neymann (1952). On the basis of his data set, Neymann showed that there existed a high correlation between the number of storks per 10,000 women and the number of babies per 10,000 women. He concluded that '... although there is no evidence of storks actually bringing babies, there is overwhelming evidence that, by some mysterious process, they influence the birth rate'.

Neymann's results would thus satisfy Friedman's criterion based upon prediction. This simply shows again the futility of trying to create universal rules to guide our research. But there are also some other issues lurking in this example. On the basis of his 'research', Neymann has identified a question: how do storks influence the birth rate of humans? Should this question now be the focus of investigation? Or is some lateral thinking required? Perhaps we are really dealing with a case of *reverse causality*. Storks do like to nest on chimney tops. In other words, they are attracted to areas where there are people. Perhaps it is humans who influence the stork population, not vice-versa. We may have a high correlation between two variables X and Y. However, this does not enable us to identify whether X causes Y or Y causes X or indeed if the relationship is pure chance. Such argumentation may seem ridiculous, but it does highlight the problems associated with utilizing prediction as the criterion for model selection.

Reflections

When I have taught post-graduate econometrics, I set an applied project relatively early in the course in order that students may become aware of the sorts of problems that are involved in applied work, as outlined above. When it becomes clear to the students that statistical work is highly subjective and hence highly problematic, I seek to dispel their despair by reading to them the following passage from Alfred Marshall's *Principles of Economics*.

> If we shut our eyes to realities we may construct an edifice of pure chrystal by imaginations, that will throw lights on real problems at all like our own. Such playful excursions are often suggestive in unexpected ways: they afford good training to the mind: and seem to be productive only of good, so long as their purpose is clearly understood.

Social science research is really a library of stories. Each story represents the conjectures of its author (or authors) at a particular moment of time. Those conjectures reflect the author's history in terms of educational, family and work experiences. These experiences are, in turn, dependent upon the histories of others. The conjectures may appear as a result of pure whim, personal experience or derived from the ideas of others. They may relate to a particular moment in time in which case they cannot form the basis of a universal theory or explanation of what is going on. The story is based upon the conscious and subconscious thought processes of its author. It can never be a complete and correct reflection of reality which can only be viewed incompletely and with uncertainty. The aim of the story is to inform readers as to how the author interprets the world.

Statistical and econometric practice involves turning the story into a cartoon. Characters in a cartoon are representations of the characters in the narrative (or theory). Simplification is introduced to highlight what the author believes to be the most important issues and points adjudged to be unimportant are eliminated. For example, a cartoon is two-dimensional, whereas reality is three-dimensional. Similarly, in statistical analysis the main elements of the conjecture form the equation to be estimated (i.e. the cartoon). Everything is assumed to be random and relegated to an error term, and like the narrative upon which it is based, the cartoon is designed to inform about the artist's (i.e. researcher's) thoughts. People will interpret the cartoon from their own perspective. Perhaps their thoughts diverge from the author's intent, therefore, discussions take place, workshops and conferences are set up. These enable researchers to inform each other about their different stories and cartoons.

Research in the social sciences is indeed an enigma. The most optimistic of us believe that the world can be made a happier and more enjoyable place not only for ourselves but for others. Indeed these were the objectives of the Enlightenment. But as we seek to achieve these objectives, we run the risk that we become more interested in the process of drawing the cartoon than in the story that it was originally designed to represent. Although workshops and conferences are designed to inform, they also provide the incentive for participants to refine their language and cartoon representations to such an extent that their meaning is only understood by themselves.

There is the danger that the cartoon becomes the reality rather than reality itself. People who are not members of the club are unable to comprehend. This asymmetry in understanding then provides a platform for the club to exercise control over the uninformed, and because the language of the club is perceived by the outsiders to have a higher, scientific status, the club is accorded prestige and trust. Councils of Wise Men are established to inform elected politicians. The elected politicians may then seek to impose the cartoon on reality. In a sense we have developed a generalization of Lucas' critique, discussed earlier. Research is part of a social process that feeds back on itself in complex ways that the researcher must be consistently on guard to identify.

It is appropriate to end our discussion of uncertainty where we began. As Schumpeter wrote,

> . . . a science is any kind of knowledge that has been the object of conscious efforts
> to improve it. (p. 7)

This definition does not seek to privilege one particular research practice or methodology over any other. Nor does it seek to exclude. Provided that we are prepared to accept the universality of the uncertainty that conditions our work, then to my mind, this statement represents an optimistic platform from which to launch our search for knowledge and understanding. Uncertainty conditions our work in many ways: the practices which we have inherited from the past, the environments in which we have lived, the nature of our education and our perceptions of the problems faced in the world about us.

Some might claim that such reflexivity is a recipe for disaster since it can only encourage inaction. I will conclude this chapter by arguing the contrary position and suggesting that as researchers we could do well to adopt the following three principles:

1. No research practice or research methodology should view itself as superior to any other. If progress is to be made in our uncertain world, then it is necessary to recognize that there can only be a plurality of understandings and consequently no such thing as a universal truth.

2. If one is prepared to adopt the first principle, then the logical implication is that any research project should investigate the use of different research methods and methodologies. For example, in an attempt to understand the causes and effects of unemployment, we might seek to use the methods of both the economist and the grounded theorist. The former conjectures a model with a particular structure and then investigates whether that model captures the data generation process. The latter seeks to develop a theory from the ground up by becoming involved with the subjects of investigation, in this example, the unemployed. With high levels of unemployment throughout the industrial world, it would be folly to restrict lines of investigation.

3. This final principle follows from the previous two. If they are accepted, then a logical implication is that we should seek to promote inter-disciplinary research. Despite the good will that develops in common room and staff

club discussions concerning this objective, actual implementation has become more rather than less difficult. In the 1980s and 1990s, universities throughout the world have been suffering from funding cut backs. Departments must battle with university management and with each other for adequate funding. The end result has been a firming up rather than a weakening of disciplinary walls.

What is required before we can effectively implement these principles is a research project into the nature of the discourses that characterize social and economic research. Such a project might include in its agenda the following questions:

1   What are the rules of the discourse. That is, what practices do they privilege and what practices do they exclude?
2   What rules decide when a new proposition or method is to be accepted within the discourse?
3   What rules constrain the issues to be discussed. What topics are excluded?
4   How are the internal rules of a discourse repackaged so as to achieve influence, control over others and perhaps elimination of others who do not have allegiance to the discourse.
5   What institutions are set up to control the discourse?

By seeking to understand these questions, we can better understand the artificial boundaries that divide disciplines and prevent their associated university departments from achieving progress in understanding.

References

FRIEDMAN, M. (1953) 'The Methodology of Positive Economics' in *Essays in Positive Economics*, Chicago, University of Chicago Press, pp. 3–43.

HENDRY, D. and MIZON, G. (1985) 'Procrustean Econometrics: Or Stretching and Squeezing Data' in GRANGER, C. (Ed) Oxford, Oxford University Press.

KEYNES, J.M. (1930) *A Treatise on Money*, London, Macmillan.

KEYNES, J.M. (1936) *The General Theory of Employment, Money and Interest Rates*, London, Macmillan.

KEYNES, J.M. (1973) *The General Theory and After: Part II — Defence and Development*, edited by MOGGRIDGE, D. London, Macmillan.

KNIGHT, F. (1921) *Risk, Uncertainty and Profit*, New York, Harper and Row (1965 reprint).

LUCAS, R. (1976) 'Econometric Policy Evaluation: A Critique', in BRUNNER, K. and MELTZER, A. (Ed) *The Phillips Curve and Labor Markets*, vol. 1, Amsterdam, North-Holland.

MARSHALL, A. (1961) *Principles of Economics* (ninth variorum edition with annotations by C.W. Guillebaud) London, Macmillan.

NEYMANN, J. (1952) *Lectures and Conferences on Mathematical Statistics and Probability*, second edition, Washington, DC, US Department of Agriculture, pp. 143–54.

POPPER, K. (1965) *The Logic of Scientific Discovery*, New York, Harper and Row.

SCHUMPETER, J. (1954) *History of Economic Analysis*, New York, Oxford University Press.

TINBERGEN, J. (1951) *Business Cycles in the United Kingdom, 1870–1914*, Amsterdam, North-Holland.

Notes on Contributors

David Avison is Professor of Information Systems at the University of Southampton. He is President of the UK Academy of Information Systems and Vice-chair of an International Federation of Information Processing working group. He is joint editor of the McGraw-Hill series in Information Systems and joint editor of Blackwell Scientific's *Information Systems Journal*. He has published sixteen books as well as numerous papers in academic journals. He has given plenary addresses at recent information systems conferences in the Netherlands, Australia, Bahrain, the United Kingdom and the United States. His research areas include information systems development and he is one of the co-authors of the Multiview methodology.

Dean Bartlett is Research Fellow in the Management Research Centre at the University of North London Business School. He is author of *Stress: Perspectives and Processes* (Open University Press) and has written about psycho-legal aspects of advocacy in the *Handbook of Psychology in Legal Contexts* (John Wiley, 1995). His main research interest is in applying qualitative methods to issues in management including managerial cognition and decision-making. He is currently involved in an ESRC research project examining the management of innovation.

Alan Hamlin is Reader in Economics at the University of Southampton. His publications include *Ethics, Economics and the State* (Wheatsheaf, 1986); *The Good Polity* (with P. Pettit, Blackwell, 1989); *Market Capitalism and Moral Values* (with S. Brittan, Elgar, 1995); *Ethics and Economics* (Elgar, 1996) and articles in economics, politics and philosophy journals including *Economics and Philosophy, Ethics, The Journal of Political Philosophy* and *Political Studies*.

David Hand is Professor of Statistics and Head of the Statistics Department at the Open University. He has published numerous articles and fourteen books including, most recently, *Construction and Assessment of Classification Rules* (John Wiley, 1997). His research interests include multivariate statistics, the foundations of statistics and the process of statistical consulting. His application interests include finance, medicine and psychology.

George McKenzie is Professor of Finance and Director of the Centre for International Finance at the University of Southampton. He has published five monographs including *Banks and Bad Debts* (John Wiley, 1995) and *New Methods for Measuring Economic Welfare* (Cambridge University Press, 1983) and articles in several journals including *Applied Financial Economics, The Journal of Banking* *and Finance, The American Economic Review, The Journal of Political Economy*, and *The Review of Economic Studies*. He is Research Co-ordinator in the School of Management and is Co-director of the MSc in International Banking and Financial Studies.

Joe Nandhakumar is Lecturer in Information Systems in the School of Management at the University of Southampton. Prior to joining the university, he worked for several years in software development and accounting projects in multinational companies in Europe. He has published widely on issues relating to the social and organizational aspects of information systems, especially the relationship between information and communication technologies, and social organizational change.

Joan Orme is Reader in Social Work studies at the University of Southampton. She is author of *Workloads: Measurement and Management* (Avebury/CEDR, 1995) and has co-authored *Managing People in the Personal Social Services* (John Wiley, 1987) and *Care Management* (BASW/Macmillan, 1993). She has also contributed chapters on research supervision and equal opportunities and research to *A Handbook for Research Students in Social Sciences*. edited by Graham Allan and Chris Skinner (Falmer Press, 1991).

Sheila Payne is Research Development Officer in the School of Occupational Therapy and Physiotherapy and Director of the Health Research Unit at the University of Southampton. She has co-authored *Psychology for Nurses and the Caring Professions* (Open University Press, 1996) and articles in several journals including *Social Science and Medicine, Palliative Care*, and the *Journal of Advanced Nursing*. Her main research interests are psychosocial oncology, psychological aspects of palliative care and health psychology. She is a member of the South and Wales Region of the HNS Responsive Grants Committee.

Jackie Powell is Senior Lecturer and Head of Social Work Studies at the University of Southampton and Associate Director of the Centre for Evaluative and Developmental Research (CEDR). She is also the Director of the Personal Research Programme in the Department of Social Work Studies and Joint Convenor of the Faculty Research Training Scheme. Her main interests include evaluative research, the impact of changing organizational styles and patterns of services on professional practice, and the relationship between social work and the social sciences. She has co-authored two books *Changing Patterns of Mental Health Care* (Avebury, 1992) and *Disability: Britain into Europe* (Avebury, 1994) and articles in *The British Journal of Social Work* and *Social Services Research*.

David Scott is Lecturer in Educational Research at the London University Institute of Education. He has published widely in edited volumes and refereed journals including *Forum, Curriculum, Journal of Policy Studies* and *Research Papers in Education*. He edited *Control and Accountability in Educational Settings* and *Undertaking Educational Research* and is the current Editor of the *Curriculum Journal*.

His current research projects include coursework and coursework assessment in the GCSE, Language in Higher Education, INSET, Library Use in the Primary School and Educational Experiences and Career Aspirations of Afro-Caribbean 16–30 year olds.

Pat Usher is the Academic Registrar at La Sainte Union College of Higher Education in Southampton. She lectures on Gender Differentiation and Feminist Approaches to Knowledge Creation in the School of Education and the Faculty of Social Sciences at the University of Southampton and is also a tutor at the Open University. Her current research concerns sexual harassment and abuse of power in the workplace.

Robin Usher is Reader in Education in the School of Education at the University of Southampton. He is author of *Adult Education as Theory, Practice and Research: The Captive Triangle* (Routledge, 1985); *Postmodernism and Education: Different Voices, Different Worlds* (Routledge, 1994) and co-editor of *Understanding Educational Research* (Routledge, 1996). He is currently Head of the School of Education and was until recently Research Co-ordinator of the Faculty of Educational Studies and course director of the Faculty's Research Training Programme.

Index

academic discipline 87
Academy 10–13, 14, 18, 20
action research 91–2, 196–209, 210
Agar, M. 173
alienated knowledge 117
Allport, G.W. 164
American Census Bureau 135
anthropology 90, 97
anti-monopoly legislation 16
Antill, L. 202, 204
Archer, M.S. 170
Archimedes 32
architecture 30
Aristotle 11, 12–15, 20, 45, 92, 177
Arrow, K. 57
assumptions 43–4, 54, 75–6, 82–3, 105
Atkinson, P. 161
Audit Commission 113
Avison, D. 87–100, 112, 196–209
axial coding 191–3

Backhouse, J. 95
Bacon, F. 14, 15, 16, 17
Bailey, R. 113
Baker, C.B. 181
Ball, S. 166
Baroudi, J.J. 89, 90, 96
Barthes, R. 38
Bartlett, D. 173–95
Baudelaire, C. 17
Baudrillard, J. 27
Becker, G. 72–3, 75–83
Begg, D. 73
belief 12
Benbasat, I. 197
Berg, B.L. 173
Bernard, J. 52
Bhaskar, R. 155, 168
binary oppositions 19–20, 31, 33, 50
biography 139, 151

biology 76, 77–8
biplots 135
Blau, F. 72
bootstrap method 131
Box, G.E.P. 127
Brake, M. 113
Brannen, J. 145
Briggs Report 102
British Psychological Society 175
British Sociological Association 163
Bryant, I. 150
Bryman, A. 144
Buchanan, J. 57
Buckingham, R.A. 88
Bulmer, M. 147, 157
Burgess, R.G. 161, 163, 164, 165

Cantley, C. 145–6, 147
capitalism 30
Carlen, P. 116, 118
Carlisle, M. 156
case studies 91–2, 115, 157–9, 207
casino analogy 222–5
Catchpole, C.P. 200, 203
category development 185–94
censorship 120
Centre for Study of Public Choice 57
ceteris paribus 82
Checkland, P.B. 196, 198
child rearing 76–8, 79
Cicero 13
civil servants 67
coding 185–94
cognitive psychological model 103
cognitivism 178
Collier, J. 197
commitments 103
common sense 15
community care 143, 148
comparative advantage 78

comparisons 186–7
compensation principle 81
competition 16
computer science 89, 94, 95, 124
Comte, A. 16
concept-indicator model 189
conceptual study 91, 92
conditioning 131, 132
confidentiality 163–4, 211, 214–15
conformity 167
conspiracy theory 28
constant comparative method 107
constitutional political economy 59
consultancy 207
contextual issues 36
control theory 188
Corbin, J. 178, 179–82, 184–6
Corner, J. 109
cost-benefit analysis 82
coursework 157–8
covert research 163
Cox, D.R. 127
criminal justice system 116
critical epistemology 90
critical theory 151
cultural anthropology 97
culture, definitions 97
Curnock, K. 150

Darlington Health Authority 201
data analysis 92, 94, 104, 155–72
    grounded theory 106–7, 183–94
    statistics 124–36
data collection 155–72
data triangulation 108
death 106
deconstructivism 20, 39, 51
deduction
    logic 63
    methods 17
    reason 14–16, 71
definitions 11–12
Denzin, N.K. 174
Department of Health 109
Derrida, J. 19
Descartes, R. 10, 14–17, 20, 221–32
    deductive reasoning 71
    rationality 63
deviance 20, 48

diagnosis 133, 134
disciplinary power 48
disciplines 85–6
discourse analysis 216
discrimination 21
dissonance 118–19
diversity 96
division of labour 73, 76–8, 81
divorce 80–1
domination 20
Dornbusch, R. 73
Down's syndrome 134
dualism 45–6, 50, 52, 178

Eco, U. 27–31, 35, 40–1
ecological correlation 134
econometrics 224–5
economics 56–70, 71–83, 221–32
economics of scale 76
Efron, B. 131
egoism 68
Electronic Revolution 9, 19
elites 11, 102, 104
emotion 83
empiricism 29, 30, 35
    approach 15
    investigation 63
    knowledge 31
    model 147
    science 173–5, 176–7
engineering 89, 147
English Revolution 14
enigma variations 221–32
Enlightenment 10, 13–16, 18, 22
    assumptions 54
    epistemology 46
    knowledge-making 42–3, 44
    model 147
epistemology 10, 13, 21
    conspiracy theory 28
    Enlightenment 46
    feminism 47–50, 114
    interpretivism 115–16, 210
    knowledge-making 42–3
    modernism 45
    participant observation 212–13
    philosophy 58
    pluralism 104–6
    positivism 89

postmodernism 30
practice 112, 113
randomized control trials 110
rationalism 63–4
science 176–7
social work 116, 119, 141, 143–4
uncertainty 221
equality 21
ethics 56–7, 61, 63, 162–4, 217–19
ethnicity 116, 120–1
ethnography 90, 91, 144
discourse analysis 216
education 156, 158, 166
grounded theory 185
European Community 16
Everitt, A. 113, 115, 142
examinations 155–72
Examinations Board 156
executive information systems (EIS)
210–18
existence 11
experimentation 82, 105

falsification 12, 17, 176, 224, 227–8
family behaviour 71–83
federalism 57
feminism 21–2, 42–55
positivism 115, 119
praxis 116, 120
social work 113–14, 117–18, 151
fertility rates 78
Field, P.A. 105
Finch, J. 148
Fischer, S. 73
Fisher randomization test 128
Fitzgerald, G. 92, 199
Flax, J. 21, 45
flip-flop technique 187
Foucault, M. 20, 33, 43, 48, 53
foundationalism 33
French Revolution 14
Freud, S. 45
Friedman, M. 221–32, 229
Fruin, D.J. 113
funding 109
futures research 91

Gadamer, H-G. 19, 43
Game, A. 37

Gaunilo 14, 15
Geach, P. 61–2
gender 44, 51, 73, 76–80
education 158
managerialism 120–1
social work 114, 116
General Certificate of Secondary Education
(GCSE) 156, 158
Giddens, A. 213
Glaser, B.G. 106, 157, 178–84, 187, 190,
194
goal displacement 168
God 13–14, 20
Goldberg, E.M. 113, 115
government 56, 113
grand plans 28
Gray, P. 95
Greek philosophy 9–13, 18–19, 177
grounded theory 90–1, 106–7, 173–95
group comparisons 126–9
Guba, E.G. 105, 116, 119–20, 147, 176,
178

Halberg, M. 119
Hamlin, A. 56–70
Hammersley, M. 158, 161
Hand, D.J. 124–36, 135
Hanson 176
Hanvey, C. 114
Hardiker, P. 150
Harding, S. 50
Harris, K. 167–8
Harrod, R. 224
Hawker, R. 110
health policy 21
health professionals 104
Hekman, S. 21, 45
Hendry, D. 225
Henkel, M. 151
hermeneutics 19, 31, 46, 91
Hicks, J. 75
Holman, B. 148
Honigmann, J.J. 157
household management 72
Howe, D. 146
Hugman, R. 144
Hult, M. 197, 198
humanism 48
Hume, D. 15–16, 66

Húngler, B. 105
hyper-reality 30
hypotheses 34, 124–36

illuminative evaluation 144
income generation 102
individualism 58, 61–3
individualization 116
individuals 129–35
induction
  grounded theory 181, 193
  investigation 63
  methods 17
  reasoning 15
  science 176
inductive-deductive process 12, 15
Industrial Revolution 9, 14, 19
infinite regression 63
inflation 17
information superhighway 30
information systems (IS) 87–96, 112
  action research 196–209
  participant observation 210–20
information technology (IT) 88–9
integration 193
interactionism 109
interpretation 19, 30
interpretivism 14, 45–6, 49, 115–16, 210
  information systems 89–90
  participant observation 216
  social work 143
  statistics 135
intertextuality 38
interviews 165–6
investigator triangulation 108
invisible hand 66–7

jackknife method 131
Jameson, F. 30
Jordan, B. 142–3
Joseph, K. 156
judges 67
jurisprudence 116

Kaplan, 173
Keen, P.G.W. 89
Kelman, 64
Keynes, J.M. 221–2, 224–6
Knight, F. 224

knowledge
  community 34
  empiricism 31
  feminism 114
  managerialism 120
  Plato 11
  power 28, 32–3, 48, 53, 150–1
  power differential 116–17
  praxis 113
  sensory experience 9, 12
Körner 201
Kuhn, T. 18, 31, 38, 176
  disciplines 86
  paradigm shifts 46

laboratory experiments 91
labour force 76–8, 81
Lakatos 176
Land, F. 95
Lane, R. 83
language 29–30, 36–7, 83
Lather, P. 21, 38–9, 41
Lawler, J. 108
Lazarus 103
leisure time 79–80
Lennung, S. 197, 198
Levy, P. 174, 175
Lewin, K. 197
liberal feminism 46
Liebenau, J. 95
Lincoln, Y.S. 105, 116, 119–20, 147, 178
local government 56
Locke, J. 15–16
logic 11, 63
London School of Economics (LSE) 114
longitudinal studies 91
Longworth, G. 92
Lucas, R. 226–7, 231

MacDonald, G. 120
McHale, B. 29
Mackay, L. 103
McKenzie, G. 8–23, 71–83, 221–32
managerialism 115, 120–1
Mann-Whitney-Wilcoxon test 128
mapping 125
marginalization 20
marriage 80–1, 83
Marshall, A. 221–32, 230

Marshall, C. 175
Marxism 16, 48, 113
Mason, D. 198
mathematics 11, 14–15, 91, 124
Mayo, E. 197
Melia, K.M. 107
methodologies
  Academy 11
  feminism 50–3, 114
  grounded theory 183–94
  individualism 61–3
  information systems 91, 92–3
  language 83
  multiview 200–7
  participant observation 212–13
  practice 112, 113
  science 18
  social work 118–19
  socialization 42
  triangulation 108
  uncertainty 222–32
microeconomics 56
Mies, M. 112, 118, 149
mind 13
Mitchell, J.C. 159
Mizon, G. 225
Modern Times 14, 16–18
modernism 28–30, 42, 45, 52, 115
monitoring 115
morality 56, 66–7
Morse, J.M. 105, 181, 184
motivation 64, 67, 68
Mulhall, A. 102
multivariate statistics 134
Multiview 94, 200–7
Munn-Giddings, C. 144
Murray, H. 196

Nandhakumar, J. 210–20
National Health Service (NHS) 101, 201, 202
Newton, I. 83
Neymann, J. 229
Nobel Prize 72, 75
normalization 48
North American Free Trade Area 16
Northern Education Association 156
numerical research 115
nursing research 101–11

object-oriented methodologies 92–4
observation 30, 90
Occam's razor 68
Oliver, M. 148
ontology 3, 10, 119, 155, 176
open coding 190, 192
opportunity cost 72, 77–8, 80
optimal scaling methods 135
organization theory 89
Orlikowski, W.J. 89–90, 96
Orme, J. 21, 112–23
orthodoxy 9, 43–7, 115

paradigm shifts 46
parents 157
Pareto efficiency 80–1
participant observation 90, 108, 144, 166–7, 210–20
participative methodologies 92–4
partnership 147–9
patriarchy 21, 44, 47, 116
Payne, S. 101–11, 173–95
phenomenology 91, 103, 168, 182
Phillips, D.C. 175, 176
philosophy 58
Plato 11–13, 14, 15, 21
pluralism 50, 65, 104–6, 145–6, 207
policy-making 57
Polit, D. 105
politics 48–9, 56–70, 120, 145, 204
Popper, K. 17, 63, 176, 228
populations 129–35
positivism 14, 30–1, 35, 45–6, 176
  characteristics 174–5
  education 155
  family behaviour 83
  feminism 115, 119
  information systems 89–90
  science 198–9
  social work 116–18, 141, 144, 149–50
  triangulation 108
  values 120
post-positivism 155, 156, 177
post-structuralism 155, 156
postgraduate training 109
postmodernism 18–22, 27–41, 44–5, 118, 155–6
poverty 65, 148
Powell, J. 112–14, 139–54

power 28, 32–3, 48, 53, 150–1
  differential 116
  discourses 20
  postmodernism 48
  rationality 42–55
practice 112–23
pragmatism 182
praxis 113–14, 116, 119–20, 150
predictability 229
prejudice 19, 21, 71
principal-agent problems 68
production lines 19
professionalism 117–18
professionalization 103–4
prototyping 92, 93, 94
psychoanalysis 44, 83
psychology 105
public choice theory 57–61, 67–8
public service tradition 67
public spirit 64

qualitative methods 119, 139–40, 144–5,
    155–72
  grounded theory 173–5
  research 105, 106–8
quality of life assessment 135
quantitative methods 105, 144–5
quasi-likelihood 129

radical feminism 46–7
random effects model 131
randomized control trials 110
rape 83
rationalism 45–6, 48, 177
rationality 42–55, 58, 63–9
Ravn, I. 148–9
reason 11, 15
reductionism 93, 117, 177–8
Rees, S. 139, 146–7, 149, 151
reflexivity 35–6, 39–40, 43, 51
  education 155–6
  family behaviour 71
  postmodernism 49
  social work 115, 142, 147, 151
  uncertainty 229–32
Regional Health Authorities 110
Reinharz, S. 50, 52
religious institutions 104
Renaissance 177

Research Assessment Exercise 104
Robinson, W.S. 134–5
Rolfe, G. 102
Rose, G. 134
Rossman, C.B. 175
rules 9–10

Sainsbury, E. 146
St Anselm of Canterbury 14
St Augustine 13, 14, 20
sampling 191
Samuelson, P. 75
saturation 190
Sawicki, J. 21
Schein, E.H. 97
Schon, D.A. 141–2
schools 155–72
Schumpeter, J. 15, 221–2, 231
science 14, 20, 32–3, 198–9
  empiricism 173–5
  hypotheses 124–36
  methodology 18
  paradigm shifts 46
  philosophy 176
  politics 120
  postmodernism 43
Scott, D. 155–72
Scott, J. 50
screening 133, 134
self-interest 66
semiology 88
Sen, A. 57
sensory experience 9, 12
sexism 43–4
Sheldon, B. 141
Shotter, J. 37
Silverman, D. 174–5
Simons, H. 160
Simpson's paradox 132
single-minded model 65, 67
Smith, A. 16, 76
Smith, D. 141
Smith, G. 145–6, 147
social anthropology 97
social care practices 139–54
social choice theory 57
social control 48
social work 112–23, 139–54
socialization 42, 67

sociology 89, 90, 94, 97
Socrates 13
software 128, 185
soul 12, 20
specialization 76–7
Spinoza, B. 63
Stanley, L. 115, 119
statistics 115, 117, 124–36, 176, 221–32
status 103
Stenhouse, L. 165
Stern, P.N. 179–81
story-telling 27–41
strategic methodologies 92, 93
Strauss, A.L. 106, 157, 178–86, 190, 194
structured methodologies 92–4
sub texts 37–8, 49
sufficiency aspect 68
surrogacy 44
surveys 91, 92
Susman, G. 197
symbolic interactionism 182, 184
systems methodologies 92, 94

t-tests 126–8
Tavistock Institute 197
taxation 56, 65
Taylor, F.W. 197
textual strategy 29, 34
Thatcher, M. 61
theory
  development 167–8
  integration 193
  sampling 191
  triangulation 108
Thyer, B. 149
Tinbergen, J. 224
trade 14, 16
tradition 19, 42–3
training 56, 78
triangulation 108–9, 144

Trist 196
Turner, B.A. 180, 190

unalienated knowledge 119
uncertainty 12, 221–32
unemployment 12–13, 17
Ungerson, C. 115
Universities Funding Council 109
University of California 179
University of Southampton 87
University of York 56
Usher, P. 21, 42–55, 112, 114, 117–19
Usher, R. 1–7, 18, 27–41, 150
utilitarianism 15

values 32–3, 120
Vaux, C. de 16
verificationism 176, 224, 227–8
vocational model 103–4

Waddell Committee 156
wages 78
Wallace, A. 146–7, 149
Warmington, A. 197
waterfall model 204
Weber, M. 17, 72–3, 221–32, 225
welfare benefits 56
Willcocks, L. 198
Wilson-Barnett, J. 109
Wiseman, J. 57
Wolcott, H. 160
women's studies 39
Wood-Harper, A.T. 92, 199–200, 202, 204–5
Woods, P. 157, 160
working women 78–80
Worrall, A. 150
Wright Mills, C. 174

Yeatman, A. 52